Digital Video: Production Workflows and Techniques

Digital Video: Production Workflows and Techniques

Edited by
Grayson Rogers

STATES
ACADEMIC PRESS
www.statesacademicpress.com

Published by States Academic Press,
109 South 5th Street,
Brooklyn, NY 11249, USA

ISBN: 978-1-63989-155-9

Cataloging-in-Publication Data

Digital video : production workflows and techniques / edited by Grayson Rogers.
    p. cm.
Includes bibliographical references and index.
ISBN 978-1-63989-155-9
1. Digital video. 2. Image processing--Digital techniques. 3. Digital media.
4. Multimedia systems. I. Rogers, Grayson.
TK6680.5 .H36 2022
006.696--dc23

For information on all States Academic Press publications
visit our website at www.statesacademicpress.com

Contents

Preface

Digital video is programmed digital data which electronically illustrates moving visual images. In contrast, analog video represents moving visual images using analog signals. Digital video consists of a series of digital images displayed in rapid succession. Digital video can be copied without any degradation in quality, unlike analog video. It can be stored on digital media storage or streamed over the Internet to end users who can watch the content on a desktop computer screen or digital smart TV. Digital video content such as TV shows and movies typically includes a digital audio soundtrack. The ever growing need of advanced technology is the reason that has fueled the research in the field of digital video in recent times. This book explores all the important aspects of this field in the present day scenario. For all those who are interested in digital video technology, it can prove to be an essential guide.

This book is a comprehensive compilation of works of different researchers from varied parts of the world. It includes valuable experiences of the researchers with the sole objective of providing the readers (learners) with a proper knowledge of the concerned field. This book will be beneficial in evoking inspiration and enhancing the knowledge of the interested readers.

In the end, I would like to extend my heartiest thanks to the authors who worked with great determination on their chapters. I also appreciate the publisher's support in the course of the book. I would also like to deeply acknowledge my family who stood by me as a source of inspiration during the project.

Editor

IP Datacast and the Cost Effectiveness of its File Repair Mechanism

Bernhard Hechenleitner
Salzburg University of Applied Sciences
Austria

1. Introduction

Internet protocol datacast (IPDC) (ETSI, 2006a) is a framework for the distribution of digital data services to wireless, mobile handsets via a broadcast infrastructure based on digital video broadcasting for handhelds (DVB-H). The technical extensions of DVB-H (ETSI, 2004; Faria et al., 2006) to the widely used terrestrial DVB transmission system called DVB-T (ETSI, 2009a; Reimers, 2005) allow for specific requirements of rather small mobile devices, like a smaller screen size compared to television sets, or their dependency on accumulators for electricity and therefore their special need for low power consumption. As a broadcasting infrastructure does not automatically offer the possibility of data transmission in the "upstream" path from a mobile device to the sender, in the context of IPDC this sole one-way system is enriched with upstream paths using cellular networks or wireless local area networks (WLAN) – two types of networks which are typically used by mobile devices. Using these upstream paths for interactivity or signalling purposes, handsets are given the possibility to inform the sender about lost data segments allowing it to retransmit portions of data already sent.

This chapter will give an introduction into the digital video broadcasting (DVB) technology, especially into the DVB transmission system useful for mobile devices called DVB-H. It will describe the architecture of IP datacast, which is based on DVB-H, and the protocols used by this technology. One means of using IPDC is the broadcasting of binary data to a number of receivers using IP multicast protocols. In order to achieve correct reception of all of the sent binary data, a signalling mechanism has been specified, which enables receivers to inform the sender about lost or irreparable data fragments. This so-called file repair mechanism allows the setting of different parameters which affect the amount of data which can be corrected at the receiver and therefore have impact on the retransmission costs. The main topics of the research presented in this chapter are studies on the parameterization of the IPDC file repair mechanism and the effects of retransmissions on financial repair costs. In order to accomplish these studies, a simulation model has been designed and implemented which simulates an IP datacast network including a state-of-the-art error model for the wireless transmission channel and a versatilely parametrizable implementation of the file repair mechanism

2. Digital video broadcasting

The systems, procedures and protocols necessary for the distribution of digital television and other media services are contained in the general term "digital video broadcasting". The specifications describing all of these components are worked out by the Digital Video Broadcasting Project, which is a consortium of over 270 broadcasting network operators, equipment manufacturers, regulatory bodies and others (DVB Project Office, 2009a). The predecessor of the DVB Project was the European Launching Group (ELG), which constituted in 1991 with the goal to introduce an open and interoperable digital television system in Europe. The DVB Project consists of several organizational parts. One of them is the Commercial Module, which is responsible for determining market requirements. Another one, the Technical Module, drafts the technical specifications necessary for implementing these requirements. Once a specification is finished by the corresponding working groups within the Technical Module, it has to be approved by the Steering Board. If this approval is successful, the specification is handed over to the European Telecommunications Standards Institute (ETSI) for formal standardisation. Although the work on DVB started in Europe, it has become a very successful solution worldwide, with more than 230 million DVB receivers (DVB Project Office, 2009a).

2.1 DVB transmission systems

The set of specifications of the DVB Project contains a multitude of technical solutions for the distribution of DVB services, some of them are shortly described in the following paragraphs.

DVB-S/DVB-S2

DVB-Satellite (DVB-S) and DVB-Satellite 2nd generation (DVB-S2) are digital satellite transmission systems. The first digital satellite TV services using DVB-S started in 1994. Currently, more than 100 million receivers are deployed conforming to this technology (DVB Project Office, 2008a). Due to the progress in many related technical areas like channel coding, modulation, error correction and media compression, the second generation digital satellite system DVB-S2 was published in 2005, taking advantages of these improvements thus creating the basis for commercially viable high-definition television (HDTV) services. As it is expected that both systems will coexist for several years, DVB-S2 was created with backwards compatibility in mind. Through the use of hierarchical modulation, legacy DVB-S receivers will continue to operate while additional capacity and services will be delivered to the second generation receivers (DVB Project Office, 2008a).

DVB-C/DVB-C2

DVB-Cable (DVB-C) and DVB-Cable 2nd generation (DVB-C2) are the first and second generation digital cable transmission systems specified by the DVB Project. Generally, the two systems make use of the wired infrastructure of cable TV providers, which mainly consists of hybrid fibre-coaxial (HFC) systems. DVB-C was published by ETSI in 1994 and the second generation DVB-C2 is expected to be published in 2009. Comparable to the satellite system, DVB-C2 among other things makes use of improved error correction and modulation schemes. As an example, data rates of up to about 80 Mbps per 8 MHz channel can be achieved when using 4096-quadrature amplitude modulation (DVB Project Office, 2009b).

DVB-T/DVB-T2

Concerning the terrestrial broadcasting of digital TV services, the corresponding first and second generation transmission systems developed by the DVB Project are called DVB-Terrestrial (DVB-T) and DVB-Terrestrial 2nd generation (DVB-T2). The first version of the specifications was published in 1997, and the first TV service using DVB-T was launched in the United Kingdom in 1998. In the meantime, more than 90 million receivers have been sold in more than 35 countries (DVB Project Office, 2009c). The second generation system provides improved modulation and error correction techniques and is expected to be published in the second quarter of 2009 (DVB Project Office, 2009d).

DVB-H

The approach of analogue switch-off (ASO) in many countries worldwide leads to the installation of digital terrestrial television (DTT) infrastructures. In Europe, as in many other parts of the world like in Australia, Asia and South America, this DTT infrastructure is based on DVB-T, mainly focused on fixed receivers. To make this system also available for mobile end systems, extensions have been specified under the designation DVB-Handheld (DVB-H). These typically small handheld devices have special characteristics like comparatively small screen sizes and special requirements like low power consumption. To meet these features and needs, appropriate extensions to the DVB-T specifications were needed (see section 2.2). Concerning DVB-H services, the main focus was on video streaming including mobile TV and file downloads (DVB Project Office, 2009e). A huge number of DVB-H trials have taken place all over the world, and full service has been launched in 14 countries (DVB Project, 2009a).

DVB-IPDC

A set of necessary components has to be built on top of the broadcasting infrastructure in order to make mobile TV services successful. Such components include e.g. an electronic service guide (ESG) for the announcement of the services offered or a framework for the purchase of specific services. These complementary building blocks have been specified within DVB-IP datacast (DVB-IPDC), which is intended to work with the DVB-H physical layer (DVB Project Office, 2008b). As a general set of system layer specifications, DVB-IPDC can be implemented for any other Internet protocol (IP) (Postel, 1981) capable system. A special property of mobile TV systems is the expected availability of an additional bidirectional connection based on 3G cellular or WLAN networks. This provides the possibility of individualization of certain services.

DVB-SH

To extend the coverage area of DVB-H based mobile TV systems, the hybrid satellite/terrestrial DVB-Satellite services to handheld (DVB-SH) transmission system has been specified. The main distribution is achieved by using satellite transmission, with terrestrial gap fillers servicing areas with poor satellite reception characteristics. DVB-SH is an extension to the DVB-H infrastructure and can be used as a transmission layer for IPDC based services. In April 2009, a satellite for the construction of a DVB-SH network targeting several European markets was launched (DVB Project Office, 2009f).

2.2 Digital video broadcasting – handhelds

As DVB-H is generally based on DVB-T, this section first of all describes the transmission system of DVB-T, followed by the extensions that constitute DVB-H.

DVB-T Transmission System

The basic transmission system that is used by both DVB-T and DVB-H was specified by the Moving Picture Experts Group (MPEG). It is called the MPEG-2 transport system and was published by the International Organisation for Standardisation (ISO) as an international standard (ISO/IEC, 2007). The basic building blocks of this system are shown in figure 1. The media encoder applies specific operations on the audio and video streams to reduce the necessary capacity for transmitting them. These are in general lossy encoders based on MPEG specifications. For example, using MPEG-2 video encoding, a standard definition television (SDTV) video signal can be compressed to about 4 – 6 Mbps instead of 166 Mbps without compression (Reimers, 2005). The compressed media streams are called elementary streams (ES) and are input to the packetizer, which divides each stream into packets of variable length up to 64 kB, depending on the content of the stream. A compressed media stream packetized in this way is called packetized elementary stream (PES). As these relatively large PES data segments are not suitable for broadcasting a number of audio and video programs within one data signal, they are further broken down into smaller data chunks called TS packets by the transport stream (TS) multiplexer. Each TS packet has a fixed length of 188 bytes consisting of a 4 bytes header and 184 bytes payload, which carries the particular parts of the PES packets. A single service program can consist of multiple audio, video and other data streams represented as streams of TS packets, and the combination of several TV programs plus additional signalling data is multiplexed by the TS multiplexer into a complete data stream called MPEG-2 transport stream.

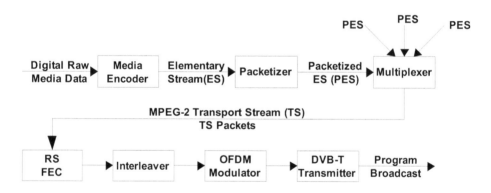

Fig. 1. Basic building blocks of the MPEG-2 transport system.

In the course of media encoding and compression, redundancy is removed from a media stream and the resulting data stream is rather fragile with respect to disruptions during the broadcast. Therefore, some redundancy has to be added systematically to be able to react on transmission errors and correct the received data stream. In DVB, primary error protection is achieved by using the Reed-Solomon (RS) forward error correction (FEC) block code. For each 188 bytes long TS packet, 16 bytes of checksum (or parity data) computed by the used RS code is added, resulting in a total length of 204 bytes. This FEC code allows the repairing of up to 8 bytes per TS packet. Packets containing more than 8 errors can not be corrected but still reliably detected and flagged as erroneous (Reimers, 2005).

Concerning DVB-T, the resulting stream of error protected TS packets is interleaved to counteract error bursts, and in the convolutional encoder additional error protection is added. After a further subdivision and interleaving of the data stream depending on the type of modulation, which can be quadrature phase-shift keying (QPSK), 16-quadrature amplitude modulation (QAM), or 64-QAM, the resulting signal is passed on to the orthogonal frequency-division multiplexing (OFDM) modulator. DVB-T supports the two OFDM transmission modes 2K and 8K, which make use of 2048 and 8192 subcarriers respectively mapped on a channel with a bandwidth of 8, 7 or 6 MHz. While the 2K mode provides larger subcarrier spacing (about 4 kHz compared to about 1 kHz using 8K mode), the symbol length is shorter (about 250 µs versus 1 ms). For mobile devices, the 2K mode is less susceptible to the Doppler effects due to its larger carrier spacing. On the other hand, the 8K mode allows greater transmitter spacing because of longer guard intervals and is therefore the preferable mode for single frequency networks (SFN). More specific technical details of the modulation and coding techniques of DVB-T can be found in (Reimers, 2005).

Extensions of DVB-T

DVB-H was specified as a set of extensions to DVB-T focussing on small, mobile receivers. Due to limited energy supply and more difficult signal reception conditions, two main extensions to DVB-T were defined: an access scheme called time slicing and an additional FEC mechanism. With time slicing, which is mandatory in DVB-H, the DVB-H data streams are not sent continuously but in bursts. This allows the receiver to power off between these bursts, thus saving energy. Depending on the bit rate of a DVB-H stream, these power savings can be up to about 90% (ETSI, 2009b). The second extension, which is an optional extension, is called multiprotocol encapsulation forward error correction (MPE-FEC) and is described in more detail in the next paragraph. Both extensions work perfectly upon the existing DVB-T physical layer and therefore DVB-H is totally backwards compatible to DVB-T (Faria et al., 2006). Nonetheless, some extensions to the physical layer were specified as well, among these the new 4K transmission mode, which is a complement to the existing 2K and 8K modes and is a compromise between mobility and SFN cell size.

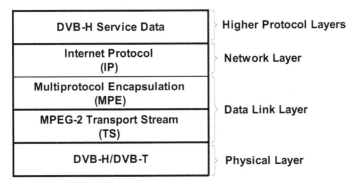

Fig. 2. DVB-H protocol stack adapted from (ETSI, 2009b).

All DVB-H payloads are carried within IP packets or other network layer protocol data units which are further encapsulated using multiprotocol encapsulation (MPE). Each IP packet is encapsulated into one MPE section and a stream of MPE sections build an elementary stream, which is further processed as described above and which is therefore finally mapped to a stream of TS packets that can be multiplexed into an MPEG-2 transport stream (see figure 2).

Multiprotocol Encapsulation Forward Error Correction

All DVB-H user data is transported in IP packets, each of them encapsulated in one MPE section. Each MPE section consists of a 12 bytes header, an IP packet as payload (max. 4080 bytes) and 4 bytes checksum. To further protect the IP data, an additional FEC code may be applied on the data. By using multiprotocol encapsulation forward error correction (MPE-FEC), some parity data is calculated and transmitted to the receivers which in turn can use this redundancy to correct corrupt data segments. The FEC code used by MPE-FEC is the Reed-Solomon (RS) block code RS(255,191). For a more detailed explanation of this FEC code see (ETSI, 2009b) and (Reimers, 2005).

An MPE-FEC frame is a logical data structure containing two data tables: the application data table (ADT) which consists of 191 columns and the Reed-Solomon (RS) data table which consists of 64 columns containing the parity bytes calculated by the FEC code (see figure 3). The number of lines can be 256, 512, 768 or 1024. As each cell in the two tables contains one byte, the size of a MPE-FEC frame either is 47.75 kB, 95.5 kB, 143.25 kB, or 191 kB.

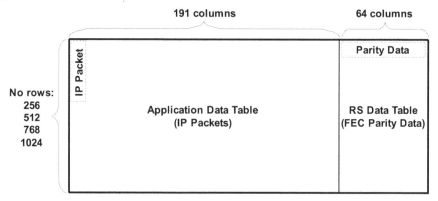

Fig. 3. MPE-FEC frame.

The IP packets plus optional padding are inserted into the ADT column by column. The RS code is applied on this data to calculate 64 parity bytes per ADT line, contained in the RS data table of the MPE-FEC frame. Concerning the data transmission, each IP packet of the MPE-FEC frame is transported within an MPE section, followed by the parity data. Each RS data table column is transported within an MPE-FEC section. The corresponding protocol stack is shown in figure 4.

2.3 IP datacast

IP datacast is a set of specifications for mobile TV systems based on IP capable systems. IPDC is specifically defined as a complement to DVB-H transmission systems, in this context called DVB-IPDC or IPDC over DVB-H. In the following, IPDC is taken short for IPDC over DVB-H. The basic building blocks of IPDC, which are described in this section, generally define how any types of digital content and services are described, delivered and protected.

Building Blocks of IPDC

An inherent part of the IPDC architecture is the possible combination of a unidirectional broadcast path realized by DVB-H and a bidirectional unicast interactivity path realized by e.g. cellular or WLAN data connections. In this way, an IPDC receiver, which is mainly built into a mobile phone, cannot only receive broadcast services but can make use of individual services or signalling through the interactivity path.

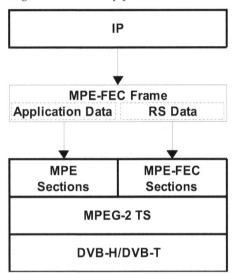

Fig. 4. DVB-H protocol stack using MPE-FEC.

The most important building blocks of IPDC are (DVB Project Office, 2008b):

- Electronic service guide (ESG): the ESG describes the services offered by an IPDC system as structured information, based on the extensible markup language (XML).
- Service purchase and protection (SPP): the SPP framework provides protocols and mechanisms for rights management and the encryption of digital content.
- Content delivery protocols (CDP): CDP is the set of protocols used by IPDC for media streaming and file delivery services.

Content Delivery Protocols

The set of protocols used for the delivery of the various mobile TV services, including media streaming and general file delivery, is called content delivery protocols (CDP) and is specified in (DVB Project, 2009b). As shown in figure 5, IPDC uses a complex stack of protocols, which can be divided in two subgroups: IP multicast based protocols for unidirectional delivery and IP unicast based protocols for interactive services, service additions or additional signalling purposes. Audio and video real-time media streams are delivered using the real-time transport protocol (RTP) and the RTP control protocol (RTCP) (Schulzrinne et al., 2003). The delivery of arbitrary binary data objects (like applications, ring tones and the like) is conducted via the file delivery over unidirectional transport (FLUTE) protocol (Paila et al., 2004), which is based on asynchronous layered coding (ALC), one of the Internet Engineering Task Force's (IETF) base protocols for massively scalable reliable multicast distribution (Luby et al., 2002). The number and types of binary data objects to be distributed within a FLUTE session as well as other metadata are described by the XML-based file delivery table (FDT), which itself is distributed using FLUTE. Summing up, the most important protocol stacks are: RTP/UDP/IP multicast for real-time streaming of audio and video, FLUTE/ALC/UDP/IP multicast for the distribution of binary objects and HTTP/TCP/IP unicast for interactivity services.

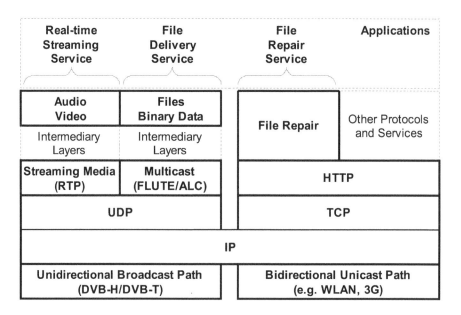

Fig. 5. IPDC content delivery protocols.

Blocking and Encapsulation

For the delivery of binary data objects using FLUTE/ALC/UDP/IP multicast, the procedure for splitting and encapsulating a binary data object for transmission via an IPDC/DVB-H system is basically as follows (ETSI, 2004; ETSI, 2006b). First, the binary object is split into source blocks and encoding symbols by a blocking algorithm as shown in figure 6. The algorithm used depends on the FEC mechanism used at the application layer. For the research done within this work (see section 4), no special application layer FEC (AL-FEC) mechanism was used[1]. Therefore, the binary object is simply split into several source blocks, with each source block consisting of several encoding symbols. The number of encoding symbols per block depends on the chosen encoding symbol size. Next, each symbol produced by the blocking algorithm is encapsulated in a FLUTE/UDP/IP packet and handed over to the MPE and MPEG-2 TS layers. Finally, if additional MPE-FEC is enabled, the procedures described in section 2.2 are applied.

---

[1] More specifically, this scheme is called the "compact no-code FEC scheme" or "null-FEC" (Watson, 2009).

3. IPDC file repair mechanism

IPDC is a general system for the distribution of arbitrary digital services to as many receivers as are within the coverage area. One specific service is the transmission of binary data objects, such as individual songs, which are to be received error-free. In this context the file repair mechanism, which is part of the IPDC specification, allows for the signalling of transmission errors from individual receivers to the sender. This section describes the technical details and procedures of this mechanism as well as the formulas for the calculation of financial retransmission costs due to multiple transmissions of data segments.

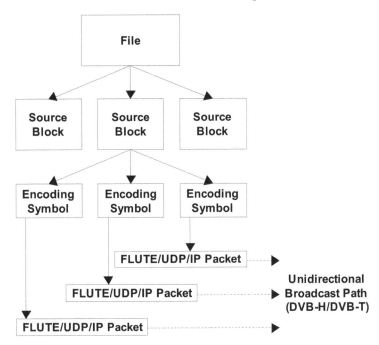

Fig. 6. Blocking and encapsulation.

3.1 File repair procedure

The IPDC file repair mechanism, specified in (DVB Project, 2009b), is part of IPDC's so-called associated delivery procedures (ADP). ADPs specify procedures for returning reception information (called "reception reporting procedures") and procedures for carrying out file repairs (called "post-repair procedures"). The former procedures are used for signalling the complete reception of one or more files as well as reporting some statistics about a streaming session. The latter ones are shortly called "file repair mechanism" and their basic purpose is the correction of lost or unrecoverable data segments of a file delivery or FLUTE session. One or more file repair servers accept file repair request messages from the receivers and either answer these requests directly via unicast 3G or WLAN connections (called "point-to-point" or ptp repair) or indirectly by repeating the requested segments via the IPDC/DVB-H broadcast infrastructure (called "point-to-multipoint" or ptm repair), thus delivering the requested repair data to all receivers once again.

The simplified basic procedure of the file repair mechanism is as follows (DVB Project, 2009b). First, a receiver identifies lost or unrecoverably erroneous data fragments or encoding symbols, respectively. Then, after the file transmission is finished, the receiver calculates a random time value called "back-off time". After the back-off time has expired, the receiver sends its file repair requests to the file repair server. Finally, the file repair server replies with a repair response message, which either contains the requested encoding symbols within a ptp repair session or the session description for the ptm repair session.

Concerning the transmission of file repair requests a time window is defined, which begins after the data session has ended. During this window the receivers send their requests at random times, represented by the individual back-off times of the single receivers. All file repair request messages should be transmitted within an HTTP 1.1 GET request (Fielding et al., 1999) to the file repair server via the bidirectional unicast interactivity path. If more than one GET request is necessary, they should be sent without intermediary waiting times. Erroneous data fragments are specified by their source block numbers (SBN) and encoding symbol IDs (ESI). In case of a ptp file repair session, all requested fragments are sent to the receivers via HTTP responses using the interactivity path. In case of a ptm file repair session, all requested fragments are sent via a FLUTE file delivery session based on IPDC/DVB-H.

Example of a File Repair Request Message

In the following example taken from (DVB Project, 2009b) and shown in figure 7, an HTTP GET message to the file repair service "ipdc_file_repair_service" at the server with the fully qualified domain name (FQDN) "www.repairserver.com"[2] is shown. This message represents a file repair request message concerning the binary data object "latest.3gp", which is a downloadable news video file hosted at the server with the FQDN "www.example.com". In this example, the receiver was not able to correctly receive two packets with SBN = 5, ESI = 12 and SBN = 20, ESI = 27. The corresponding MD5 message-digest algorithm (Rivest, 1992) value of the file is used to identify a specific version of the file.

```
GET    /ipdc_file_repair_service?fileURI=www.example.com/news/latest.3gp
       &Content-MD5=ODZiYTU1OTFkZGY2NWY5ODh==
       &SBN=5;ESI=12&SBN=20;ESI=27 HTTP/1.1
```

Fig. 7. Example of an IPDC file repair request message.

Example of a ptp Repair Response Message

In the following example adapted from (DVB Project, 2009c) and shown in figure 8, an HTTP response message from a file repair server is shown. The repair server uses a ptp repair strategy by directly answering the file repair request within the same HTTP session as the request. This HTTP response contains the two requested symbols in two separate groups.

---

[2] Therefore, the uniform resource locator (URL) of the service is "http://www.repairserver.com/ipdc_file_repair_service".

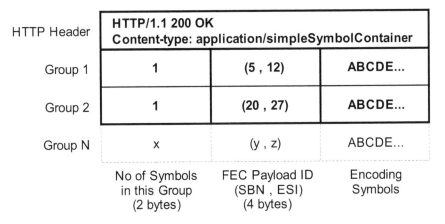

HTTP Header	HTTP/1.1 200 OK Content-type: application/simpleSymbolContainer		
Group 1	1	(5 , 12)	ABCDE...
Group 2	1	(20 , 27)	ABCDE...
Group N	x	(y , z)	ABCDE...
	No of Symbols in this Group (2 bytes)	FEC Payload ID (SBN , ESI) (4 bytes)	Encoding Symbols

Fig. 8. Example of an IPDC ptp file repair response message.

3.2 Cost calculation

Due to the two file repair strategies, different file repair costs may result. Costs may be declared regarding the transmission volume or bytes that result from retransmitted data segments or regarding financial costs that result from transmitting the repair data via the broadcast or interactive paths, respectively. After a file transmission is finished, a file repair server can calculate the expected ptp and ptm repair costs and therefore decide which file repair strategy to choose in order to minimize the repair costs. In case of a ptp repair session, only one repair round is normally sufficient for the receiver to correct all erroneous data segments. For ptm sessions, further rounds could be necessary until all receivers have received complete and error-free data. The cost estimation is done during the time window for file repair requests, which consists of a predefined, fixed value and a random part, the maximum back-off time. At a fraction of the maximum random part of the repair request window, defined by the parameter α, the file repair server executes the calculation of the expected costs, based on the repair requests received until this point in time. After the time window for file repair requests has expired, the actual cost of one round of a file repair session can be calculated.

Projected Financial Repair Costs

The projected financial repair costs of a ptp repair session are defined by formula (1), which is specified in (DVB Project, 2009b).
The following parameters are used:

- c_u defines the financial cost of the transmission of a single byte via the used ptp network
- N_{sym} specifies the expected number of requested symbols to repeat
- s_{sym} defines the average size of an encoding symbol in bytes
- N_{req} defines the expected number of repair request messages
- s_{req} specifies the average size of a repair request message in bytes

The expected numbers of repair requests (N_{req}) and requested symbols (N_{sym}) are calculated by dividing the numbers of repair requests (n_{req}) and requested symbols (n_{sym}) the repair server accepted until the time of the expected cost calculation (t) by α. This calculation is based on the assumption that the repair requests are uniformly randomly distributed over time.

$$C_{ptp(expected)} = c_u \cdot N_{sym} \cdot s_{sym} + c_u \cdot N_{req} \cdot s_{req} \tag{1}$$

Concerning a ptm repair session, it is assumed that the repair server conducts ptp repair until time t and then switches over to ptm repair mode. A service operator should further assume that the ptm repair session contains the whole file to achieve complete reception. Therefore, formula (2) taken from (DVB Project, 2009b) can be used for the calculation of the projected ptm financial repair costs.

The following additional parameters are used:
- c_m defines the cost of the transmission of a single byte via the used ptm network
- S defines the size of the whole file in bytes
- s_{an} specifies the size of a ptm repair session announcement in bytes

$$C_{ptm(expected)} = c_m \cdot (S + s_{an}) + c_u \cdot N_{req} \cdot s_{req} + c_u \cdot n_{sym} \cdot s_{sym} \tag{2}$$

Actual Financial Repair Costs

When the time window for file repair requests has expired, the total cost for one round of a file repair session can simply be calculated by using formulas (1) and (2) and replacing the estimated values for the number of repair requests (N_{req}) and the number of requested symbols (N_{sym}) therein by their actual values n_{req} and n_{sym} respectively.

4. Simulations of the IPDC file repair mechanism

The study shown in this section deals with a simulation framework developed to examine the IPDC file repair mechanism. More specifically, it is used to examine resulting financial ptp and ptm repair costs in different simulation scenarios. The research shown focuses on the broadcast transmission of time-uncritical binary data objects, such as applications, images, ring tones, songs, or other data using an existing IPDC/DVB-H infrastructure. These data objects need to be delivered lossless, therefore the transmission relies on the IPDC/DVB-H file repair mechanism. For the examination of different aspects of this file repair mechanism, a simulation framework has been developed. The framework is based on the open source simulation tool OMNeT++ (Varga, 2009) and implements current error models for the wireless transmission channel as well as additional forward error correction measures (MPE-FEC, see section 2.2). It supports the simulation of both ptp and ptm file repair sessions, which are basically depicted in section 3.1. The calculations of expected and actual financial file repair costs are based on the formulas specified in (DVB Project, 2009b) and described in section 3.2.

The most important research questions of the study concerning the transmission of a single file to a varying number of receivers were:
- What are the financial file repair costs of both ptp and ptm repair sessions?
- What are the effects of different MPE-FEC frame sizes on the repair costs?
- What are the influences of different encoding symbol sizes on the repair costs?

In the context of this study, the costs for the first rounds of file repair sessions are compared. For ptp repair sessions, one round should be sufficient because each receiver gets its individual repair data from the repair server via an individual bidirectional connection. For ptm sessions, further rounds could be necessary until all receivers have received complete and error-free data.

4.1 Simulation topology

Figure 9 shows the general topology used for conducting the simulations. The component *Sender* represents the IPDC/DVB-H sender, which broadcasts binary data objects to the receivers. The broadcast transmission is represented by the component *PacketBroadcast*. This component simply replicates a packet sent by the sender for each receiver. The component *Receiver* incorporates the error model for the transmission channel and the optional MPE FEC error correction (see section 2.2). In this example, two receivers send file repair requests to the component *FileRepairServer* which receives file repair requests from the receivers and conducts cost calculations (see section 3.2).

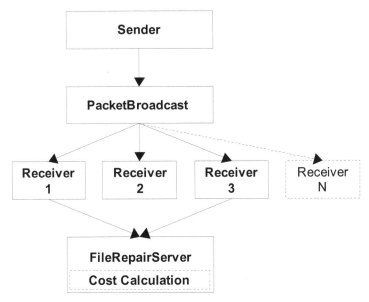

Fig. 9. Simulation topology.

The following parameters can be set for the component *Sender*: size of the data object to be transmitted (file size), size of an encoding symbol (each encoding symbol is the payload of a FLUTE packet), number of encoding symbols per source block, sum of additional protocol overheads (FLUTE/ALC, UDP, IP), and MPEG-2 TS data rate.

The component *Receiver* allows the configuration of the following parameters: file size, encoding symbol length, number of encoding symbols per source block, number of rows of the MPE-FEC frame (optional), DVB-T transmission mode (2K, 4K or 8K), minimal distance from sender in km, offset time and random time period for sending file repair requests after the transmission is finished.

Figure 10 shows the most important parts of the component *Receiver* in more detail. Each encoding symbol is transported within a FLUTE packet, which itself is mapped to TS packets of the used MPEG-2 TS. The error model described below is applied to the received stream of TS packets. Depending on the states of the error model, this results in no or several erroneous TS packets. If MPE-FEC is used, some or all of these erroneous TS packets can be recovered. Unrecoverable encoding symbols are listed in the table of erroneous symbols and can be requested at the file repair server after the transmission of the file is finished.

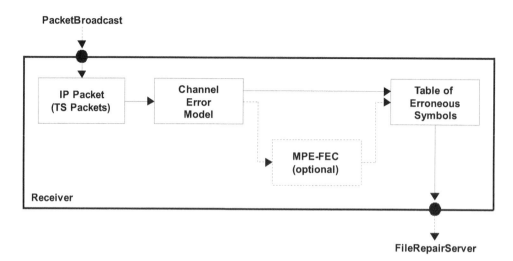

Fig. 10. Details of the component Receiver.

The following parameters can be set for the component *FileRepairServer*: number of receivers, cost for the transmission of a single byte via the ptp network, cost for the transmission of a single byte via the ptm network, offset time and maximum back-off time for receiving file repair requests after the transmission is finished, fraction of the maximum back-off time for the calculation of estimated repair costs (α), file size, average symbol size, average size of a file repair request, size of a ptm repair session announcement, estimated success rate for a receiver using a ptm repair session, and fraction of receivers without a ptp connection.

Error Model of the Transmission Channel

To simulate erroneous data segments, an error model had to be implemented into the transmission system of the simulation framework. The error model used is based on the so-called four-state run length model described in (Poikonen & Paavola, 2006) and (Poikonen & Paavola, 2005). This model operates on the resulting MPEG-2 transport stream of the DVB-T data transmission (see section 2.2) and produces streams of erroneous TS packets by using the four states *Good (short)*, *Bad (short)*, *Good (long)* and *Bad (long)*. If the model is in the states *Bad (short)* or *Bad (long)*, erroneous TS packets are generated, and if the model operates in the other two states, correct TS packets are produced.

According to the state diagram of this model (Poikonen & Paavola, 2006), the probabilities for remaining in a state denoted as *long* are very high. Therefore, whenever the error model switches over to one of these states, it will remain there for a rather long period of time compared to the states denoted as *short*, leading to long sequences of erroneous or error-free TS packets. With these settings, the model has shown to produce a good approximation to error streams measured using the COST 207 Six-tap Typical Urban (TU6) multi-path channel model (COST, 1989). See (Poikonen & Paavola, 2006) for a comparison.

Modified ptm Repair Cost Formula

For the simulations done within this study, a modified formula (3) for the calculation of the ptm repair costs (see section 3.2) was used. This formula focuses on the characteristic that only distinctive erroneous symbols have to be retransmitted in a ptm repair session instead of the whole file as specified in the original formula for ptm sessions in (DVB Project, 2009b). Therefore, the parameter n_{dsym} denotes the number of distinctive requested symbols. For the calculation of the actual financial ptm repair costs, the estimated value for the number of repair requests (N_{req}) is replaced by the actual value denoted by n_{req}.

$$C_{ptm(expected)} = c_m \cdot s_{an} + c_u \cdot N_{req} \cdot s_{req} + c_m \cdot n_{dsym} \cdot s_{sym} \qquad (3)$$

Simulation Parameters

For all simulations done within this study, the size of the transmitted object (file size) was 4 MB. This is for example the typical size of an MPEG-1 audio layer 3 (MP3) encoded sound file. MPE-FEC either was disabled or enabled, using 256, 512 or 1024 rows for the corresponding MPE-FEC frames. With these settings, it was possible to compare the effectiveness of different MPE-FEC settings with regard to the resulting number of repair requests and therefore with regard to the resulting transmission overheads and repair costs. The size of an encoding symbol either was 100 bytes, 500 bytes or 1400 bytes. This allowed for the comparison of the effects of very small, medium-sized, and large FLUTE packets on the effective repair costs. The cost for the transmission of a single byte via the ptm network was based on the pricing published by an Austrian DVB-H provider which bills EUR 39700 excluding 20% value added tax (VAT) per 100 kbps stream per year[3] for nationwide coverage. This is equivalent to EUR $1.225 \cdot 10^{-7}$ per byte. The cost for the transmission of a single byte via the ptp network was based on the pricing published by an Austrian mobile network operator that bills EUR 10 including 20% VAT per 1 GB per month[4] for nationwide coverage. This equates to EUR $1 \cdot 10^{-8}$ per byte. After one-third of the time window for repair requests, the calculation of the projected repair costs was done by the file repair server. Other parameters, e.g. concerning values for the DVB transmission mode and TS data rate were set to typical, technical parameters of current DVB-H trial services (DVB Project, 2009a) or according to examples in (DVB Project, 2009b) and (DVB Project, 2009c).

4.2 Simulation results

Figure 11 shows the financial repair costs for a transmitted file of size 4 MB without MPE-FEC for up to 1000 receivers. Whereas the costs for ptp sessions rise almost linearly with the number of receivers, the costs for ptm sessions quickly converge to a maximum. This maximum represents the correction of the whole file. These different behaviors are due to the fact that in a ptp repair session each requested symbol has to be transmitted to the requester individually, whereas in a ptm session only distinctive requested symbols are repeated, independent of the number of different requests for one and the same symbol.

Figure 12 shows the file repair efficiencies of the ptp and ptm repair sessions for up to 5000 receivers. The file repair efficiency is defined in (DVB Project, 2009b) as the number of receivers with successful recovery divided by the cost of the transmission of repair data. For ptp sessions, the number of receivers with successful reception is given by the total number of receivers, because it is assumed that all receivers will be successful. For ptm sessions, it is

---

[3] http://www.ors.at/bekanntmachungen/301.pdf (18.06.2009)
[4] http://www.a1.net/privat/breitband (18.06.2009)

assumed that there will be a fraction of the receivers that are still not able to recover the file after the first round of the ptm repair session. In the simulations done, it is assumed that 90 % of the receivers will be able to recover the file after the first round of the ptm session. Due to the fact that the ptm repair costs are independent of the number of receivers, ptm sessions result in higher efficiencies, especially when there are many receivers.

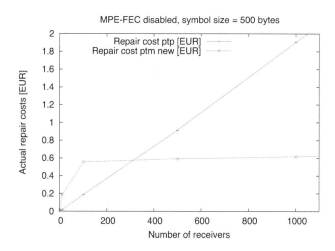

Fig. 11. File repair costs without MPE-FEC.

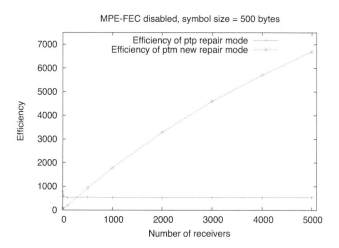

Fig. 12. Efficiencies of the different file repair methods.

Figure 13 compares the expected and actual file repair costs for ptp and ptm repair sessions without MPE-FEC. It can be seen that the expected costs are very close to the final costs, although the calculation of the expected costs was done at only one-third of the repair request window ($\alpha = 0.33$).

The results of the simulations which explore the impact of MPE-FEC for additional forward error correction are shown in figures 14 and 15. Figure 14 compares the resulting amount of necessary repair data for ptp repair sessions depending on the used MPE-FEC frame size. As can be seen clearly, the bigger the MPE-FEC frame size, the lower the amount of erroneous data. This is due to the fact that the probability of being able to recover a single IP packet is higher when the MPE-FEC consists of more rows, because the shorter the frame the higher the probability that an IP packet spans several columns.

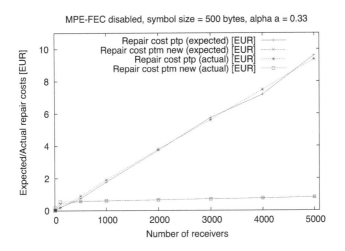

Fig. 13. Expected vs. actual file repair costs.

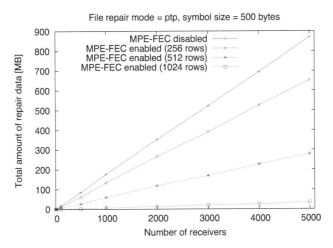

Fig. 14. Effects of MPE-FEC on ptp repair.

Concerning ptm sessions, the amount of repair data converges to the file size including protocol overheads. The bigger the used MPE-FEC frames, the more slowly this convergence happens (see figure 15).

Figure 16 compares the ptp and ptm repair costs for the two cases of disabled and enabled MPE-FEC. As can be seen, ptp can outperform ptm, when MPE-FEC is used with the maximum MPE-FEC frame size due to ptp's lower transmission cost per byte.

Figures 17 and 18 show the comparison of ptp and ptm repair costs using maximum MPE-FEC frame size and different symbol sizes. For ptp repairs, the usage of a symbol size of 500 bytes yields better results than using a bigger symbol size of 1400 bytes or a very small symbol size of only 100 bytes.

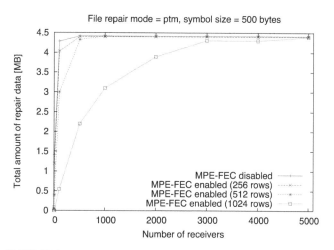

Fig. 15. Effects of MPE-FEC on ptm repair.

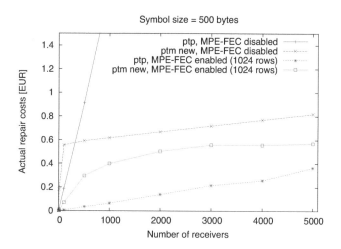

Fig. 16. File repair costs with/without MPE-FEC.

For large symbols, the probability of spanning several MPE-FEC frame columns is higher than for shorter symbols. As the number of bytes per row which can be corrected is limited by the used RS code, a symbol contained in only one column can more likely be corrected than a symbol distributed over several columns. Very small symbols have a misbalanced ratio between protocol headers and payload. Each symbol is prefixed with 52 bytes of FLUTE/UDP/IP encapsulation overheads. Therefore, very small symbol sizes intrinsically result in increased repair costs per user data.

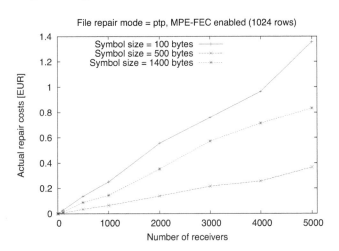

Fig. 17. Effects of encoding symbol size on ptp repair costs.

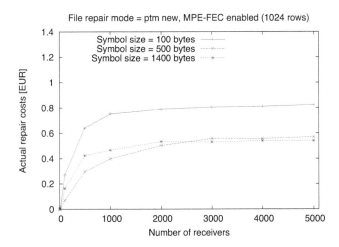

Fig. 18. Effects of encoding symbol size on ptm repair costs.

The results depicted in figure 18 dealing with ptm repairs show once again the negative effects of very small symbol sizes. As the amount of repair data for this repair mode converges to the file size, the symbol size with the most efficient payload/header ratio produces the lowest repair costs if a large number of receivers is considered. Summing up the results of both figures, the usage of medium-sized symbols is recommended.

5. Conclusions

IP datacast over DVB-H is one possible technical system to deliver mobile multimedia services, which are gaining more and more importance. This chapter gave an overview of the different digital video broadcasting transmission systems, including DVB-H and IP datacast. An IPDC/DVB-H infrastructure can provide different services, such as real-time streaming services for mobile TV or file delivery services for the distribution of arbitrary files to all receivers within the service area. Concerning the latter services, a file repair mechanism was specified for enabling the retransmission of data segments which were received erroneous at the receivers. In order to understand the technical details of the file repair mechanism and its technical context, the relevant building blocks and protocols were described in detail within the chapter.

A considerable part of the chapter deals with a simulation study to examine the financial costs of file repair sessions based on IPDC's file repair mechanism. This examination was done using a simulation framework, which incorporates the basic IPDC/DVB-H transmission and file repair procedures as well as a current error model concerning the DVB-H transmission channel. Simulations concerning the transmission of a file to a variable number of receivers with varying values for several critical parameters such as the use of MPE-FEC for error correction, the size of MPE-FEC frames, or the size of encoding symbols were executed. Three of the most important results of the simulations are as follows. First, the file repair costs of ptp repair sessions rise (almost) linearly with the number of receivers, whereas the file repair costs of ptm repair sessions rapidly converge to the costs of retransmitting the whole file. For a high number of receivers and without MPE-FEC for additional error correction, ptp repair costs are considerably higher than ptm repair costs. Second, MPE-FEC can drastically reduce the amount of repair data necessary for data recovery, especially concerning ptp repair sessions. The bigger the used MPE-FEC frame, the lower the rising of the file repair costs, especially concerning ptp repair sessions. The biggest MPE-FEC frame size (1024 rows) provides the best results. Depending on the number of receivers, the ptp repair mode can outperform the ptm repair mode, if MPE-FEC is used. Third, the size of the encoding symbols has a strong impact on the repair costs. Neither very big symbols nor very small symbols lead to optimal results. It is recommended to use medium-sized symbols of about 500 bytes.

6. References

COST (1989). *Digital land mobile radio communications*, Commission of the European Communities

DVB Project (2009a). *DVB-H: Global Mobile TV*, online, accessed 18th June 2009. Available at http://dvb-h.org/

DVB Project (2009b). *IP Datacast over DVB-H: Content Delivery Protocols (CDP)*, DVB BlueBook A101 Rev.1. Available at http://dvb-h.org/

DVB Project (2009c). *Digital Video Broadcasting (DVB); IP Datacast over DVB-H: Content Delivery Protocols (CDP) Implementation Guidelines*, DVB BlueBook A113 Rev.1. Available at http://dvb-h.org/

DVB Project Office (2008a). *2nd Generation Satellite – DVB-S2 (DVB Fact Sheet)*. Available at http://www.dvb.org/technology/fact_sheets/

DVB Project Office (2008b). *Internet Protocol Datacast – DVB-IPDC (DVB Fact Sheet)*. Available at http://www.dvb.org/technology/fact_sheets/

DVB Project Office (2009a). *Introduction to the DVB Project (DVB Fact Sheet)*. Available at http://www.dvb.org/technology/fact_sheets/

DVB Project Office (2009b). *2nd Generation Cable – DVB-C2 (DVB Fact Sheet)*. Available at http://www.dvb.org/technology/fact_sheets/

DVB Project Office (2009c). *Digital Terrestrial Television – DVB-T (DVB Fact Sheet)*. Available at http://www.dvb.org/technology/fact_sheets/

DVB Project Office (2009d). *2nd Generation Terrestrial – DVB-T2 (DVB Fact Sheet)*. Available at http://www.dvb.org/technology/fact_sheets/

DVB Project Office (2009e). *Broadcasting to Handhelds – DVB-H (DVB Fact Sheet)*. Available at http://www.dvb.org/technology/fact_sheets/

DVB Project Office (2009f). *Satellite Services to Handhelds – DVB-SH (DVB Fact Sheet)*. Available at http://www.dvb.org/technology/fact_sheets/

ETSI (2004). *Digital Video Broadcasting (DVB); Transmission System for Handheld Terminals (DVB-H)*, ETSI EN 302 304 V1.1.1

ETSI (2006a). *Digital Video Broadcasting (DVB); IP Datacast over DVB-H: Architecture*, ETSI TR 102 469 V1.1.1

ETSI (2006b). *Digital Video Broadcasting (DVB); IP Datacast over DVB-H: Content Delivery Protocols*, ETSI TS 102 472 V1.2.1

ETSI (2009a). *Digital Video Broadcasting (DVB); Framing structure, channel coding and modulation for digital terrestrial television*, ETSI EN 300 744 V1.6.1

ETSI (2009b). *Digital Video Broadcasting (DVB); DVB-H Implementation Guidelines*, ETSI TR 102 377 V1.3.1

Faria, G. et al. (2006). DVB-H: Digital Broadcast Services to Handheld Devices. *Proc. IEEE*, Vol. 94, No. 1, pp. 194-209

Fielding, R. et al. (1999). *Hypertext Transfer Protocol -- HTTP/1.1*, IETF RFC 2616, The Internet Society

ISO/IEC (2007). *Information technology -- Generic coding of moving pictures and associated audio information: Systems*, ISO/IEC 13818-1:2007

Luby, M. et al. (2002). *Asynchron Layered Coding (ALC) Protocol Instantiation*, IETF RFC 3450, The Internet Society

Paila, T. et al. (2004). *FLUTE - File Delivery over Unidirectional Transport*, IETF RFC 3926, The Internet Society

Poikonen, J. & Paavola, J. (2005). *Comparison of Finite-State Models for Simulating the DVB-H Link Layer Performance*, Technical Report, University of Turku

Poikonen, J. & Paavola, J. (2006). Error Models for the Transport Stream Packet Channel in the DVB-H Link Layer. In: *Proceedings of the IEEE International Conference on Communications 2006 (ICC '06)*, Vol. 4, pp. 1861-1866

Postel, J. (1981). *Internet Protocol*, IETF RFC 791, USC/Information Sciences Institute

Reimers, U. (2005). *DVB – The Family of International Standards for Digital Video Broadcasting*, Springer, Berlin Heidelberg New York

Rivest, R. (1992). *The MD5 Message-Digest Algorithm*, IETF RFC 1321, MIT Laboratory for Computer Science and RSA Data Security, Inc.

Schulzrinne, H. et al. (2003). *RTP: A Transport Protocol for Real-Time Applications*, IETF RFC 3550, The Internet Society

Varga, A. (2009). *OMNeT++ Community Site,* online, accessed 18th June 2009. Available at: http://www.omnetpp.org/

Watson, M. (2009). *Basic Forward Error Correction (FEC) Schemes*, IETF RFC 5445, IETF Trust

2

Trick Play on Audiovisual Information for Tape, Disk and Solid-State Based Digital Recording Systems

O. Eerenberg and P.H.N. de With
NXP Semiconductors Research, CycloMedia
Technology /Eindhoven University of Technology
The Netherlands

1. Introduction

Digital video for consumer applications became available in the early 1990s, enabled by the advances in video compression techniques and associated standards and their efficient implementation in integrated circuits. Convergence of transform coding and motion compensation into a single hybrid coding scheme, resulting in various standards in the early 1990s, such as MPEG-1 (ISO/IEC11172-2, 1993), MPEG-2 (ISO/IEC13818-2, 2000) and DV (CEI/IEC61834, 1993). These standards are capable of compressing video at different quality levels with modest up to high compression ratios and differing complexity. Each of the previous standards has been deployed in a digital storage system, based on different storage media.

The above hybrid coding schemes, distinguish intraframe and interframe coded pictures. The former, also labelled as I-type pictures, can be independently decoded so that it can be used for video navigation. The latter coding form result in P-type and B-type pictures requiring surrounding reference pictures for reconstruction. The availability of these reference pictures cannot be guaranteed during fast-search trick play, which makes these pictures unsuitable for certain navigation functions. Digital consumer storage standards are equipped with locator information facilitating fast-search trick play. The locator information considers the data dependencies and enables the system entry points for proper decoding. These mechanisms form the basis for selectively addressing coded data and the associated data retrieval during trick play.

This chapter discusses trick play for push- and pull-based architectures and elaborates on their implementation for tape, optical and disk-based storage systems. Section 2 introduces traditional and advanced video navigation. Section 3 presents the concepts of low-cost trick play. Section 4 elaborates on trick play for tape-based helical-scan digital video recording. Section 5 discusses trick play in relation with three popular optical-storage systems. Section 6 introduces trick play for push- or pull-based personal video recording deploying a hard-disk drive or solid-state disc. The chapter concludes and presents a future outlook in Section 7.

2. Navigation methods

Video navigation is defined as video playback in non-consecutive or non-chronological order as compared to the original capturing order. Video navigation can be divided into traditional fast forward or fast rewind playback and advanced search methods, which are modern forms of video navigation. The former is found in analogue and digital video recorders. The latter has become possible for random accessible media such as disc and silicon-based memories. This section covers the basic aspects of traditional video navigation and presents two forms of advanced video navigation. The navigation methods are presented without implementation aspects. Implementation aspects will be discussed in consecutive sections addressing tape, optical disk, silicon-based storage solutions.

2.1 Traditional video navigation

For traditional video navigation a distinction is made between fast search and slow search mode, also known as trick play. Let Ps be the relative playback speed, which is unity for normal play, then fast-search trick play is obtained for $Ps > 1$ and slow-motion trick play for $Ps < 1$. Although this is a firm seperation between fast search and slow motion, there is an overlapping area for playback speeds in the vicinity $L_b < Ps < U_b$ of normal play.

Fast-search video navigation is characterized in the sense that the pictures forming the trick-play sequence are derived from the normal-play sequence by applying a temporal equidistant sub-sampling factor, which corresponds to the intended playback speed Ps. In practice, Ps is limited but not restricted to integer values.

Slow-motion search is obtained by repetitive display of each normal-play picture. The amount of repetitions is equal to the reciprocal of Ps. Again, practical values for Ps are limited but not restricted to integer values. Although the basic operation to obtain slow motion has low costs, a distinction is made between slow motion on progressive video and interlaced video. When video originates from an interlaced video source, repetition of an interlaced picture may result in motion judder. Such a situation occurs when the spatial area contains an object that is subject to motion between the capture time of the odd and even field, forming a single frame picure. Repetition of such an interlaced picture causes the object repetetively traveling along the trajectory, which is perceived by the viewer as motion judder (van Gassel et al., 2002).

The above solutions for trick play are based solely on using resampled video information. For playback speeds in the vicinity of unity, there is an alternative implementation for trick play, that builds on also re-using the normal play audio information. For this situation, time-scaled normal-play audio information is used to create an audiovisual trick-play sequence. To maintain audibility of the time-scaled audio information, pitch control is required. The playback speeds Ps that can be used for this type of trick play depend heavily on aspects of the normal play sequence such as speed of the oral information and the algorithm used for processing the audio signal. Algorithms for time- and pitch-scaling can be divided into frequency-domain and time-domain methods. Good results are obtained using Pointer Interval Controlled OverLap and Add (PICOLA) (ISO/IEC 14496-3, 1999), an algorithm that operates in the time-domain on mono-channel audio signals for playback speeds in the range $0.8 \le Ps \le 1.5$ for audiovisual content with spoken text. This form of trick play indicates that Ps does not need to be limited to integer-based values.

2.2 Advanced video navigation

Traditional video navigation methods are adequate for navigation in video sequences with a duration of a few minutes. Navigation becomes already a daunting task when a two-hour movie is searched for a particular scene. Increasing the playback speed Ps up to a factor 50 or even higher, does not result in a better navigation performance. There is a twofold reason for this. First, at high playback speeds, pictures forming the trick-play video sequence are less correlated. As a result, it is difficult for the viewer to interpret each individual picture. Lowering the refresh rate by a factor three, which means that each picture is rendered three times and maintaining the playback speed Ps, results in an increment of the normal-play temporal sub-sampling factor, thereby effectively tripling Ps. For example, if Ps is equal to 50, this value will be scaled to 150. A typical scene duration lasts 3–4 seconds. With a Ps of 150, the trick-play sequence may not contain information of all scenes, which makes this approach less suitable for fast search. A more effective method to navigate through hours of video is *hierarchical* navigation, which is based on the usage of mosaic screens to obtain an instant overview of a certain time interval (Eerenberg & de With, 2003). When descending the hierarchy, the mosaic screens contain images that correspond to a smaller time interval, increasing the temporal resolution. Images used for the mosaic screen construction can be either based on a fixed temporal sub-sampling factor, or based on the outcome of a certain filter e.g. a scene-change detection filter. Mosaic screens based on fixed temporal sub-sampling, results in selection of normal-play pictures that in traditional video navigation are used to create a trick-play video sequence. When using these pictures for hierarchical navigation, the navigation efficiency (presence of many similar sub-pictures) of the lowest hierarchical layer depends on the applied temporal sub-sample factor. The usage of scene-change algorithms results in the selection of normal-play pictures that are effective from information point of view. This becomes apparent when only a single picture of a scene is used for construction of a mosaic screen, avoiding the navigation efficiency problem of equidistant temporal sub-sampling.

Hierarchical video navigation forms a good extension on traditional video navigation, but involves user interaction for browsing through the individual mosaic screens. Another advanced video navigation method which minimizes user interaction, is obtained when combining normal-play audiovisual information and fast-search video trick-play (Eerenberg et al., 2008). Time- and pitch scaling of audio information to create an audiovisual navigation sequence is only effective for trick-play speeds about unity, as indicated in Section 2.1. Although the human auditory system is a powerful sensory system, concatenation of normal-play audio samples corresponding to the time interval of a picture selected for fast-search trick play, is not an effective approach. The auditory system requires depending on the audio type, e.g. speech or music, hundreds of milliseconds of consecutive audio to become effective with respect to interpretation of the received audio signal. Based on this observation, an audiovisual trick-play method is proposed, in which normal-play audiovisual fragments are combined with fast-search video, resulting in a double window video with corresponding audio. The strength of this navigation method is that the viewer is not only provided with a course overview of the stored video information via the fast-search video trick-play sequence. Additonally, the viewer is also provided with detailed audiovisual information via the normal-play fragments. The duration of the normal-play fragments can be freely chosen obeying the minimal duration required by the auditory system to recognize well-known audio content or interpret new audio information. For the former situation, an audio fragment duration of about 1 second is suitable for recognition the origin of that particular fragment. For the latter situation, a longer duration is required leading to a practical value of 3 seconds.

3. Low-cost trick play

The basic principles of traditional trick play have been presented in Section 2. This section discusses low-cost trick play for fast search as well as slow motion in the context of the applied storage architecture. Section 3.1 will discuss two types of architectures. In digital consumer recording systems, trick play is a low-cost feature, resulting in the need for simple high-efficient signal processing algorithms fulfilling the cost requirement. Low-cost trick play is in general characterized by signal processing in the compressed domain, avoiding expensive transcoding. This involves selection and manipulation of coded pictures, which is covered in succeeding sections.

3.1 Impact of pull and push-based architectures on trick play

The chosen architecture of the storage system influences the involved trick-play signal processing. A digital storage system can have either a pull- or a push-based architecture. In a pull-based architecture, the video decoder pulls the data from the storage medium, whereas in a push-based architecture the video decoder receives the audiovisual information at a certain rate. For traditional trick play, there is a difference in performance due to the different architectures. Moreover, a push-based architecture allows two approaches. The first approach is based on a solution provided by the MPEG-2 system standard (ISO/IEC13818-2, 2000). This involves trick-play signalling information provided by the Packetized Elementary Stream (PES) header. This information is used to control the output of the video decoder during trick play. The second solution applies signal processing in the compressed domain, avoiding the usage of previous MPEG-2 system signalling information (van Gassel et al., 2002). Although the first solution is described by MPEG-2, its usage is optional and not obligatory (ETSI_TS_101154, 2009). The second solution is a generic approach, which delivers a compliant MPEG-2 video stream. This makes it an attractive solution from the video decoder point of view.

3.2 Influence of video encoding parameters on trick play

Modern compression schemes such as MPEG-2 or H.264, achieve high compression ratios by exploiting spatial and temporal correlation in the video signal. Compression of pictures exploiting only spatial information are intraframe compressed, whereas pictures that exploit temporal correlation are interframe compressed. The latter can be split in two categories: uni-directional (P-type) and bi-directional (B-type) predictive pictures. In a compressed video sequence, the distance between two successive intraframe compressed pictures is expressed by N, which is also known as the Group-Of-Pictures (GOP) length, whereas the distance between P-type predictive pictures is expressed by M. For the situation that $M>1$, the number of B-type pictures preceding a P-picture is equal to $M-1$. For the common situation that N is an integer multiple of M, the construction of trick play sequences in simplified because P-pictures are a sub-integer fraction of the GOP length N.

In general, trick play for digital consumer storage equipment is a low-cost feature, which limits the amount of involved signal processing. Low-cost trick-play algorithms deploy pictures that are selected from the compressed normal-play sequence. For fast-search trick play, the minimum fast-forward search speed is equal to M, whereas other fast-forward speeds are obtained for speed-up factors equal to N, or an integer multiple of N. Note that there is basically a gap between speed-up factor M and N if $N \gg M$. This gap is caused by the fact that

P-type pictures can only be decoded if the reference (anchor) picture has been decoded. For typical video compression applications such as Digital Video Broadcast (DVB), or digital recording, the GOP size $N=12$ and P-picture distance $M=3$, resulting in fast-search speed-up factors $Ps=\{ 3, 12, 24, ..., 12n \}$, with $n=\{1, 2, 3... \}$. Fast-search trick play in reverse direction is obtained in a similar way, but for a speed-up factor equal to M, buffering is required to store the decompressed pictures to facilitate reordering. This is required to match (potential) motion with the reverse playback direction, as the decoding is always performed in the positive time direction. This forward decoding direction introduces an extra delay, which occurs only once when switching to the reverse search mode with speed-up factor equal to M.

From the concept point of view, trick play in the compressed domain is equal for push or pull-based architecture. However, from a compliancy point of view, they are different. In a pull-based architecture, the decoder retrieves either fragments containing the intended intraframe compressed pictures, or the whole compressed video sequence at a higher rate. For either case, there will most probably be a frame-rate and bit-rate violation. From trick-play point of view, a high quality is perceived by the viewer both for low and high search speeds.

For push-based architectures, fast-search trick play based on concatenation of normal-play intraframe compressed pictures may cause a bit-rate violation. A low-cost method to overcome this bit-rate violation is the usage of repetition pictures, i.e. interframe compressed pictures, of which the decoded result is identical to the reference image (anchor picture), which is the last transmitted intraframe or P-type interframe picture, see Fig. 1. A repetition picture precedes the transmission of an intraframe coded picture. Multiple repetition pictures are involved when the transmission time exceeds two or more display periods, where one display period is equal to the reciprocal of the frame rate. For the situation that the normal-play video is MPEG-2 coded, a repetition picture has an extreme small size of 342 Bytes for a picture size 720×576 and 4:2:0 sampling format. The transmission time for such a compressed picture is negligible compared to the display period, leaving the remaining time for transmission of intraframe compressed data. This concept introduces fast-search trick play with a reduced refresh rate, so that the frame rate is not jeopardized. This concept yields a proper result for progressive as well as interlaced video, although motion judder may be introduced for interlaced video. Motion judder is avoided when the two fields that form the repetition pictures are field-based coded, where

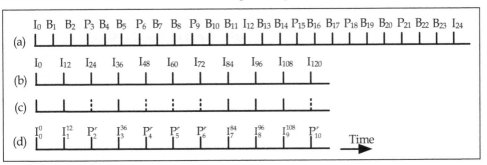

Fig. 1. Low-cost MPEG-compliant fast-search trick play. (a) Normal play compressed pictures with absolute picture index, (b) Intraframe compressed normal-play pictures, (c) Sub-sampling of the normal-play sequence, using a speed-up factor of 12, where the dashed lines indicate the skipped pictures, (d) MPEG-compliant trick play for speed-up factor 12 equipped with repetition pictures to avoid bit-rate violation.

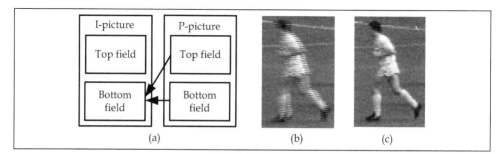

Fig. 2. Effect of "interlace kill". (a) Predictive picture causing top and bottom field to have equal content. (b) Snapshot of I-picture region constructed of two fields from different time instances. (c) Snapshot of the same region after applying the "interlace kill" feature.

both fields refer to the same reference field, resulting in an "interlace- kill" operation see Fig. 2 (van Gassel et al., 2002). In this operation, one field is removed and replaced by the remaining field.

The reference field depends on the search direction and is bottom field for forward and top field for the reverse search direction. The result of the required decoding operation is that after decoding, both fields are equal, eliminating the possibility of motion portrayal. Using the MPEG-2 coding format, the bit cost for such a predictive-field coded picture is 954 Bytes, with a picture size of 720×288 pixels and 4:2:0 sampling format. The coding of two involved field pictures results in a total of 1,944 Bytes, including the required picture header and corresponding extension header.

3.3 Slow-motion for push-based storage systems

Slow-motion trick play is based on repetitive display of a picture. The number of display periods that a normal-play picture is displayed, is defined by Eqn. (1), where D_p indicates the number of display repetitions and Ps the slow-motion speed factor, giving

$$D_p = \frac{1}{Ps}. \tag{1}$$

Also here, there is a difference between push- and pull-based architectures. In a pull-based architecture, the video decoder outputs the decoded image data D_p times. In a push-based architecture, a slow-motion sequence is derived on the basis of the normal-play compressed video sequence. The slow motion operation requires that newly created display periods, are filled up with the repetition of normal-play pictures. For progressive video, all newly created frame periods are inserted after each original frame. Repetition of normal-play I-type and P-type pictures is achieved by uni-directional coded B-type repetition pictures. Any normal play B-type picture is repeated via repetitive transmission and decoding of the original B-picture. Special attention is required for the repetition of normal-play anchor pictures when they are originating from an interlaced video source. To avoid corruption of the decoder reference pictures, only uni-directional B-type coded "interlace-kill" pictures can be used for repetition of the normal-play anchor pictures, as they do not modify the anchor picture memory.

Anchor pictures maintaining their proper content is a basic requirement for the slow-motion decoding process, as each predictive-coded normal-play picture may use reference data from two or more fields. The basic problem is that an "interlace-kill" operation can only be applied to the anchor pictures, which are intraframe or P-type predictive normal-play pictures. There is no low-cost algorithm for removing interlacing to process the B-type coded pictures, when they are frame-based coded. For the situation that B-type pictures are field based, only one field out of two B-type field pictures is used. As a result, frame-based B-type coded pictures can only be used once, if the video originates from an interlaced source.

Slow motion results in $N \cdot D_p$ pictures per normal-play GOP. For the situation that the video originates from an interlaced video source, a display error D_e occurs as indicated in Eqn. (2), the display error per normal-play GOP. From Eqn. (2), it becomes clear that for $M=1$, which conforms to MPEG-2 simple profile, no display error occurs, as indicated by

$$D_e = N(D_p (1-\frac{1}{M})-(1-\frac{1}{M})). \tag{2}$$

In order to avoid a speed-error, normal-play anchor pictures which are displayed D_p times, must be displayed an additional A_r times, as specified in Eqn. (3), resulting in

$$A_r = D_p (M-1)-(M-1). \tag{3}$$

4. Digital tape-based helical-scan video recording

This section discusses Digital Video (DV) and Digital Video Home System (D-VHS), two tape-based Video Cassette Recording (VCR) standards developed in the 1990s. The DV standard differs from the D-VHS standard in the sense that video coding, on tape storage and trick play form an integral approach. The standardization of D-VHS followed a two-step approach. First, a basic recording engine was established capable of storing an MPEG-2 transport stream. In the second stage of the standardization process, trick play was added to this system. This section is divided in three sections. Section 4.1 discusses the impact of helical-scan recording on trick play. Section 4.2 elaborates on the DV trick-play solution. Finally, Section 4.3 presents trick play for the D-VHS STD mode.

4.1 Helical-scan video recording
Tape has been a popular storage medium for many decades due its good price/storage capacity ratio and the high capacity storage per volume unit. Tape-based video recorders apply helical-scan recording, where the magnetic heads are mounted on a rotary head wheel inside a cylindrical drum, and the tape is helically wrapped around it. Such a recording solution provides a large recording bandwidth, due to the fast rotation speed of the scanner and the relatively slow tape speed. This concept creates high-density recording with modest sized cassettes and sufficient playing time. The heads mounted on the rotary wheel have a different azimuth and write the information in slanted tracks on tape, resulting in a high track density, due to partial overlapped writing. Moreover, each track forms a fixed bit-rate channel, see Fig. 3 (a).

During playback, the heads with the proper azimuth scan the corresponding tracks on tape, a process that is controlled by the tracking servo. During normal play, see Fig 3 (b), all information that was recorded on tape is read from tape. A different situation arises for trick play. During fast-search trick play, the tape travels at a higher speed along the scanner. As a result, the heads that scan the tape, under control of the tracking servo, follow a different path when compared to normal play, see Fig 4 (a). The tracking servo controls the scanner scan-path via adaptation of the tape speed and allows for two concepts. The first concept is based on speed-lock. Here the heads scan the fast travelling tape, where there is no guarantee which head scans the tape at a particular moment. The second concept is phase-lock. In this concept, the scanner is positioned such that at the beginning of the scan path, the head with a particular azimuth scans the track with the corresponding azimuth. The impact of the different servo approaches has its influence on the available trick-play bit rate. For the situation that the more complex phase-lock servo system is deployed, there is no need for duplicating the trick-play data, which results in a higher available trick-play bit rate because the head starts at the track with the corresponding azimuth, see Fig. 4 (b). For the situation that a speed-lock servo system is used, trick-play data needs to be stored multiple times, such that it reads once during fast search, see Fig. 4 (c).

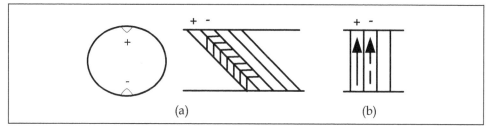

(a)   (b)

Fig. 3. Helical-scan recording. (a) Two-head scanner and corresponding azimuth tracks, (b) Simplified track diagram showing normal scan path, the non-dashed arrow indicates scan path of `+` head and dashed arrow indicates scan path of `-` head.

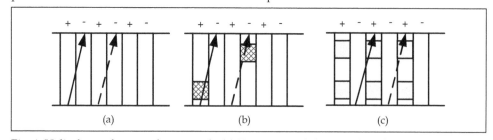

(a)   (b)   (c)

Fig. 4. Helical-scan fast search scan path. (a) Fast scan path for speed-up factor $Ps=2$, (b) Example of trick-play data location for phase-lock-based servo solution, (c) Example of trick-play data location for speed-lock-based servo solution.

The obtained trick-play quality is not only influenced by the applied servo system, but also by the applied video compression scheme. In the DV recording system, tape and compression related aspects have been combined, thereby facilitating trick play on the basis of re-using normal-play compressed video information. D-VHS is a recording system where storage part (bit engine) and compression have been separated, resulting in a trick-play solution that facilitates individual trick play (virtual) channels for various trick-play speed-up factors and their corresponding directions.

4.2 Trick play for digital video

The DV system (CEI/IEC61834, 1998) is a recording standard intended for 25-Hz (PAL) and 30-Hz (NTSC) television standards and was first announced in 1993 (Matsushita et al., 1993). The applied video compression was largely guided by system aspects such as editing on a picture basis, robustness for repetitive (de-)compression, number of tracks to store a compressed picture, very high forward and backward search on tape, overall robustness and high picture quality. In order to understand the DV trick-play mechanism, a brief system overview is presented, which introduces the essential aspects that enable trick play.

4.2.1 System architecture

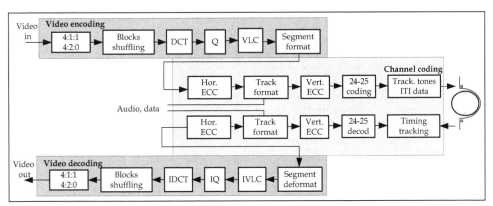

Fig. 5. Block diagram of complete processing of consumer DV recording system.

Figure 5 depicts the block diagram of the DV recording system. At the left-hand side, video enters the system and is compressed using a 4:2:0 sampling format for 25-Hz video or 4:1:1 sampling format in the case of 30-Hz video. Prior to compression, the video data is shuffled increasing the normal-play quality and enabling trick play. The compression is based on intraframe coding, using a Discrete Cosine Transform (DCT), and subsequent quantization and Variable-Length Coding (VLC) of the transformed video data. The compressed video or uncompressed audio data together with signalling information is packetized into Sync Blocks (SB), which are protected with parities from the Reed-Solomon-based horizontal forward error correction. To further improve the system robustness, a vertically-oriented error-correction layer is added, calculating parities over multiple SBs within a track, which are stored in dedicated parity SBs. Finally, the SBs are stored on tape using a highly efficient DC-free 24 -25 channel code with embedded tracking tones required for tracking purposes. For a 25-Hz frame rate, a picture is stored using 12 consecutive tracks or 10 tracks for a 30-Hz frame rate.

4.2.2 DV video compression and sync block mapping

DV video compression is based on macroblocks (MB) constructed from luminance and chrominance DCT blocks, see Fig. 6. Each macroblock contains a full-color area of 256 pixels, where the physical dimensions differ between 32×8 rectangular (30 Hz) and 16×16 square for (25 Hz).

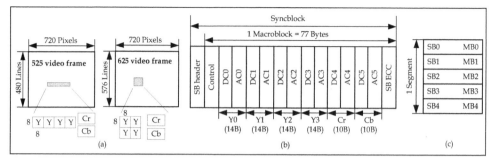

Fig. 6. DV Macroblocks. (a) Construction of macroblocks for 25-Hz and 30-Hz video, (b) SB data format showing fixed predetermined positions of low-frequent DCT coefficients, (c) Five pre-shuffled macroblocks forming a single segment.

The number of DCT blocks differ for a 25-Hz or 30-Hz system, but result in an equal number of 135 macroblocks per track (one MB per SB), which leads to a uniform recording concept that lowers the system costs. Segments are constructed from 5 pre-shuffled MBs, see Fig. 6 (c), to smoothen the coding performance and create a fixed bit cost per segment.

The compression of a segment is realized by applying a feedforward coding scheme, resulting, which high robustness and individual decodability of each segment. Although the segments are of fixed length, this does not mean that the macroblocks constructing the segment are also fixed-length coded. The optimal mapping of macroblocks on sync blocks is achieved when each macroblock is stored in a single sync block. This also enables the highest search speed (up to 100 times), due to individual decodability. By applying a fixed mapping, see Fig 6 (b) of the DCT low-frequency coefficients on a sync block, each sync block is individually decodable at the expense of a somewhat lower PSNR, due to the fact that some high-frequency coefficients may be carried by neigboring sync blocks belonging to the same segment.

The trick-play quality is determined by two factors: the trick play speed-up factor and the data shuffling. The system is designed such that the picture quality gradually deteriorates with increasing search speed. For very high search speeds (50-100 times), the reconstructed picture is based on individually decoded MBs, which are found in the individually retrieved SBs. In this mode, the vertical ECC cannot be deployed and therefore the decoder relies only on a very robust storage format where the low-frequency information of each DCT block is available on fixed positions inside the SB. For lower tape-speeds, larger consecutive portions of a track can be retrieved, so that full segments can be decoded in full quality and individual MB from partial segments. The shuffling is organized such that the quality is further increased in this playback mode. Figure 7 (b) depicts that consecutive segments contain MBs that are neighbors, which form a superblock resulting in a larger coherent spatial area from the same image. Hence, the lower the tape speed, the more neighboring MBs are successfully retrieved and the larger the coherent area that is constructed.

Figure 7 (a) depicts how the individual MBs of one segment are chosen. It can be seen that within one segment, MB data is sampling the full image both horizontally and vertically. This ensures a smoothening of the data statistics, enabling a fixed bit cost per segment. Moreover, the shaded area in the upper-left corner indicates a superblock with that is constructed from the neighboring MBs, deploying a pattern as depicted in Fig. 7 (b).

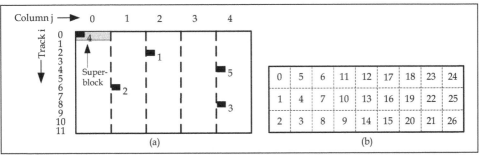

Fig. 7. DV tracks. (a) Selection of MBs for segment construction and assignment of picture areas on tracks, (b) Ordering of macroblocks in repetitive clusters, called superblocks.

4.3 Trick play for D-VHS STD mode format

D-VHS (ISO60774-5, 2004) is a tape-based recording system, following the push-based architecture and developed in two stages. The first stage covers the record and playback of MPEG-2 compressed normal-play information (Fujita et al., 1996), whereas the second stage addresses trick-play aspects. The D-VHS standard describes three recording modes, each intended for a specific data rate, resulting in a format for STanDard (STD) mode, Low-Speed (LS) mode and High-Speed (HS) mode. The first two recording modes share the same trick-play speed-up factors ±4, ±6, ±12 and ±24, whereas the HS recording mode supports the speed-up factors ±3, ±6 and ±12. This section describes high-end and low-cost trick-play signal processing for the STD mode format supporting speed-up factors ±4, ±12 and ±24.

4.3.1 Trick play based on information carried by a virtual channel

Trick play for the D-VHS STD mode assumes that the recording system deploys a phase-lock tracking servo (track select). The standard describes areas within the tracks, which are allocated for a particual trick-play speed-up factor for forward as well as reverse playback direction. These trick-play regions form a pattern, which is repetitive modulo 48 tracks, see Fig. 8. For a particular playback direction, i.e. forward or reverse, the trick-play regions corresponding to a particular trick-play speed-up factor, form a virtual information channel. This channel is only present during fast search at a particular speed-up factor and corrsponding direction. During record, a track is filled with 336 sync blocks, see Fig. 9 (b), which are data units of 112 Bytes. Each Sync Block (SB) consists of synchronization information, main data area and inner parity based on a Reed-Solomon forward error correction, see Fig. 9 (a). Two main data areas store a time-stamped TS packet, which is constructed of a 4-Byte header containing the time stamp and a single TS packet of 188 Bytes. The physical storage position depends on the SB number and corresponding time stamp value.

Each SB, regardless whether it contains normal-play or trick-play data, is protected by means of inner parity. The corresponding inner parity is stored at the last Byte positions of a SB. To increase the playback robustness, a second Reed-Solomon forward error correction is applied. The corresponding parity data (outer parity) are stored in the last SBs of a track. The usage of outer parity information for trick play is optional. In a push-based architecture, the isochrone nature of the stored audiovisual information is reconstructed at playback with the aid of time stamps. Time stamping is a method that captures the position of an MPEG-2

Transprt Stream (TS) packet on the time axis. At playback, the time stamp is used to position the TS packet at the proper time location. This reconstructs the isochrone behavior of the TS sequence, which enables the usage of an external MPEG-2 decoder connected via a digital interface (IEC61883-4, 1994). Time stamping in D-VHS, is based on a more accurate 27-MHz clock (±20ppm versus ±40ppm in broadcast), which is locked to the incoming TS stream. D-VHS stores this time stamp together with the TS packet in either two consecutive SBs or in two separated SBs, with trick play SBs in between. The trick-play virtual information channel contain an MPEG-2 compliant TS stream. The isochronous playback of such a trick-play sequence requires the presence of time stamps. Moreover, these time stamps are also used for adequate placement of the TS packets in the virtual channel.

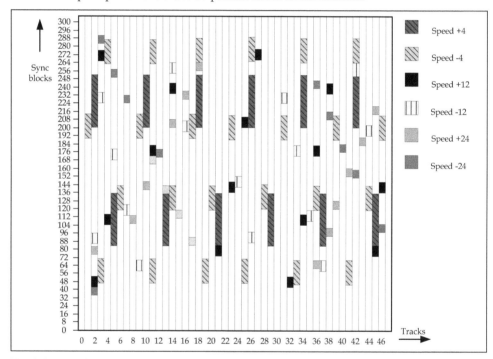

Fig. 8. D-VHS STD-mode trick play regions for speed-up factors: ± 4, ± 12 and ± 24.

Due to the tight relation between the time stamp and the physical storage location, the drum rotation phase needs to be synchronized during record and playback. Synchronization is essential because the local time stamp generator is reset modulo three revolutions of the scanner. Trick play in D-VHS is based on retrieving scattered fragments from various tracks. For the situation that the drum rotates at 1,800 rpm (30 Hz), the sync blocks allocated for each trick-play speed-up factor, result in a capacity of 2,301,120 bits/sec, see Table 1, regardless the playback direction. Trick-play data can be divided into two categories: high-end and low-cost. The former is characterized by high video quality and a refresh rate equal to the frame rate, regardless of the involved implementation cost. The latter is determined by minimizing the involved system costs. In any case, as trick play is in general a low-cost feature, the amount of signal processing should be bounded.

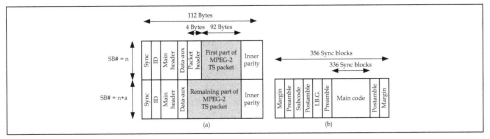

Fig. 9. D-VHS sync block. (a) MPEG-2 TS packet mapped at two SBs, (b) 336 SBs containing normal play, trick play, or padding data constructing one track.

Scanner revolution (Hz)	Trick play channel bit rate (bits/s)
30	2,301,120
29.97	2,298,821.17

Table 1. Channel bit rate for 30-Hz and 29.97-Hz scanner frequency.

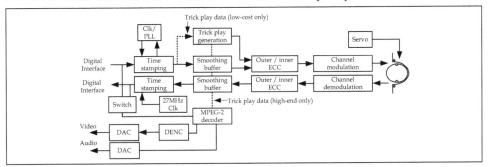

Fig. 10. D-VHS block diagram. The dashed connections indicate the information flow for the two trick-play flavors.

A basic functional block diagram that enables both high-end and low-cost trick-play implementation, is depicted in Fig. 10. The difference between the two concepts is only in the selection of normal-play pictures for the lowest forward trick-play speed, while the remaining processing steps are equal.

High-end trick play is implemented in the following way. During record of the normal play sequence, the normal play sequence is decoded and the decoded pictures are made available to the trick-play functional block, indicated by the dashed line, see Fig. 10. During trick play, the stored trick-play sequence is de-smoothed and reconstructed based on the time stamps. Low-cost trick play requires de-multiplexing of the normal-play sequence and video elementary stream parsing to locate the intraframe-compressed normal-play pictures. Due to the low trick-play bandwidth, see Table 1, high-end trick play is based on Common Intermediat Format (CIF) resolution. Almost 90,000 bits are available on a per picture basis for video with 25-Hz frame rate. Images of CIF-based resolution can be coded with sufficiently high quality using fixed bit-cost compression, resulting in a Peak Signal-to-Noise Ratio (PSNR) between 30 dB and 40 dB, depending on the spatial complexity, see Fig. 11 (b).

For low-cost trick play, the available bandwidth during trick play is not sufficient to enable a full refresh rate and preserve the picture quality when re-using normal-play intraframe-coded pictures. Hence, the concept for low-cost trick play is based on using transcoded normal-play intraframe-compressed pictures. Transcoding resulting in lower bandwidth can be obtained in two ways: removing picture energy (AC coefficients, see Table 3) or reduced refresh rate. Table 2 indicates the normal-play intraframe-compressed bit cost for various encoder settings. The minimum intraframe bit cost that remains when removing all AC energy is depicted in Table 3.

Normal play bit rate (Mbit/s)	Number of pixels per line	GOP parameters		Average intraframe bit cost (bits)	Minimum intraframe bit cost (bits)	Maximum intraframe bit cost (bits)
		N	M			
9.4	720	12	3	770,084	430,896	1,099,696
3.4	480	12	3	281,126	45,984	564,568
5.0	528	12	1	417,819	68,344	640,244
8.0	720	12	3	578,032	451,616	909,848

Table 2. Normal-play MPEG-2 intraframe bit cost for various bit rates, frequently used GOP structures, 576 lines per image, 25-Hz frame rate and 4:2:0 sampling format.

Normal play bit rate (Mbit/s)	GOP parameters		Average intraframe bit cost (bits)	Minimum intraframe bit cost (bits)	Maximum intraframe bit cost (bits)
	N	M			
9.4	12	3	108,326	83,600	122,488
3.4	12	3	77,329	53,944	97,200
5.0	12	1	55,012	48,032	60,176
8.0	12	3	78,915	75,336	81,840

Table 3. Transcoded DC-only bit costs for various bit rates, frequently used GOP structures, 576 lines per image, 25-Hz frame rate and 4:2:0 sampling format.

The normal-play intraframe-compressed pictures, as depicted in Table 2, result in refresh rates varying between 3 Hz and 8 Hz, which is insufficient from trick play perception (fast changing images) point of view. The DC-only intraframe-compressed pictures as depicted in Table 3, result in refresh rates up to 25 Hz, which is sufficient for trick-play perception, but the pictures lack detail due to the strong energy removal. An acceptable solution is obtained when the refresh rate is reduced to 8.3 Hz. In order to create an MPEG-2 compliant trick-play sequence, repetition pictures with or without "interlace kill" are applied, see also Section 3, resulting in a fixed bit cost of roughly 270,000 bits per trick-play GOP, see Fig. 11 (a). Various approaches have been reported to reduce AC energy from the intraframe-compressed normal-play pictures. The approaches vary between selecting the number of AC coefficients based on the amplitude of the AC coefficients (Ting & Hang, 1995) by means of prioritization (Boyce & Lane 1993), or on the basis of the differential DC value between successive DCT blocks (US6621979, 1998). Based on the concepts for low-cost trick play, the final trick-play quality depends on the normal-play quality and associated factors, due to the re-use of pictures. This results for luminance-only information, in a 25-dB PSNR for DC-only trick-play pictures, up to the original normal-play PSNR, when the spatial content of the pictures are of low complexity.

The trick-play information channel is filled with a multiplex of six individual transport streams, which are all derived from a single information stream, in this case the lowest fast-forward sequence. During trick-play, the higher and all supported reverse speeds are derived from fragments belonging to that particular trick-play sequence. Once the fixed bit-cost trick-play GOP for speed-up factor $Ps=+4$, is available (regardless whether high-end or low-cost), the trick-play video sequences for the other forward trick-play speed-up factors ($Ps=+12$ and $Ps=+24$) are derived from this trick-play sequence by the "search speed data selection" block, see Fig. 11 (c), via sub-sampling in the compressed domain of the fixed bit-cost GOPs.

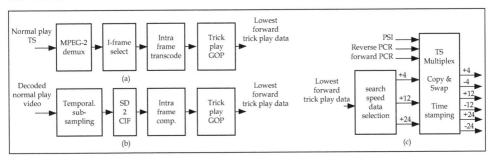

Fig. 11. D-VHS trick-play processing. (a) Low-cost trick-play video elementary stream generation, (b) High-end trick-play video elementary stream generation, (c) MPEG-2 TS multiplexing, time stamping and reverse trick-play generation.

The six trick-play streams are constructed as follows, assuming that the lowest search speed GOP is available, see Fig. 11 (a) and (b) . The functional block "TS multiplex Copy & Swap Time stamping", see Fig. 11 (c), performs three final operations on the forward trick-play elementary streams. The first operation is multiplexing the elementary streams into MPEG-2 Transport Streams (TS). The second operation is to copy and swap the TSs creating the trick-play sequences for the reverse search direction. Due to the fact that MPEG-2 decoding uses an increasing time axis, the reverse trick-play sequences are generated with a declining time axis. The swap operation on TS data is required to read the GOP in the correct order during trick play. Finally, the TS packets are equipped with a time stamp, such that the TS packets are properly mapped on the corresponding trick-play regions.

5. Trick play for optical storage systems

Optical storage systems differ from the traditional tape-based storage system in the sense that they offer random access to the stored audiovisual information, enabling trick-play generation at playback using the stored normal-play audiovisual information. Although no separate trick-play sequences are stored on the storage medium, additional information is stored facilitating trick play. In this section, trick play is described for two optical standards: SuperVCD and DVD.

5.1 Super Video Compact Disc (SuperVCD or SVCD)

SuperVCD is the successor of Video Compact Disc (VCD) and is also known as SVCD, offering up to 800 MByte storage capacity, using a 780 nm laser. This standard appeared on the market in the early 1990's (IEC62107, 2000). SuperVCD utilizes better audio and video quality compared to VCD, which used MPEG-1 video compression at Common Intermediat Format (CIF) resolution with a fixed bit rate of 1.1458 Mbit/s and MPEG-1 layer 2 audio at 256 kBit/s. The improved video quality of SuperVCD was later obtained by going to higher spatial resolution 480×576 (H×V) at 25 Hz for PAL TV system and 480×480 (H×V) at 29.97 Hz for the NTSC TV system. To code the interlaced video more efficiently, MPEG-2 video coding is applied in combination with variable bit rate. Multi-channel audio has been added to the system to increase the audio quality. Figure 12 depicts the SuperVCD reference model. From Fig. 12, it can be seen that the amount of data delivered by the CD module differs for MPEG sectors and data sectors, which is caused due to unequal error protection resulting in a higher (14%) storage capacity for an MPEG sector and less protection of the MPEG-compressed data. The layout of an SVCD consists of a lead-in, program area and a lead-out area, as depicted in Fig. 13 (a).

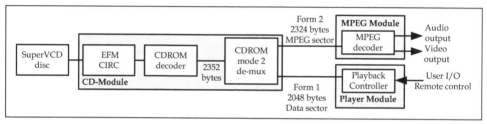

Fig. 12. SuperVCD system reference Model.

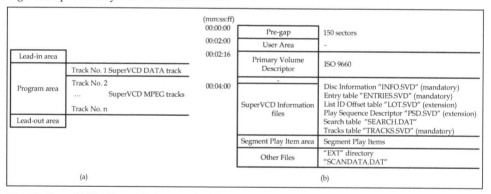

Fig. 13. SuperVCD disc and data track. (a) SuperVCD disc layout, (b) Data track layout example.

The program area is split into a SuperVCD data track and SuperVCD MPEG tracks. The former track stores additional information required by the SuperVCD player. The latter contains the MPEG-2 Program Stream containing the audiovisual information, which can be sub-divided into parts or chapters and are stored on the SuperVCD directory "MPEG2". SuperVCD is based on a pull-based architecture. Traditional trick play for such a system, as discussed in Section 3, can be on the basis of using only normal-play intraframe pictures or intraframe pictures in combination with uni-directional coded pictures. In SuperVCD, only intraframe-compressed pictures are used to realize traditional trick play. Traditional trick play on a SuperVCD stored program is established by means of locator information indicating the start position of an intra-coded picture. Furthermore, due to the random access of the stored information, a new navigation feature has been added to the system enabling to jump forward or backward in a stored program. To support this new form of navigation, another list with locator information is available.

Traditional trick play on a SuperVCD stored program is established by means of the "SEARCH.DAT" information or via the scan information data, which is multiplexed as user data together with the video elementary stream. The presence of the "SEARCH.DAT" file depends on whether the system profile tag is set to 0x00. Due to the Variable Bit Rate (VBR) coding and buffering applied by MPEG-2, there is no longer a direct relation between playing time and the position on disc. To solve this relation problem for trick play, the "SEARCH.DAT" file contains a list with access point sector addresses, indicating the nearest intraframe compressed picture in the MPEG track on a regular incremental time grid of 0.5 seconds. The total number of entries is minimally 1 and maximally 32,767 using a storage format of (*mm:ss:ff*), where *mm*={0 ..99 } indicates the minutes part of the sector offset value, *ss*={0..59 } the seconds part of the sector offset value and *ff*={0..74} represents the fraction part of the sector offset value. This information is useful for features such as time search. It should be noted that, as indicated in Fig. 13 (b), the MPEG-2 coded information and associate data are embedded into the regular CD-Audio sectors, which form the fundamental storage framework on a CD disc. Each sector corresponds to a certain time instance indicates in minutes, seconds and fragments.

If the "SEARCH.DAT" is not present, a second information mechanism, called scan information data, is provided by the SuperVCD standard to enable trick play. Scan information data is information indicating the location of the next and previous intraframe coded picture. This information, which is transmitted using the MPEG-2 user data structure, precedes each intra-coded picture and consists of two field pairs, one pair for a video stream and one pair for a still image stream. The fields are coded as a sector offset value referencing to the start sector of the MPEG track, as indicated by the table of contents. The scan information fields share the same storage format, which is *mm:ss:ff*. The scan information data refers to an access point sector.

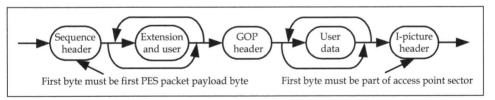

First byte must be first PES packet payload byte   First byte must be part of access point sector

Fig. 14. SuperVCD access-point sector structure.

An access point sector is an MPEG video sector, in which the first byte of a Packetized Elementary Stream (PES) packet belongs to a sequence header, see Fig. 14. MPEG-2 allows the usage of different quantization tables. MPEG-2 video encoders that use this feature will transmit the different quantization matrices in the sequence header. It is for this reason that in order to have proper trick play, these quantization matrices have to arrive at the MPEG-2 decoder, which is guaranteed by the access-point structure as depicted in Fig. 14.

Time-based jumping is another navigation method supported by SuperVCD and involves jumping forward or backward in time to the next chapter. This feature is enabled by means of the "ENTRIES.SVD" file, which stores the entry point addresses of the MPEG-2 tracks on disc. Due to the limited size of 2,048 Bytes, which corresponds to one sector, the number of entries of the "ENTRIES.SVD" file is limited to a maximum of 500.

5.2 Digital Video Disc (DVD)

The DVD is the optical media successor of the SuperVCD featuring higher recording density of up to 4.7 GByte for the basic format, using a 650 nm laser and deploying a pull-based architecture. The DVD-Video format (Taylor, 2001) specification is a video playback application of the DVD-ROM standard, applying MPEG-2 video compression and allowing MPEG-1 and run-length coding for still images. Various audio formats are supported such as Pulse Code Modulation (PCM), MPEG-1 or MPEG-2 compressed audio, or Dolby Digital multi-channel, which are packetized into a Packetized Elementary Stream (PES) and multiplexed into an MPEG-2 Program Stream. Also included in the MPEG-2 Program Stream multiplex are the real-time private stream, called Presentation Control Information (PCI), and Data Search Information (DSI), resulting in a maximum multiplexed bit rate of 10.08 Mbit/s. A player based on the DVD format, is typically connected to an standard TV display, either via baseband or modulated composite coax, or via analog component YCrCb/RGB video. Moreover, the signal can be of either interlaced or progressive nature. Figure 15 indicates the block diagram of a DVD player. A DVD player is based on a presentation engine and a navigation manager, as shown in Fig. 16. The presentation engine uses the information in the presentation data stream, see Fig. 15, to control what is presented to the viewer. For example, the navigation manager creates menus, provides user interfaces and controls branching, all on the bases of retrieved information from the DVD disc. This allows content providers to disable search-mode functions on particular DVD content, e.g. a trailer indicating that the audiovisual content is only to be used in the domestic environment. Per video title set, a particular movie can be made available as a single MPEG-2 Program Stream, or can be split up in maximally 9 parts, as indicated in Fig. 17 (a). This figure shows an example of a DVD volume layout containing a DVD-Video zone (DVD-Audio zone have been left out for simplicity). A Video Object Block (VOB) file, see Fig. 17 (b), is constructed of one or more cells containing a group of pictures or audio blocks; the cell forms the smallest addressable entity for random access. A cell, also known as scene, can be as short as 1 second, or cover the whole sequence and is uniquely identified with its cell ID and corresponding video object ID. A cell is further sub-divided into video object units, an entity containing zero or more Group-Of-Pictures (GOP). For the situation that a video object unit contains a single GOP, this GOP should start with a sequence header followed by a GOP header, which by default is followed by an intra-coded picture. Video object units are further split into packs and packets, which are compliant with the MPEG-2 Program Stream standard (ISO/IEC13818-1, 2000). Navigation data is a collection of information that determines how the physical data is accessed and controls interactive playback. The information is grouped into four categories: control, search, user interface and navigation commands, resulting in navigation information being split over five levels. The levels "program chain" and "data search" contain information required to perform navigation as discussed previously. For example, the "program chain" information enables the remote control navigation buttons "previous" and "next". The "data search" information is situated in the "navigation pack", see Fig. 17 (b) and thereby an integral part of the Program Stream.

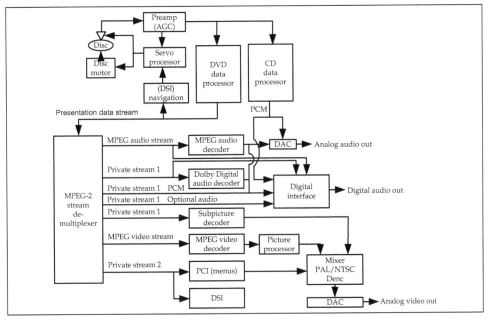

Fig. 15. DVD-Video player block diagram.

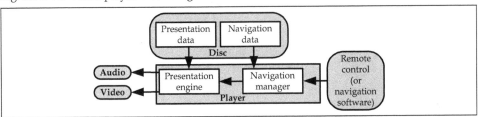

Fig. 16. DVD navigation and presentation model.

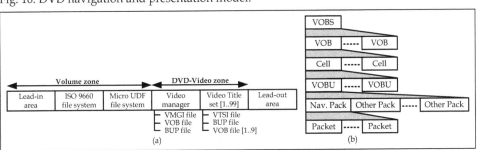

Fig. 17. DVD-Video data construction. (a) DVD volume layout containing a DVD-Video zone, (b) DVD abstraction layers on top of an MPEG-2 Program Stream.

The "navigation pack" holds for each video object unit a pointer for forward / reverse scanning, either referring to I-type or P-type pictures, which is an improvement with respect to SuperVCD that is only supporting I-type picture search.

5.3 Blu-ray Disc (BD)

Blu-ray Disc (BD, 2006) is the optical media successor of DVD, featuring higher recording density of up to 25 GByte for the basic format enabled by a 405 nm laser. BD is an optical storage system suitable for recording as well as playback-only of audiovisual information applying a pull-based architecture, see Fig. 18 (b). Video can be compressed using either: MPEG-2, MPEG-4 AVC, also known as H.264, or SMPTE VC-1 video compression. Multi channel audio is supported up to a 7.1 audio system and encoding is based on either, using Dolby Digital AC-3, DTS, or uncompressed using PCM. Besides the previous audio coding standards, three other standards are optionally supported: Dolby Digital Plus and two lossless coding methods, called Dolby TrueHD and DTS HD. The BD-ROM standard defines two platforms: a High Definition Movie (HDMV) and a Java™ platform, also known as BD-J, and these platforms categorize the BD-ROM features. In the BD-ROM system, exactly one mode, either HDMV mode or BD-J mode, is active at any given point of time during playback. HDMV supports features such as seamless multi-angle and multi-story, Language Credits, Directors Cuts, etc., see Fig. 18 (b).

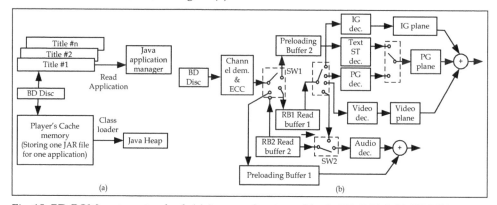

Fig. 18. BD-ROM system standard. (a) Java application tables in BD-ROM, (b) HDMV decoder model.

BD-J enables a fully programmable application environment with network connectivity, thereby enabling the content provider to create highly interactive, updateable BD-ROM titles, see Fig. 18 (a), and is based on the Java-2 Micro-Edition (J2ME) Personal Basis Profile (PBP), a Java profile that was developed for consumer electronics devices. It is assumed that the BD-ROM disc will be the primary source for media files, but it alternatives are the studio's web server and local storage. The unit of playback in BD-J is the PlayList, just as in HDMV. All features of HDMV, except Interactive Graphics (IG), which is replaced by BD-J graphics, can be used by a BD-J application. Supported features include Video, Audio, Presentation Graphics (PG), Text Subtitle component selection, media-time and playback-rate (trick-mode) control. The BD-J video device is a combination of the HDMV video and presentation graphics planes. Both video and presentation graphics will playback in the video device. BD supports traditional trick play via additional locator information, situated in the Clip Information file. Moreover, BD optionally supports Title Scene Search (TSS), a metadata-based advanced navigation method.

An AV stream file, together with its associated database attributes, is considered to be one object. The AV stream file is called a "Clip AV stream file", and the associated database attribute file is called a "Clip Information file". An object consisting of a "Clip AV stream file" and its corresponding "Clip information file" is called a Clip. A "Clip AV stream file" stores data, which is an MPEG-2 Transport Stream defined in a structure called the BDAV MPEG-2 Transport Stream. In general, a file is a sequence of data bytes. But the contents of the "Clip AV stream file" are developed on a time axis, therefore the access points into a "Clip AV stream file" are specified with time stamps. The "Clip Information file" stores the time stamps of the access point into the corresponding AV stream file. The Presentation Engine reads the clip information, to determine the position where it should begin to read the data from the AV stream file. There is a one-to-one relationship between a "Clip AV stream file" and a "Clip Information file", i.e., for every "Clip AV stream file", there is one corresponding "Clip Information file".

The Playback Control Engine in the BD-ROM Player Model uses PlayList structures, see Fig. 19 (b). A "Movie PlayList" is a collection of playing intervals in the Clips, see Fig. 20 (a). A single playing interval is called a PlayItem and consists of an IN-point and an OUT-point, each of which refers to positions on a time axis of the Clip, see Fig. 20 (a). Hence, a PlayList is a collection of PlayItems. Here, the IN-point denotes a start point of a playing interval, and the OUT-point indicates an end point of the playing interval.

In Section 3, it was discussed that traditional trick play on compressed video data depends on the GOP structure, see also Fig. 1 (a). To enable random access, BD stores an EP_map (Entry Point), which is part of the Clip Information file, for each entry point of an AV stream. Unlike the previous optical storage standards, not only information regarding the position of intraframe-compressed pictures is stored, but optionally, also information regarding the length of each GOP and the coding type of the pictures constructing a particular GOP. This information is stored in the so-called $GOP\_structure\_map$ located in the Supplemental Enhancement Information (SEI), which is stored in the user data container of the firstly decoded Access Unit (AU) of a GOP. The meaning of trick play is defined by the manufacturer of the BD-ROM Player, e.g. the manufacturer may define that $Ps=1.2$ forward play is not trick play, and instead define that $Ps>2$ forward play is considered trick play.

EP_map is a part of the "Clip Information file", and this information is mainly used for finding addressing information of data positions, where the BD-ROM player should start to read the data in the AV stream file. The corresponding access point is given to the Clip, see Fig. 19 (b), in the form of time indications, referring ultimately to a particular data byte in the AV stream. EP_map has a list of Entry Point data (EP-data) that is extracted from the AV stream, where decoding can start. Each EP-data is a pair of a PTS (Presentation Time Stamp) for an access unit and a data address of the access unit in the AV stream file. EP_map is used for two main purposes. First, it enables to find the data address of the access unit in the AV stream file that is pointed to by the PTS in PlayList. Second, it is used for facilitating fast forward and reverse trick play. The EP_map gives the relationships between Presentation Time Stamp (PTS) values and addresses in the AV stream file. The PTS entry point is called PTS_EP_start, where the actual AV stream entry point address is called SPN_EP_start, see Fig. 20 (b). In order to reduce the size of the table and to improve the searching performance, the EP_map for one stream is split in two sub-tables: EP_coarse and EP_fine. The "Clip Information file", which has a maximum file size of 2 MBytes is stored in "Clipinf", a sub-directory of "BDMV". Note that it is allowed that the CLIPINF directory contains no Clip Information file.

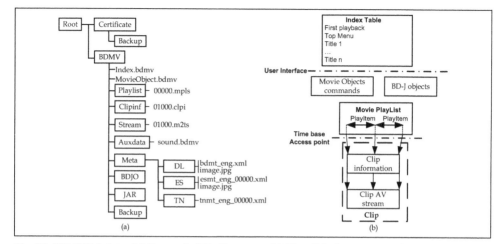

Fig. 19. BD-ROM data. (a) Example BD directory, (b) Simplified structure of BD-ROM.

If Title Scene Search is present, the corresponding information is separately stored from the content in "ES", a sub-directory of the "META" directory, which also stores other metadata, see Fig. 19 (a). The value part of the metadata filename links the file to the corresponding playlist. Other sub-directories of the "META" directory are "DL" and "TN". The directory "DL" (Disc Library) contains the disc-library metadata, which is mainly composed of two types of information: disc information and title information. Disc information contains the metadata of a disc itself, and title information includes the metadata of a title. The directory "TN" (Track/chapter Name) stores files containing metadata information regarding the names of tracks and chapters, which are sequentially stored. The track/chapter name metadata file exists per PlayList of a movie title. The corresponding metadata file is linked to the PlayList file via the value part of the file name.

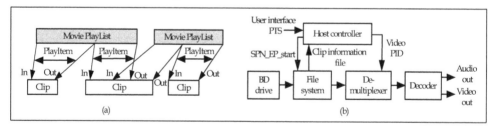

Fig. 20. Playback BD movie. (a) Movie playback using information from the PlayList, (b) Player model for I-picture search using EP_map.

6. Trick play for hard or solid-state disk based storage systems

With the advances in storage capacity and an associated firm price erosion, Hard Disk Drive (HDD) based storage systems have replaced the traditional tape-based storage media in the consumer arena. Recently, the Solid-State Drive (SSD) has made its appearance in the consumer arena, working its way into systems dominated by the HDD. Due to the enormous storage capacity of this type of media, a massive amount of audiovisual material can be stored. Efficient navigation through this data requires fast random access, enabling high-speed search and new forms of audiovisual navigation. HDD and SSD storage solutions have an advantage regarding the access time, see Fig. 21, when used for audiovisual storage applications.   For the situation that the access time of the storage medium is less than the reciprocal of the frame rate, the storage system responsiveness enables traditional trick play at full refresh rate and paves the way for advanced navigation methods.

The disk-based storage system architecture can be either push- or pull-based and is mainly determined by the context in which the storage system is deployed. A good solution is to offer both architectures, and make a choice depending on where the audiovisual decoding is performed, so that the best of both architectures is deployed. When audiovisual decoding is performed locally, the pull-based solutions give the best trick-play quality. When operated in a networked manner, trick-play quality cannot be guaranteed, as this depends on the normal-play encoding settings. It should be kept in mind, that the involved network communication is minimal for push-based architectures, in which only commands are required when changing the mode of operation, i.e. play, stop, fast search forward, etc. Moreover, when supporting both architectures, also advanced navigation features become possible, where the availability of the navigation mode depends on the location of decoding.

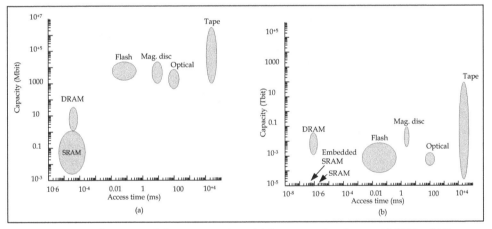

Fig. 21. Storage solutions and their access time. (a) Storage technology mid 1990s, (b) Storage technology 2009.

As a result, some advanced navigation modes may only be partly available when decoding is performed on remotely located decoders. Figure 22 depicts a functional block diagram of an HDD or SSD-based PVR, supporting both pull- and push-based playback. The pull mode requires the decoder to request for information, indicated via the dashed line. Let us elaborate on the two advanced navigation concepts introduced in Section 2. The pull-based architecture is suitable for traditional trick play and supports both advanced navigation concepts, whereas the push-based mode supports traditional trick play, hierarchical navigation and partly audiovisual trick play as discussed in Section 3.

During record, an MPEG-2 Transport Stream enters the system at the left-hand side, see Fig. 22. The CPI block adds time stamps to the incoming TS packets, which are stored together with the corresponding TS packet on disk. Furthermore, the MPEG-2 TS is de-multiplexed and the video signal is parsed.

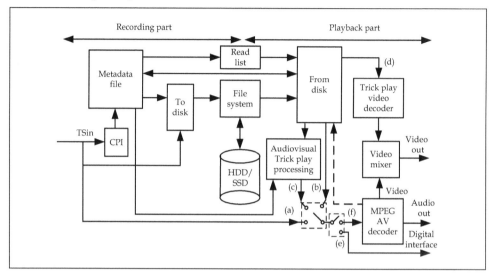

Fig. 22. Functional block diagram of HDD or SSD-based PVR. Operation modes: (a) View real-time, (b) View time-shift, (c) Traditional trick play or trick play based on normal-play AV fragments, (d) Trick play PiP to be used in combination with normal-play AV fragments, (e) AV playback according to push mode, (f) Pull-mode playback for local decoding.

During the parsing process, various characteristics of the MPEG-2 Video Elementary Stream are stored, such as relative positions of I- and P-type pictures, GOP length and transmission time of the intraframe-encoded pictures. This data is stored in a metadata file, which is stored as an extra descriptor file on the disk. Besides the information for traditional trick play, sub-pictures are derived from the normal-play video sequence and stored in the metadata file. The sub-pictures are generated in such a way that they can be used to construct mosaic screens via signal processing in the MPEG-2 domain, resulting in MPEG-2 compliant mosaic screen pictures (Eerenberg & de With, 2003). The information in the metadata file offers navigation features such as traditional trick play, but also the more advanced navigation methods for local (pull-mode) as well as remote users (push-mode).

For traditional trick play, the read-list block (using data from the metadata file) controls the disk retrieval process, resulting in fetching MPEG-2 TS fragments. These fragments are either processed by the audiovisual trick-play processing, which creates an MPEG-2 compliant signal, see Fig. 22 (c) and (e), or send the fragments directly to the local MPEG-2 decoder, see Fig. 22 (c) and (f).

For hierarchical navigation, the audiovisual trick-play block generates the mosaic screens for the pull- and push-based playback. For video navigation reinforced with audible sound, the audiovisual fragments are retrieved from disk and made available to the local decoder. A fast-search trick-play sequence is generated by means of a second video decoder, which could also be the control processor. The CIF-based trick-play sequence is merged with the normal-play video fragments by means of a video mixer.

7. Conclusions

Trick play is a feature that needs to be embedded within the design of a storage system. The system implementation should have low costs and be of suitable quality for quickly searching through the data. However, implementation of trick play differs for the various storage systems. Based on the discussed systems in this chapter, the following techniques have become apparent.

Trick play can be realized by re-use of normal-play compressed video data, or via additional dedicated trick-play information streams. Digital helical-scan recorders apply both mechanisms. For example, DV shuffles normal-play data to facilitate trick-play for a broad range of speed-up factors and D-VHS deploys dedicated virtual channel for each supported speed-up factor, which is filled with special trick-play information. The disadvantage of this solution is the reduction of the normal-play recording bandwidth, e.g. in D-VHS the reduction is about 5 Mbit/s.

Common optical-disc storage systems all deploy the re-usage of normal-play information and selectively address individual decodable pictures in the normal-play video stream. This is achieved via so-called locator information stored within the recorded stream. The optical pick-up unit is positioned, using this locator information, such that the retrieved information contains individually decodable pictures. In this way, the proper placement of the optical-pickup unit becomes a dominant factor in the random access time. As a consequence, the final trick-play quality depends on the normal-play GOP structure. The BD-based optical storage solution also optionally deploy normal-play GOP information, enabling the usage of P-type and B-type pictures for trick play. Moreover, metadata-based retrieval is facilitated by an optional descriptor file. With the current advances in optical drive technology, random access time can be avoided due the readout of the optical disc at a significant higher rate, causing the video source decoder to be the dominant factor for trick-play quality.

With the introduction of HDD-based PVRs, trick play can be deployed in full temporal quality due to the short access time, when operated in pull-mode. Both HDD and SSD-based systems deploy locator information, enabling basic and advanced forms of navigation. When operated in a push-mode, the trick-play temporal quality most probably decreases somewhat, but the decoder always receives a compliant stream for decoding, thereby making this approach suitable for networked-based storage systems. Drawback of a push-based architecture is that it limits the advanced navigation modes, as the final signal must comply with the deployed standards, when system cost should be kept low.

Future work in the field of trick play should focus on low-cost algorithms which are capable of finding useful metadata to create the metadata search files. This will facilitate searching techniques, which are based on semantic understanding of the data content, so that high-level searching becomes possible.

8. References

BD (2006). System Description Blu-ray Disc Read-Only Format, Part 3: Audio Visual Basic Specifications (3-1 Core Specifications) Version 2.01 DRAFT2

Boyce, J. & Lane, F. (1993). Fast scan technology for digital video tape recorders. *IEEE Trans. Consumer Electron.*, Vol. 39, No. 3, August 1993, pp. 186-191, ISSN 0098-3063

CEI/IEC61834 (1993). Helical-scan digital video cassette recording system using 6,35 mm magnetic tape for consumer use (525-60, 625-50, 1125-60 and 1250-50 systems

Eerenberg, O. & de With, P.H.N. (2003). System requirements and considerations for visual table of contents in PVR, *Proceedings of ICCE 2003*, pp. 24-25, ISBN 0-7803-7721-4, USA, June 2003, Los Angeles, CA

Eerenberg, O. & Aarts, R.M. & de With, P.H.N. (2008). System Design of Advanced Video Navigation Reinforced with Audible Sound in Personal Video Recording, *Proceedings of ICCE 2008*, pp. 1-2, ISBN 978-1-4244-1458-1, USA, Jan. 2008, Las Vegas, NV

ETSI_TS_101154 (2009). Technical Specification Digital Video Broadcasting (DVB); Specification for the use of Video and Audio Coding in Broadcasting Applications based on the MPEG 2 Transport Stream, Version 1.9.1, March 2009

Fujita, M.; Higurashi, S. & Hirano, S. & Ohishi, T. & Zenno, Y. (1996). Newly developed D-VHS digital tape recording system for the multimedia era. *IEEE Trans. Consumer Electron.*, Vol. 42, No. 3, (August 1996), pp. 617-622, ISSN 0098-3063

van Gassel, J.P. & Kelly, D.P. & Eerenberg, O. & de With, P.H.N. (2002). MPEG-2 compliant trick play over a digital interface, *Proceedings of ICCE 2002*, pp. 170-171, ISBN 0-7803-7300-6, USA, June 2002, Los Angeles, CA

IEC62107 (2000). Super Video Compact Disc – Disc-interchange system-specification International Standard

IEC61883-4 (2004). Digital Interface For Consumer Audio/Video Equipment Part 4: MPEG-TS data transmission

ISO/IEC11172-2 (1993). Information technology - Coding of moving pictures and associated audio for digital storage media at up to about 1,5 Mbit/s - Part 2: Video

ISO/IEC 14496-3 (1999). PICOLA Speed change algorithm, Annex 5.D.

ISO/IEC13818-1 (2000). International Standard Information technology — Generic coding of moving pictures and associated audio information: Systems, Dec. 2000

ISO/IEC13818-2 (2000). International Standard Information technology — Generic coding of moving pictures and associated audio information: Video, Dec. 2000

ISO60774-5 (2004). Helical-scan video tape cassette system using 12,65 mm (0,5 in) magnetic tape on type VHS –Part 5: D-VHS

Matsushita, Philips, Sony & Thomson. (1993). Outline of Basic Specification for Consumer-use Digital VCR

Taylor, J. (2001). *DVD Demystified*, McGraw-Hill, ISBN 0-07-135026-8

Ting, H. & Hang, H. (1995). Trick play schemes for advanced television recording on digital VCR. *IEEE Trans. Consumer Electron.*, Vol. 41 No. 4, Nov. 1995, pp. 1159-1168, ISSN 0098-3063

US6621979 (1998). Trick play signal generation for a digital video recorder using retrieved intra-encoded pictures and generated inter-encoded pictures, Patent

3

Performance Analysis of DVB-T/H OFDM Hierarchical Modulation in Impulse Noise Environment

Tamgnoue Valéry, Véronique Moeyaert, Sébastien Bette and Patrice
Mégret *University of Mons (UMONS), Faculty of Engineering, Department of
Electromagnetism and Telecommunications, Mons Belgium*

1. Introduction

DVB-T\H (Digital Video Broadcasting – Terrestrial \ Handheld) are standards of the DVB consortium for digital terrestrial handheld broadcasting and are based on Coded Orthogonal Frequency Division Multiplex (COFDM) signals as described in the documents ETSI 300 744 and ETSI EN 302 304 in 2004. Orthogonal Frequency Division Multiplex (OFDM) modulation is based on a multi-carriers scheme, instead of the single carrier modulation scheme used classically in DVB-Cable. In OFDM, the bit stream to be transmitted is serially separated and modulated in parallel over several subcarriers which increases the robustness to multipath in wireless environment.

In the DVB standard, the recommended modulation scheme is multi-carriers QAM modulation but hierarchical modulation is also proposed as an optional transmission mode where two separate bit streams are modulated into a single bit stream. The first stream, called the "High Priority" (HP), is embedded within the second stream called the "Low Priority" (LP) stream. At the receiver side, equipments with good receiving conditions demodulate both streams, while those with bad receiving conditions only demodulate HP stream. Hierarchical modulation, therefore, gives more service opportunities for receivers in good operating conditions compared to receivers in bad receiving conditions that only decode basic services.

Hierarchical modulation has been included in many digital broadcasting standards such as MediaFLO, UMB (Ultra Mobile Broadband), T-DMB (Terrestrial Digital Multimedia Broadcasting), DVB-SH (Digital Video Broadcasting - Satellite Handheld). Nevertheless, in the new version of video broadcasting, DVB-T2 (Digital Video Broadcasting- Terrestrial second version), the hierarchical modulation has been replaced by Physical Layer Pipes (PLP). Notice that, in order to provide dedicated robustness, the PLP technologies allow different levels of modulation, coding and power transmitted per service. Thus, PLP differentiates the quality in service by service basis, while the hierarchical modulation works based on receivers conditions independently of the services (DVB Document A122, 2008).

Impulse noises combined with Gaussian noises are one of the major causes of errors in digital communications systems and thus in DVB-T\H networks (Biglieri, 2003). These two kinds of noises behave in a different way to corrupt digital communications. Gaussian noise, also known as background noise, is permanently present through the network with a moderate power. On the contrary, impulse noise randomly appears as bursts of relative short duration and very large instantaneous power.

The primary purpose of this chapter is to investigate the behaviour of coupled OFDM/QAM and hierarchical modulation systems under impulse noise environment as it appears in DVB-T/H specifications. This impact is evaluated firstly by expressing Bit Error Rate (BER), when it is simulated, or Bit Error Probability (BEP) when it is calculated, of both HP bit stream and LP bit stream with impulsive impairment, and secondly by validating these expressions through simulation. The Signal to Noise Ratio (SNR) penalty induced by the presence of impulse noise in each stream is also analytically estimated and confirmed by computer simulations.

This chapter will first introduce the insights of OFDM and hierarchical modulation in DVB-T/H and will also give some examples of possible implementations. After, it will give a brief overview of impulsive noise characteristics. Then, it will describe the method to theoretically analyze the BER at the bit level in presence of impulse noise. At this level, an original method to obtain the SNR penalty on HP stream due to the introduction of LP stream is reported. And finally, the conclusion will bring some comments in next DVB-T/H technologies.

2. System model

DVB-T/H are technical standards that specify the framing structure, channel coding and modulation for terrestrial handheld television. These standards define the transmission of encoded audio and video signals using the COFDM modulation.

Many parameters, which are listed here, are settled to characterize DVB-T/H transmission stream:

- The code rate: it is the ratio of data rate of the useful bits to overall data rate (typical values are: $\frac{1}{2}$, $2/3$, $\frac{3}{4}$, $5/6$, $7/8$).
- The modulation order: non-hierarchical (4-QAM, 16-QAM, 64-QAM), hierarchical (4/16-QAM, 4/64-QAM).
- The guard interval: it is defined to guarantee the safety interval for the subsequent symbol (typical length of guard interval: $\frac{1}{4}$, $1/8$, $1/16$, $1/32$).
- The number of sub-carriers: 2k (2048), 4k (4096, only for DVB-H) and 8k (8192).
- The hierarchical uniformity parameter: 1 for uniform constellation and 2 or 4 for non-uniform constellation.

2.1 Introduction of hierarchical modulation

Hierarchical Modulation (HM) is defined to be used on quadrature modulations (QAM) and mainly consists of two separate bit streams that are modulated onto a single bit stream. The first stream, called the "High Priority" (HP), is modulated with basic quadrature modulation order (4-QAM) and the second stream, "Low Priority" (LP), is embedded on HP stream to define high order QAM modulation (M-QAM, where M is greater that 4).

The Hierarchical Modulation is designed such that HP stream is more robust against disturbances than LP stream. Therefore, only receiver with good channel condition (imposed by distance, fading, interferences, and impulse noise) can decode HP and LP streams while others can only use HP stream. This leads to differentiate service content depending of receiving conditions.

In DVB-T/H systems, Hierarchical Modulation (HM) is only defined on QAM (Quadrature Amplitude Modulation) and is denoted 4/M-QAM. Generally, square QAM is used in which M is 2^{2n}, and 2n is the number of bits per symbol. The 4/M-QAM is simply defined by its constellation diagram as depicted in fig. 1 for a 4/16-QAM. In this diagram, the HP stream is modulated with QPSK, equivalent to 4QAM, and thus specifies the quadrant in the entire constellation. The LP stream is modulated with (M÷4)-QAM, and is embedded on primary QPSK. The entire constellation is mapped with Gray coding to allow only one bit variation between adjacent symbols.

For example, in fig. 1 for 4/16-QAM, on the entire $log_2(16)=4$ bits ($i_1q_1i_2q_2$) of the 4/M-QAM symbol, the first two bits, i_1q_1, are assigned the HP stream (fig.1a), and the next $log_2(M)-2$, i_2q_2, bits are allocated to LP stream (fig. 1b).

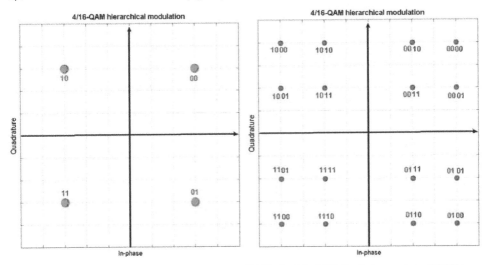

(a) HP stream (i_1q_1) modulated in QPSK

(b) Embedded LP (i_2q_2) stream into QPSK to give ($i_1q_1i_2q_2$)

Fig. 1. Illustration of construction of constellation diagram of 4/16-QAM modulation

Hence, hierarchical modulation can be view as HP stream transmitted with the fictitious symbol of QPSK defined by the first two bits (each fictitious symbol defining a quadrant), whereas the LP stream used the (M/4)-QAM modulation around these fictitious symbols.

Many parameters are used to characterize hierarchical constellation and are defined in fig. 2:

- $2d_1$ which represents the minimum distance between two fictitious symbols,
- $2d_2$ which represents the minimum distance between two neighboring symbols within one quadrant,
- $2d'_1$ which represents the minimum distance between two symbols in adjacent quadrants.

The ratio, α, of d'_1 and d_2 is the uniformity parameter and it defines the balance of power between HP stream and LP stream. As illustrated in fig. 3, the hierarchical QAM constellation is called:

- uniform constellation when α = 1,
- non-uniform constellation when α ≠ 1,.

Uniform constellation leads to equal power distribution between HP and LP while for non-uniform constellation, the power is unbalanced and is more in HP stream for growing α.

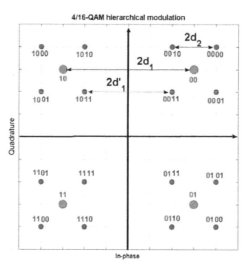

Fig. 2. Presentation of HM parameters in constellation diagram of 4/16-QAM modulation.

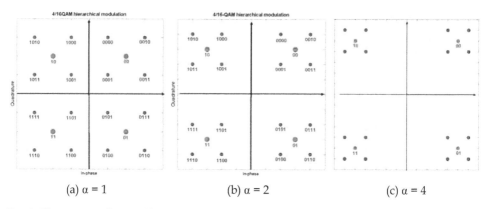

(a) α = 1   (b) α = 2   (c) α = 4

Fig. 3. Illustration of constellation diagram of 4/16-QAM modulation with various uniformity parameter (α = 1,2,4).

In the square 4/M-QAM, i.e. where the constellation order is $M = 2^{2n}$ which is the case of interest, the distances parameters are linked by this expression (Vitthaladevuni, 2001):

$$d_1 = d_1' + \left(\frac{\sqrt{M}}{2} - 1 \right) d_2 \qquad (1)$$

where M is the constellation order.

Concerning the energy distribution, it has been shown in (Vitthaladevuni, 2001) that, for square 4/M-QAM, the total average energy per symbol, E_s, is given by:

$$E_s = 2d_1^2 + \frac{2}{3}\left(\frac{M}{4} - 1\right)d_2^2 \tag{2}$$

On this expression, the average energy per symbol of HP and LP streams, E_{hp} and E_{lp}, can be written as:

$$E_{hp} = 2d_1^2 \tag{3}$$

$$E_{lp} = \frac{2}{3}\left(\frac{M}{4} - 1\right)d_2^2 \tag{4}$$

where E_{hp} represents the average energy of 4-QAM with constellation points separated by distance $2d_1$ (fictitious symbol in 4/M-QAM). Likewise, E_{lp} represents the average energy of M/4-QAM with constellation points separated by distance $2d_2$.

One important property that characterizes the hierarchical modulation is the penalty of modulation, also called modulation efficiency (Jiang, 2005, Wang, 2008) which is defined as the excess power that is needed in the HP stream to achieve the same Bit Error Probability (BEP) than in classical QPSK. In other words, it therefore quantifies the excess of power needed for receivers which are designed to deal with HP stream compared to the case where only classical QPSK is send.

2.2 Possible implementations of hierarchical modulation

Hierarchical modulation allows different kind of resources (bandwidth and bit rate) exploitation for receivers in various conditions. Therefore, it can be used to smoothly introduced new kind of services without needing new and expensive spectrum allocation. By this way, mobile reception or High Definition (HD) can complete and enhance the offer of the broadcaster (Schertz, 2003, Faria, 2006).

In the case of mobile reception scenario, the HP stream can be dedicated to broadcasting mobile programmes, while the LP stream can be devoted to broadcast traditional fixe or portable programmes. The HP stream will present sufficient robustness to achieve mobile channel communication. However, LP stream, weaker, will use less disturbed fixe or portable channel. Trade-off between mobile and fixe or portable channel will be assured by sizing uniformity parameters and error coding properties.

In the case of High Definition scenario, HP stream can be used for Standard Definition (SD) programmes, while LP stream can transmit HD programmes. Users with HD receivers will access broadcasted enhanced HD programmes and others, with no HD capabilities, will continue to enjoy traditional broadcasted SD programmes.

2.3 Introduction of OFDM modulation

OFDM is a parallel transmission scheme where the bit stream to be transmitted is serially separated and modulated with several sub-carriers. In practice, OFDM systems are implemented using the combination IFFT (Inverse Fast Fourier Transform) at the emitter side and FFT (Fast Fourier Transform) at receiver part (Proakis, 2001). Basically, the information bits are mapped into N baseband complex symbols c_k using quadrature modulation scheme as shown in fig. 4. The block of N complex baseband symbols, considered in the frequency domain, is changed by means of an IFFT that brings signal into the time domain. The sequence of complex received symbols r_l, after sampling and assuming ideal channel, is given by:

$$r_l = \frac{1}{\sqrt{N}} \sum_{k=0}^{N-1} c_k e^{j\frac{2\pi kl}{N}} + n_l \qquad 0 \le l \le N-1 \qquad (5)$$

where c_k is the M-QAM complex symbol of the nth sub-carrier, n_l is the channel noise (jointly impulsive and Gaussian noises in this case), and N is the number of sub-carriers.

The estimated baseband complex M-QAM symbol is recovered by performing a FFT that transforms the received signal in frequency domain, and it is given by:

$$\hat{c}_k = \frac{1}{\sqrt{N}} \sum_{l=0}^{N-1} r_l e^{-j\frac{2\pi kl}{N}} = c_k + \frac{1}{\sqrt{N}} \sum_{l=0}^{N-1} n_l e^{-j\frac{2\pi kl}{N}} = c_k + z_k \qquad 0 \le k \le N-1 \qquad (6)$$

where z_k denotes an additive noise term which is in fact the frequency conversion of n_l.

From relation (2), it can be seen that the noise in the kth QAM symbol depends on all noise samples present during the OFDM symbol. In fact, the noise, and particularly the impulse noise, is spread over the N QAM symbols due to the FFT operation.

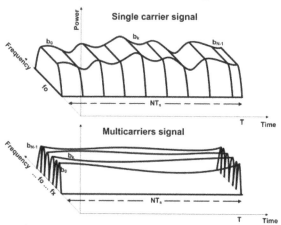

Fig. 4. Representation of OFDM modulation

2.4 Introduction of OFDM hierarchical modulation
OFDM hierarchical modulation is the combination of an OFDM system and some hierarchical QAM modulation as illustrated in fig. 5. It is constituted by a concatenation of a hierarchical QAM modulator and an OFDM modulator.

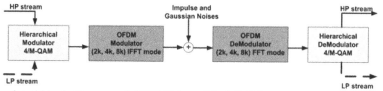

Fig. 5. Simulated block diagram of OFDM hierarchical QAM system

In DVB-{T, H} systems, OFDM modulation uses 2k (2048), 4k (4096), 8k (8192) subcarriers. Further, Hierarchical Modulation (HM) is defined based on QAM (Quadrature Amplitude Modulation) and it is denoted 4/M-QAM.

2.5 The Middleton class-A model

Impulse noise is basically defined with three statistical properties: the duration, the inter-arrival and the voltage amplitude. Middleton class-A is a complete canonical statistical model of joint impulse and Gaussian noise where the properties are defined by a compound Poisson process (Middleton, 1979, Berry, 1981). For this model, the in-phase and quadrature Probability Density Function (PDF) of voltage $f_n(x,y)$ is given by:

$$f_n(x,y) = e^{-A_A} \sum_{q=0}^{\infty} \frac{A_A{}^q}{q!} \cdot \frac{1}{2\pi\sigma_q^2} \exp\left(-\frac{x^2+y^2}{2\sigma_q^2}\right) \tag{7}$$

where $\sigma_q^2 = \dfrac{(q/A_A + \Gamma)}{1+\Gamma}$, $\Gamma = \dfrac{\sigma_g^2}{A_A\sigma_i^2}$, A_A is the impulsive index, Γ is the mean power ratio

of the Gaussian component and the impulsive component, σ_g^2 and σ_i^2 are respectively the variances of Gaussian and impulse noises.

Specifically, A_A corresponds to the product of the average rate of impulse generation and the mean duration of typical impulses. Small values of A_A and Γ give predominance to impulse type of noise while large values of A_A and Γ lead to a Gaussian type of noise.

3. Bit error probability of OFDM hierarchical QAM calculation

3.1 Bit error probability of hierarchical 4/M-QAM calculation

In hierarchical modulation, the bit error probability must be determined at the bit level. In fact, a noise can lead to error in the LP bits and not disturb the HP bits. Bit error probability of hierarchical QAM HP and LP streams has been presented in scientific literature (Vitthaladevuni, 2001, 2004), and here the principles will be described.

For square 4/M-QAM (M=2^{2n}), the entire bit stream is ($i_1q_1i_2q_2...i_nq_n$) in which the HP stream is (i_1q_1) and the LP stream is ($i_2q_2...i_nq_n$). The BEP of HP bits is given by (Vitthaladevuni, 2001, 2004):

$$P_{hp}(M) = \frac{1}{2}\left[P(i_1,M) + P(q_1,M)\right] \tag{8}$$

where $P(i_1,M)$ and $P(q_1,M)$ represent respectively the bit error probability of the first in-phase and quadrature bits of 4/M-QAM hierarchical modulation.
The symmetry of the constellation diagram reduces equation (8) to:

$$P_{hp}(M) = P(q_1,M) = P(i_1,M) \tag{9}$$

On the other hand, the BEP of the LP bits is obtained by (Vitthaladevuni, 2001, 2004):

$$P_{lp}(M) = \frac{\sum_{k=2}^{(1/2)\log_2 M} P(i_k, M) + P(q_k, M)}{\log_2(M) - 2} \tag{10}$$

where $P(i_k, M)$ and $P(q_k, M)$ represents the BEP of kth in-phase and quadrature LP bits of 4/M-QAM hierarchical modulation.

Using again the symmetry of the constellation diagram, this equation is rewritten as:

$$P_{lp}(M) = \frac{2\sum_{k=2}^{(1/2)\log_2 M} P(q_k, M)}{\log_2(M) - 2} = \frac{2\sum_{k=2}^{(1/2)\log_2 M} P(i_k, M)}{\log_2(M) - 2} \tag{11}$$

Equations (9) and (11) show that, due to the symmetry, the bit error probability of HP and LP streams only depends on only in-phase bits, or on only quadrature bits. Therefore, in-phase bits were chosen to make error probability calculation. The in-phase bits constellation diagram which corresponds to the reduced diagram is constructed and depicted in fig. 5 for 4/16-QAM. There, a symbol is defined by i_1-i_2-i_3-..., where the dashes represent the positions in quadrature axis.

In the next part, the development of error probability for the 4/16-QAM, which can be generalized to 4/64-QAM and widely to 4/M-QAM, will be described.

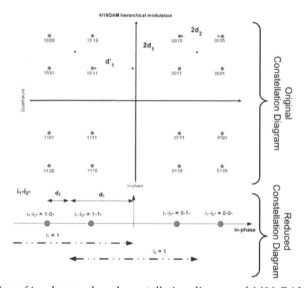

Fig. 6. Construction of in-phase reduced constellation diagram of 4/16-QAM

3.2 Case of 4/16-QAM hierarchical modulation

Before calculating the bit error probability of HP stream, we express here $P(i_1, 16)$:

$$P(i_1, 16) = P(i_1 = 1)P(error / i_1 = 1) + P(i_1 = 0)P(error / i_1 = 0) \tag{12}$$

where $P(i_1=x)$ is the probability that bit i_1 is equal to x, and $P(error/i_1=x)$ is the conditional probability to have an error if bit i_1 is equal to x.

Fig. 6 shows the reduced diagram of 4/16-QAM and two kinds of symbols with probability ½ can be transmitted when i_1=1: 1-0- and 1-1-. Similarly, when i_1=0, the two kinds of symbols with probability ½ can be transmitted: 0-0- and 0-1-. Derived from (12), the expression of $P(i_1,16)$ is thus given by:

$$P(i_1,16) = P(i_1 = 1)\left[1/2\,P(error/1-0-)+1/2\,P(error/1-1-)\right]$$
$$+ P(i_1 = 0)\left[1/2\,P(error/0-0-)+1/2\,P(error/0-1-)\right] \tag{13}$$

where $P(error/x-y-)$ is the conditional probability to have an error if the transmitted symbol is equal to $x-y-$.

Fig. 7a shows that when the bit i_1 is 1 and the emitted symbol is 1-0-, error appears when displacement on the reduced constellation diagram is greater than d_1+d_2 on the right. Likewise, fig. 7a shows that when the bit i_1 is 1 and the emitted symbols is 1-1-, error appears if the displacement is greater than d_1-d_2 on the right. Similar analysis when i_1=0 leads to express $P_{hp}(16)$ as:

$$P_{hp}(16) = P(i_1,16) = \frac{1}{2}\left[1/2\int_{d_1+d_2}^{+\infty} f(x)dx + 1/2\int_{d_1-d_2}^{+\infty} f(x)dx\right]$$
$$+ \frac{1}{2}\left[1/2\int_{-\infty}^{-d_1-d_2} f(x)dx + 1/2\int_{-\infty}^{-d_1+d_2} f(x)dx\right] \tag{14}$$

where $f(x)$ is the PDF of voltage amplitude of noise.

Thus, by using equation (7) to express the PDF of voltage amplitude noise $f_n(x)$, the bit error probability of HP stream can be written as:

$$P_{hp}(M) = \frac{1}{2}\left(\frac{1}{2}Y(d_1' + 2d_2) + \frac{1}{2}Y(d_1' + 2d_2)\right) \tag{15}$$

where $Y(d) = \int_{-\infty}^{d} f_n(x)dx$, and expressed by:

$$Y(d) = e^{-A_A}\sum_{k=0}^{+\infty}\frac{A_A^k}{k!}\cdot\frac{1}{2}\cdot erfc\left(\frac{d}{\sigma_k}\right)$$

In the other hand, the bit error probability of LP in-phase bits is obtained by calculating $P(i_2,16)$. It is given by:

$$P(i_2,16) = P(i_2 = 1)P(error/i_2 = 1) + P(i_2 = 0)P(error/i_2 = 0) \tag{16}$$

Based on reduced constellation diagram, it becomes:

$$P(i_2,16) = P(i_2 = 1)\left[1/2\,P(error/1-1-)+1/2\,P(error/0-1-)\right]$$
$$+ P(i_2 = 0)\left[1/2\,P(error/1-0-)+1/2\,P(error/0-0-)\right] \tag{17}$$

The fig. 7.b shows that when the bit i_2 is 1 and the emitted symbol is 1-1-, error appears when displacement on the reduced constellation diagram is greater than $2d_1-d_2$ on the right and d_2 on the left. Equally, fig. 7.b shows that when the bit i_2 is 1 and the emitted symbols is 0-1-, error appears if the displacement is greater than d_2 on the right and $2d_1-d_2$ on the left. Similar analysis when i_2=0 leads to express $P_{lp}(16)$ as:

$$P(i_2, M) = \frac{1}{2}\left[1/2\left(\int_{-\infty}^{-d_2} f(x)dx + \int_{2d_1-d_2}^{+\infty} f(x)dx \right) + 1/2\left(\int_{-\infty}^{-2d_1+d_2} f(x)dx + \int_{d_2}^{+\infty} f(x)dx \right) \right]$$
$$+ \frac{1}{2}\left[1/2 \int_{d_2}^{2d_1-d2} f(x)dx + 1/2 \int_{-2d_1+d2}^{-d_2} f(x)dx \right] \quad (18)$$

where $f(x)$ is the PDF of voltage amplitude of noise.
Thus, by using equation (7) to express the PDF of voltage amplitude noise $f_n(x)$, the bit error probability of LP stream can be written as:

$$P_{lp}(16) = \frac{1}{2}\left(Y(d_2) + \frac{1}{2}Y(2d_1' + d_2) - \frac{1}{2}Y(2d_1' + 3d_2) \right) \quad (19)$$

where $Y(d) = \int_{-\infty}^{d} f_n(x)dx$, and expressed by:

$$Y(d) = e^{-A_A} \sum_{k=0}^{+\infty} \frac{A_A^k}{k!} \cdot \frac{1}{2} \cdot erfc\left(\frac{d}{\sigma_k} \right)$$

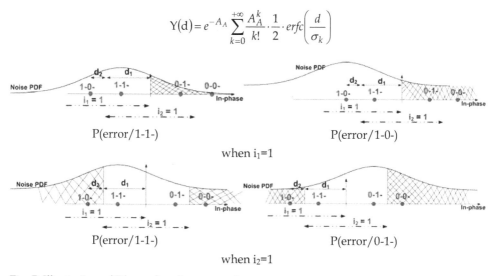

Fig. 7. Illustration of P(error/x-y-) computation

Fig. 8a and 8b depict the error probability of HP and LP stream of hierarchical 4/16-QAM with α is equal to 1 and 4 and when the noise is given by Middleton class-A noise. Globally, the HP stream is less protected than the classical QPSK while the LP stream is less protected than the M-QAM with same constellation diagram.

When α is equal to 1, the HP and LP curves of error probability (red and green) are almost the same. They are around the curve of pure 16-QAM (blue), and far from the curve of pure 4-QAM (black).   However, when α is equal to 4, the HP and LP curves are different. HP curve of error probability (blue) is close to the curve of pure 4-QAM (black).

This seems logic because when α grows, the energy of the constellation is more concentrated on HP stream and on base 4-QAM in the entire constellation. In fact, when α is increased, the energy of fictitious symbols grows (d_1 increases), expression (3). In contrary, the energy of refinement symbols diminishes (d_2 decreases), expression (4). Moreover, impulse noise induced a plateau in the error probability curve as it is the case of classical QAM (derived from Miyamoto, 1995).

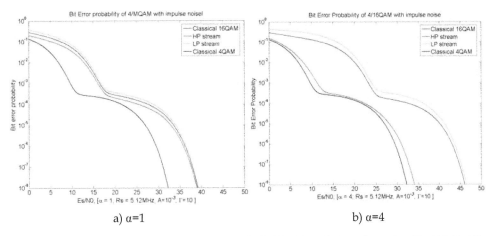

a) $\alpha=1$ b) $\alpha=4$

Fig. 8. Analytical curves of error probability of 4/16QAM with impulse noise (A=10⁻³, Γ=10)

3.3 Analysis of modulation penalty

Hierarchical modulation allows transmission of two different streams on the same transmission channel: one hp stream based on 4-QAM, and one LP stream build above the 4-QAM. Therefore, HP 4-QAM stream differs from pure 4-QAM by a quantity called the penalty modulation.

One calculation method exists in the scientific literature (Jiang, 2005), but does not lead to exact value at high Signal to Noise Ratio (SNR) which is the case in practice.

A new calculation method has been suggested to compute penalty of modulation (Tamgnoue, 2007). For that, we define:

- SNR as the signal to noise ratio of the hierarchical modulation;
- MNR (Modulation Noise Ratio) as the signal to noise ratio of the HP stream considering the introduction of LP stream.

To estimate the MNR, the worst case symbols are selected in the constellation diagram. These symbols correspond to the nearest symbols to the middle of the constellation diagram as illustrated in fig. 9. Thus, SNR and MMR are respectively obtained as:

$$SNR = \frac{2d_1^2 + \frac{2}{3}\left(\frac{M}{4} - 1\right)d_2^2}{2\sigma_N^2} \tag{20}$$

and

$$MNR = \frac{2\alpha^2 d_2^2}{2\sigma_N^2} \tag{21}$$

Therefore, the penalty denoted P_{mnr} is given by (Tamgnoue, 2007):

$$P_{mnr} = \frac{SNR}{MNR} = \left(1 + \frac{\left(\sqrt{M}/2\right) - 1}{\alpha}\right)^2 + \frac{\frac{1}{3}\left(\frac{M}{4} - 1\right)}{\alpha^2} \tag{22}$$

This penalty is function of M and α, whereas it does not depend on SNR. It grows with M and it is in inverse proportion to α.

The fig. 10.a and fig. 10.b depict the calculated penalty in term of error probability. In these figures, the calculated penalty is in green, and the modulation penalty estimated from curves of error probability is depicted in red. Globally, the penalty does not changes significantly and is constant when probability error varies.

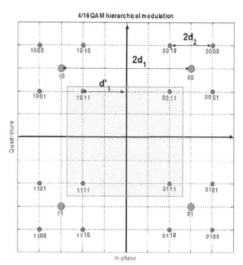

Fig. 9. Penalty analysis in constellation diagram

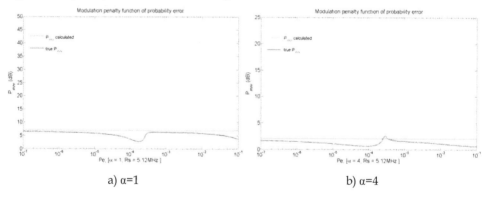

a) $\alpha=1$ b) $\alpha=4$

Fig. 10. Analytical curves of modulation penalty of 4/16QAM with impulse noise ($A=10^{-3}$, $\Gamma=10$)

3.4 Bit error probability of OFDM hierarchical 4/M-QAM calculation

At the receiver side, the noise in hierarchical symbol is given by:

$$z_k = \frac{1}{\sqrt{N}} \sum_{l=0}^{N-1} n_l e^{-j\frac{2\pi kl}{N}} \qquad 0 \le k \le N-1 \qquad (23)$$

where n_l is the noise in the transmission channel.

Therefore, error probability OFDM hierarchical 4/M-QAM is the same as 4/M-QAM where the noise in presence is given by z_k. PDF of z_k is thus needed.

Like presented by Huynh (Huynh, 1998), lets define:

$$u_k = \frac{1}{\sqrt{N}} n_l e^{-j\frac{2\pi kl}{N}} \tag{24}$$

Given the circular symmetry of the PDF of n_l, the PDF of u_k is given by:

$$f_u(x,y) = e^{-A_A} \sum_{q=0}^{\infty} \frac{A_A^q N}{q!} \cdot \frac{1}{2\pi\sigma_q^2} \exp\left(-\frac{(x^2+y^2)N}{2\sigma_q^2}\right) \tag{25}$$

Following the approach discussed by Ghosh (Ghosh, 1996), it is supposed that u_k are independent random variables. Using the characteristic function method, the PDF of z_k is thus given by:

$$f_{z'}(x,y) = e^{-A_A N} \sum_{q=0}^{\infty} \frac{(A_A N)^q}{q!} \cdot \frac{1}{2\pi\sigma_{z'q}^2} \exp\left(-\frac{x^2+y^2}{2\sigma_{z'q}^2}\right) \tag{26}$$

where $\sigma_{z'q}^2 = \frac{q/(A_A N) + \Gamma}{1+\Gamma}$ and $\Gamma = \frac{\sigma_g^2}{(A_A N)\frac{\sigma_i^2}{N}}$.

It is thus similar to general Middleton class-A equation when A_A becomes $A_A N$ and σ_i^2 becomes σ_i^2/N.

However, the hidden hypothesis surrounding this expression is that only when one pulse of duration equal to one QAM symbol impedes the entire OFDM symbol. It means that this pulse has been spread in all the N subcarriers, so duration grows N time and power decreases by a factor N.

In the general case, pulse will have duration of N_i in term on number of QAM symbols and an OFDM symbol will contain X_{imp} pulses. Therefore, PDF of z_k, $f_z(x,y)$, will become (Tamgnoue, 2007):

$$f_z(x,y) = e^{-A_A} \sum_{q=0}^{\infty} \frac{A_z^q}{q!} \cdot \frac{1}{2\pi\sigma_{zq}^2} \exp\left(-\frac{x^2+y^2}{2\sigma_{zq}^2}\right) \tag{27}$$

$$A_z = \frac{N}{N + D_{imp}/A_A} \tag{28}$$

$$\sigma_{zq}^2 = \frac{(q/A_z + \Gamma_z)}{1+\Gamma_z} \tag{29}$$

$$\sigma_{zg}^2 = \sigma_g^2 + \frac{(X_{imp}-1)A_A\sigma_i^2}{X_{imp}} \tag{30}$$

$$\Gamma_z = X_{imp}\Gamma + (X_{imp} - 1) \tag{31}$$

In the case of OFDM 4/16-QAM, the expression of error probability of HP and LP stream, by using equation (27) to express the PDF of voltage amplitude noise $f_z(x,y)$, are given by:

$$P_{z/hp}(M) = \frac{1}{2}\left(\frac{1}{2}Y_z(d_1' + 2d_2) + \frac{1}{2}Y_z(d_1' + 2d_2)\right) \tag{32}$$

and,

$$P_{z/lp}(16) = \frac{1}{2}\left(Y_z(d_2) + \frac{1}{2}Y_z(2d_1' + d_2) - \frac{1}{2}Y_z(2d_1' + 3d_2)\right) \tag{33}$$

where $Y(d) = \int_{-\infty}^{d} f_z(x)dx,$ and expressed by:

$$Y(d) = e^{-A_z}\sum_{q=0}^{+\infty}\frac{A_z^k}{q!}\cdot\frac{1}{2}\cdot erfc\left(\frac{d}{\sigma_{zq}}\right).$$

The fig. 11.a and fig. 11.b depict the error probability of HP and LP stream of OFDM hierarchical 4/16-QAM with α is equal to 1 and 4 when the noise is given by Middleton class-A noise. For comparison purpose, the curves of simple hierarchical QAM are added on the figures.

It appears directly that the plateau has vanished due to the introduction of OFDM. It is a general observation which has already been studied in classical OFDM/QAM systems in presence of impulse noise (Zhidkov, 2006, Abdelkefi, 2005, Suraweera, 2004, Huynh, 1998, Ghosh, 1996). OFDM/QAM is proved to be more robust against impulse noise than classical single carrier QAM systems. This advantage appears because the impulse noise energy is spread among OFDM subcarriers. However, this spreading effect turns into disadvantage if the impulse noise energy becomes too strong.

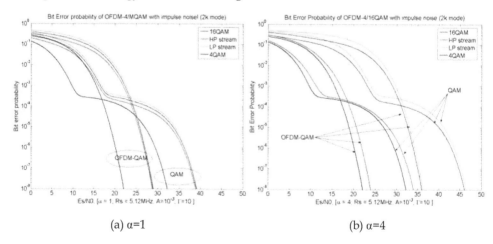

(a) α=1   (b) α=4

Fig. 11. Analytical curves of error probability of OFDM hierarchical 4/16QAM with impulse noise ($A_A=10^{-3}$, $\Gamma=10$).

In the same figures, when α is equal to 1, the HP and LP curves of error probability of OFDM 4/16-QAM are almost the same. However, when α is equal to 4, the HP and LP curves are different. HP curve of error probability (blue) is close to the curve of pure OFDM with 4-QAM (black).

4. Simulation results

4.1 Impulse noise simulation

For analysis purpose, DVB has defined impulse noise model which is based on gated Gaussian noise (ETSI TR 102 401, 2005). In this model of impulse noise, an impulsive event comprises a train of bursts and each burst contains many impulses. The impulsive events are defined by their patterns which are therefore characterized by: burst duration, burst inter-arrival time, pulse duration, impulse inter-arrival time. This pattern is used as a gate and applied to Additive White Gaussian Noise (AWGN) to obtain gated Gaussian noise. By this way, 6 patterns have been defined an used to resilience evaluation of impulse noise.

But this model does not fit directly to Middleton class-A model which is a statistical analytical model. Nevertheless, to transform this model according to analytical Middleton model, the pattern parameters have been taken as statistical parameters and some links have been defined between them. As illustrated in fig. 12, the pattern has been built in such a way that the mean values of the duration and inter-arrival time are linked with the constraint that their ratio equals the Middleton impulsive index A_A. The duration has been given by a Rayleigh distribution while the inter-arrival has been given by the Poisson distribution. The amplitude has been statistically obtained with Rayleigh distribution. On the top obtained impulse noise, AWGN has been added to simulate the Gaussian contribution with the constraint that the ratio of mean Gaussian noise power and impulse noise power is equal to the mean power ratio Γ.

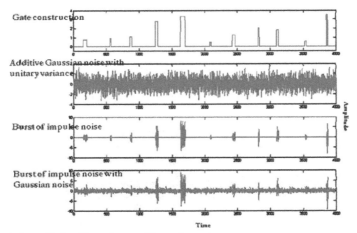

Fig. 12. Simulation of joint Gaussian and impulse noise.

4.2 Results analysis

The fig. 13.a and fig. 13.b depict some analytical and simulated bit error probability of HP and LP stream of OFDM hierarchical 4/16-QAM in presence of impulse noise. The values of the parameters of impulse noise are given by the impulse noise test pattern #3 specified in validation Task Force Report (ETSI TR 102 401, 2005, Lago-Fernández, 2004). In this figure, we illustrate simulation points by markers, analytical curves of BEP with both impulse and Gaussian noise by solid lines and analytical curves of BEP with Gaussian noise by dashed lines.

We observe that the simulated results are very close to analytical curves. Generally, HP stream is more robust than classical OFDM QAM which is also more robust than LP stream. The parameter α =2 leads to a good compromise between the strength of HP stream and the weakness of LP stream.

Compared to the case where the noise is purely Gaussian, we observe a right shift in the BEP curve. This shift corresponds to the penalty induced by impulse noise. For the case of impulse noise test pattern #3, in 4k OFDM mode, the impulse noise penalty is the same for the two streams and is equal to 8.3 dB.

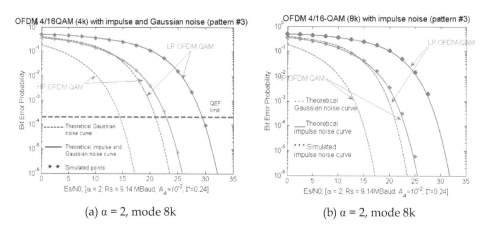

(a) α = 2, mode 8k   (b) α = 2, mode 8k

Fig. 13. Simulation of HP and LP bit error probability of 2k OFDM 4/16-QAM in presence of both impulse and Gaussian noise given by pattern #3

5. Conclusions

Hierarchical modulation is a modulation technique allowing to transmit two completely separate streams modulated in the same transmitter and on the same channel. On this, a High Priority (HP) streams are embedded within a Low Priority (LP) streams. Hierarchical modulation has been defined in many standards.

In the frame of DVT-T\H, this paper have analyzed the bit error probability of hierarchical OFDM QAM modulation in presence of both Gaussian and impulse noises. It has proved that the curve of error probability depends on the parameters of hierarchical QAM, on the number of subcarriers, and on all the noise properties (not only on the PDF of voltage). Furthermore, the power penalty induced by hierarchical modulation has been defined and analytical formula to tackle this penalty has been provided. The formulas we have derived can be used when installing a new OFDM hierarchical QAM communications. Indeed, according to the desired BEP and the impulse noise properties, transmission parameters, like the number of subcarriers, the modulation order and the signal power, can be obtained efficiently to make right use of system resources.

Analysis of bit error probability performance has show that mix of OFDM and hierarchical modulation used in DVB-T\H systems present real differentiate performance for HP streams and LP streams. It improves the spectrum and the resources utilisation and it gives features to deal with impulse noise. It offers many opportunities for operators to delivering enhanced services. For instance, operators can launch different services for different kind of receiver (fixe or mobile). Many trials are been taken around the world demonstrating the capabilities of hierarchical modulation.

6. References

F. Abdelkefi, P. Duhamel, F. Alberge, " Impulsive noise cancellation in multicarrier transmission", IEEE Trans. Commun., vol. 53, No. 1, pp. 94-106, Jan. 2005.

L. Berry, "Understanding Middleton's Canonical Formula for Class A Noise", IEEE Trans. EMC, vol. EMC-23, No. 4, pp. 337-344, Nov. 1981.

E. Biglieri, "Coding and modulation for a horrible channel," IEEE Commun. Mag., vol. 41, no. 5, pp. 92-98, May 2003.

DVB Document A122: "Framing structure, channel coding and modulation for a second generation digital terrestrial television broadcasting system (DVB-T2)", June 2008.

ETSI, EN 300 744, V1.5.1, Digital Video Broadcasting (DVB): framing structure, channel coding and modulation for digital terrestrial television, Nov. 2004.

ETSI TR 102 401 v1.1.1, "Digital Video Broadcasting (DVB); Transmission to Handheld Terminals (DVB-H); Validation Task Force Report", May 2005.

ETSI EN 302 304 v1.1.1, "Digital Video Broadcasting (DVB): Transmission System for Handheld Terminals (DVB-H)", Nov. 2004.

ETSI 300 744 v1.5.1, "Digital Video Broadcasting (DVB): Framing structure, channel coding and modulation for digital terrestrial television", Nov. 2004.

G. Faria, J.A. Henriksson, E. Stare, P. Talmola, "DVB-H: Digital Broadcast Services to Handheld Devices", Proceedings of the IEEE, Vol. 94, NO. 1, pp. 194 – 209, Jan. 2006.

M. Ghosh, "Analysis of the effect of impulse noise on Multicarrier and Single carrier QAM systems", IEEE Trans. Commun. Vol.44, pp. 145-147, Feb. 1996.

H. T. Huynh, P. Fortier, G. Delisle, "Influence of a class of man-made noise on QAM Multicarrier systems", Seventh Communication Theory Mini-conference (Globecom '98), Sydney, Australie, pp. 231-236, 8-12 Nov 1998.

H. Jiang and P. A. Wilford, "A hierarchical modulation for upgrading digital broadcast systems", IEEE Trans. Broadcasting, vol. 51, no2, pp. 223-229 , 2005.

José Lago-Fernández and John Salter, "Modeling impulsive interference in DVB-T", EBU technical review, july 2004.

Middleton, "Canonical Non-Gaussian Noise Models: Their Implications for Measurement and for Prediction of Receiver Performance", IEEE Trans. EMC, vol. EMC-21, No. 3, pp. 209-220, Aug. 1979.

Miyamoto S., M. Katayama, "Performance analysis of QAM system under Class A impulsive noise environment", IEEE Trans. EMC, vol. 37, No.2, May 1995.

JG Proakis, Digital Communications, 4th ed., McGraw-Hill, New York, 2001.

Alexander Schertz and Chris Weck, "Hierarchical modulation — the transmission of two independent DVB-T multiplexes on a single TV frequency", EBU technical review, april 2003.

H.A. Suraweera, Armstrong J., "Noise bucket effect for impulse noise in OFDM", Electronics Letters, vol. 40-10, pp. 1156- 1157, Sept. 2004.

Tamgnoue V., Moeyaert V., Bette S., Mégret P., "Performance analysis of DVB-H OFDM hierarchical modulation in impulse noise environment", 14th IEEE Symposium on Communications and Vehicular Technology in the BENELUX, Delft (The Netherlands), 15/11/2007.

Tamgnoue V., Moeyaert V., Mpongo H., Bette S., Mégret P., "Performance analysis of hierarchical modulation in presence of impulse noise", published in Proceedings (on CD-ROM) of BroadBand Europe 2007, Anvers (BE), 03/12-06/12, 2007.

Vitthaladevuni P. K., Alouini M-S., "BER Computation of 4/M-QAM Hierarchical Constellations", IEEE Transactions on Broadcasting, Vol. 47, No. 3, pp. 228-239, 2001.

Vitthaladevuni P. K., Alouini M.-S., "A closed-form expression for the exact BER of generalized PAM and QAM constellations," IEEE Transactions on Communications, vol. 52, no. 5, pp. 698–700, 2004.

Wang Shu, Kwon Soonyil, Yi, "On enhancing hierarchical modulation", 2008 IEEE International Symposium on Broadband Multimedia Systems and Broadcasting (USA-Las Vegas), pp. 1-6, March 31 2008-April 2 2008.

Zhidkov S. V., "Performance analysis and optimization of OFDM receiver with blanking nonlinearity in impulsive noise environment", IEEE Transactions on Vehicular Technology, Vol. 55, No. 1, pp. 234-242, Jan. 2006.

4

Adaptive Video Transmission over Wireless MIMO System

Jia-Chyi Wu, Chi-Min Li, and Kuo-Hsean Chen *National Taiwan Ocean University*
Department of Communications, Navigation and Control Engineering
Taiwan

1. Introduction

There has been an interesting issue in multimedia communications over wireless system in recent years. In order to achieve high data rate wireless multimedia communications, spatial multiplexing technique (Foschini & Gans, 1998; Wolniansky et al. 1998) has recently developed as one of the most noteworthy techniques as multiple-input and multiple-output (MIMO) systems. If the channel state information is perfectly available at the transmitter (Driessen & Foschini, 1999; Burr, 2003), we can maximize the channel capacity to design a realizable video transmission system. Under channel capacity limitation, the chapter presents how to employ joint source-channel coding algorithm with adequate modulation techniques to get the possibly best performance in the system design. Adaptive video coding to the varying channel conditions in real-time is well matched to MIMO systems for an optimized video transmission. An important matter in designing adaptive video transmission system is how often the feedback of the channel state information should be carried out. In fact, the feedback interval is mainly decided by the channel characteristics. For wireless fading channels, the feedback information needed to be able to capture the time varying channel characteristics for a true adaptive transmission. Song & Chen (2007, 2008) proposed adaptive algorithm design to utilized partial channel state information from receiver for layered scalable video coding (SVC) transmission over MIMO system. There are some interesting topics related in adaptive video transmission over wireless multimedia communication systems can be found in (Chen & He, 2006).

In our proposed system, we investigate the system performance of a joint MPEG-2 coding scheme with convolutional channel coding and space time block coding (STBC) techniques, associated with suitable modulation method (BPSK or QPSK), for video data transmission over a wireless MIMO system with Rayleigh fading noises. Rates assigned to MPEG-2 source code and convolutional channel code as well as space-time block code schemes are based on the feedback information from Performance Control Unit (PCU) under system channel capacity limitation, which ensures the proposed system achieved the best performance compared to a conventional designed system. In a conventional way, source coding and channel coding are designed to accomplish the best system performance respectively. With simply combining the best source coding scheme with the best channel coding scheme together, the system does not promise a better overall performance.

Consequently, the present algorithm employs joint source-channel coding scheme and MIMO concept to get the best performance in the system design over fading channel.

We are interested in the joint source-channel coding with modulation scheme design under the channel capacity constraint consideration in a MIMO system. Figure 1 shows joint source-channel codes under the combination of various source coding rates and various channel coding rates. Source coding is concerned with the efficient representation of a signal. While bit errors in the uncompressed signal can cause minimal distortion, in its compressed format a single bit error can lead to significantly large errors. For data, channel coding is necessary to overcome the errors resulted from transmission channel. We have noticed that combining source coding with adequate channel coding, we should be able to achieve a better system performance. Assuming that the overall system transmission rate $r = k/n$, where k is the source coding rate and n is the channel coding rate. In Fig. 1, we have found that a better performance (with a lower distortion) can be promised when we increase the source coding rate k, while we increase the channel coding rate n, a higher bit error rate (a lower system performance) happened under the same E_b/N_0, signal-to-noise ratio (SNR) criterion. Therefore, we would like to design a transmission system with higher source coding rate k but lower channel coding rate n to achieve a higher overall transmission rate r. Since the overall transmission rate r is under channel capacity limitation, we have to justify the concept with proper method to design transmission system.

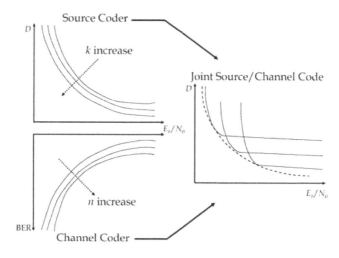

Fig. 1. Joint source and channel coding with different rates

The overall transmission rate r can be obtained by source coding rate k cooperated with channel coding rate n. We will not satisfy the system performance while we have a high source compression ratio (lower k) with strong channel protection (lower n). In turns, if we apply a low source compression ratio (higher source coding rate k with low distortion) but a high channel coding rate n (weak channel protection capability) to the system, which may result in higher bit error rate (BER) performance, we are not satisfactory with the reconstructed signal from the received high BER data. It is quite clear that we have to find a better match between source coding rate and channel coding rate to assure an acceptable system performance.

The most significant criterion in designing a transmission system is the channel capacity limitation. The available channel capacity restricts the overall transmission rate r, which is the rate between source coding rate k and channel coding rate n. We have to consider source coding rate, channel coding rate, and the corresponding modulation type all together simultaneously to cope with the channel capacity limitation. Assuming channel capacity limitation is one bit/transmission, we are asked to keep overall transmission rate $r \leq 1$ bit/channel-use, which can be achieved only with $k \leq n$. Therefore, we will keep our system rate design with $r \approx 1$ and $r \leq 1$, that is, $k \approx n$ and $k \leq n$. Furthermore, space-time block coding (STBC) algorithm was introduced (Alamouti, 1998; Tarokh et al., 1999) as an effective transmit diversity technique to resist fading effect. For a fixed number of transmit antennas, its decoding complexity increases exponentially with the transmission rate. The proposed algorithm employs joint source-channel coding scheme with STBC technique to get the best performance in MIMO systems design.

1.1 Outline
The rest of the chapter is organized as follows. Section 2 describes the system configuration adopted in this proposed algorithm. Experimental results for performance of the overall adaptive video transmission system compared with a conventional scheme over Rayleigh fading channel are shown in Section 3. Finally, a summary and conclusions are presented in Section 4.

2. System configuration
We are interested in the joint source-channel coding with modulation scheme design under the channel capacity constraint consideration in a MIMO system. We have applied the integrated transmission system design method (Daut & Ma, 1998) for digital transmission of video signals over noisy channels. To transmit a given video bit stream efficiently, we propose a joint source-channel coding system as shown in Figure 2.

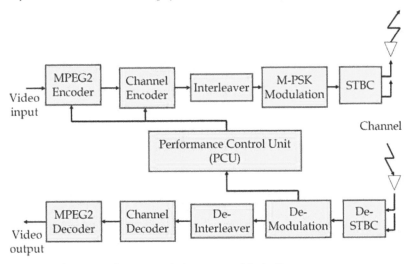

Fig. 2. Proposed adaptive video transmission system block diagram

In this proposed system, the video sequence is first source coded by a MPEG2 scheme (Sikora, 1997). In order to reduce the system complexity of decoding, after the source coding stage, we use convolutional code and STBC in channel coding. The interleaver is adopted which is effected resisting burst error in wireless channel. There are two modulation techniques employed to be selected, BPSK or QPSK. The channel capacity is limited to one bit/transmission.

2.1 MPEG2 video source coding

The proposed adaptive video transmission system has been experimentally tested using an MPEG2 source coding algorithm provided from MPEG.ORG website.

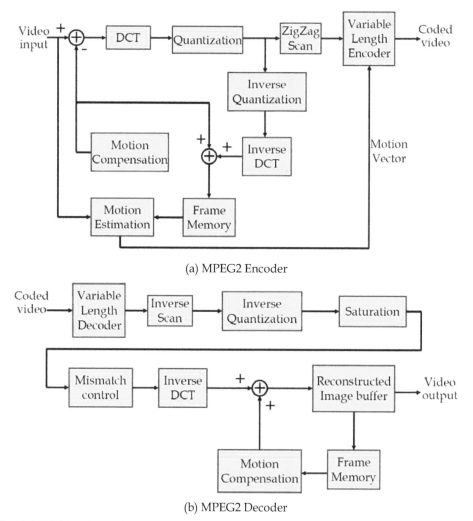

(a) MPEG2 Encoder

(b) MPEG2 Decoder

Fig. 3. MPEG2 video coding block diagram

Figure 3 shows the video coding and decoding block diagram of MPEG2 scheme, in which we can change the coding bit rate of MPEG2 to obtain the required source compression ratio. In the proposed system, there are three MPEG2 video coding rates adopted and the resulted compressed video frames compared with the original test video is shown in Fig. 4. The source coding scheme is MPEG2 format and there are 160×120 pixels in every frame. It can be seen that the video quality is better with MPEG2 coding rate 0.6659 bit/pixel (bpp) among the three tested coding rates.

Original captured video   Coding rate: 0.4994 bpp

Coding rate: 0.3986 bpp   Coding rate: 0.6659 bpp

Fig. 4. Video quality comparison of original and MPEG2 compressed test video frames

2.2 Channel coding – convolutional coding and space-time block coding

In order to reduce the channel error effect and to improve the system performance while transmitting video signals over wireless channel, we have employed the convolutional encoder and maximum-likelihood Viterbi hard decision decoder for channel error correction. Figure 5 shows a typical 1/2 recursive systematic convolutional (RSC) code scheme with generator function $G(D) = [1, (1 + D^2)/(1 + D + D^2)]$ (Proakis, 2001). After the convolutional encoding, the processed data is fed into a random interleaver to reduce burst error effect in wireless channel. The convolutional coding rates provided in this proposed system are set as 2/5, 1/2, and 2/3, respectively. The channel coding rate selected is corresponding to the MPEG2 source coding rate to satisfy the channel capacity limitation to one bit/transmission. For the system simulation, we have adopted two modulation types: BPSK and QPSK. The corresponding coding rates and modulation types are listed in Table 1. In order to receive a decent quality video sequence over wireless MIMO system with good coding gain real time, we have selected convolutional code and space time block code (STBC) for the channel coding. It has been known that a transmission system with antenna diversity can achieve reliable communication over wireless channel. Antenna diversity is achieved by employing spatially separated antennas at the transmitter and/or receiver. The advantage with multiple antennas scheme is that it results in a drastic increase in the channel capacity (Foschini & Gans, 1998). Alamouti (1998) introduced an efficient scheme which involves using two transmit antennas and one receive antenna (2×1 STBC code) for a wireless communication system. Tarokh et al. (1999) generalized the Alamouti scheme with STBC code to an arbitrary number of transmit antennas. STBC codes do not in general

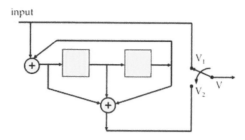

Fig. 5. Recursive systematic convolutional (RSC) encoder, coding rate = ½

Type	Transmission rate $(r = k/n)$	Channel coding rate, n (Convolutional)	Source coding rate, k (MPEG2)	Modulation type
A	0.9965 bit	2/5	0.3986 bpp	BPSK, QPSK
B	0.9988 bit	1/2	0.4994 bpp	BPSK, QPSK
C	0.9989 bit	2/3	0.6659 bpp	BPSK, QPSK

Table 1. Corresponding source-channel coding rate to achieve transmission rate, $r \approx 1$ bit.

provide any coding gain, therefore, it may need to be combined with an outer channel coding scheme to provide such coding gains. We then select convolutional code and space time block code for the channel coding. To simplify the analysis, we consider the simple STBC G_2 encoder (Alamouti, 1998). The input symbol vector of the STBC encoder is denoted as $S = [S(0), S(1), ..., S(2N-1)]^T$, where N is the number of the subcarriers. Let $S_1 = [S(0), S(1), ..., S(N-1)]^T$ and $S_2 = [S(N), S(N+1), ..., S(2N-1)]^T$, after the STBC encoder, the generated STBC G_2 coded data symbols are

$$G_2^{STBC} = \begin{bmatrix} S_1 & S_2 \\ -S_2^* & S_1^* \end{bmatrix} \begin{matrix} \text{time} \end{matrix} \quad \text{antenna} \tag{1}$$

It can be found that, at time T, the first antenna sends out symbol S_1 and the second antenna sends out symbol S_2; at time $T+1$, the first antenna sends out symbol $-S^*_2$ and the second antenna sends out symbol S^*_1. It is easy to show that the inner product of matrix G_2 is zero, which means the data within matrix G_2 are orthogonal to each other. The space diversity types applied in this proposed system are 2×2, 2×1, and 1×2, respectively. Figure 6 suggests a 2×2 STBC G_2 coded diversity transmission block diagram. The received signals can be represented as follows,

$$r_1(t) = S_1 h_1 + S_2 h_2 + n_1 \tag{2}$$

$$r_2(t+\tau) = -S^*_2 h_1 + S^*_1 h_2 + n_2 \tag{3}$$

$$r_3(t) = S_1 h_3 + S_2 h_4 + n_3 \tag{4}$$

$$r_4(t+\tau) = -S^*_2 h_3 + S^*_1 h_4 + n_4 \tag{5}$$

where S_1 and S_2 are the transmitted signals (* represents complex conjugate), $h_1 \sim h_4$ are the channel fading coefficients between transmitter antennas and receiver antennas as shown in

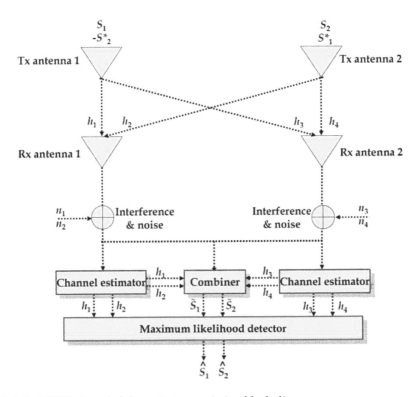

Fig. 6. A 2×2 STBC G_2 coded diversity transmission block diagram

Antennas	Rx antenna 1	Rx antenna 2
Tx antenna 1	h_1	h_3
Tx antenna 2	h_2	h_4

Table 2. Channel impulse response between transmitter and receiver

Table 2, and $n_1 \sim n_4$ are corresponding AWGN channel noise. The coefficients $h_1, h_2, h_3,$ and h_4 can be represented as the following,

$$h_i = \alpha_i e^{j\theta_i}, i = 1, 2, 3, 4 \tag{6}$$

Assuming that the channel impulse responses can be fully estimated, we then are able to reconstruct $\tilde{S}_1$ and $\tilde{S}_2$ with the received signals, $r_1, r_2, r_3,$ and r_4 by the following equations:

$$\tilde{S}_1 = h_1^* r_1 + h_2 r_2^* + h_3^* r_3 + h_4 r_4^* \tag{7}$$

$$\tilde{S}_2 = h_2^* r_1 - h_1 r_2^* + h_4^* r_3 - h_3 r_4^* \tag{8}$$

Substituting $r_1, r_2, r_3,$ and r_4 from equations (2) ~ (5) into equations (7) and (8), we have,

$$\tilde{S}_1 = (\alpha_1^2 + \alpha_2^2 + \alpha_3^2 + \alpha_4^2)S_1 + h_1^* n_1 + h_2 n_2^* + h_3^* n_3 + h_4 n_4^* \tag{9}$$

$$\widetilde{S}_2 = (\alpha_1^2 + \alpha_2^2 + \alpha_3^2 + \alpha_4^2)S_2 - h_1 n_2^* + h_2^* n_1 - h_3 n_4^* + h_4^* n_3 \tag{10}$$

Finally, we can decode S_i by applying Maximum Likelihood Detector (MLD) rule if and only if:

$$\begin{aligned}(\alpha_1^2 + \alpha_2^2 + \alpha_3^2 + \alpha_4^2)|S_i|^2 - \widetilde{S}_1 S_i^* - \widetilde{S}_1^* S_i \\ \leq (\alpha_1^2 + \alpha_2^2 + \alpha_3^2 + \alpha_4^2)|S_k|^2 - \widetilde{S}_1 S_k^* - \widetilde{S}_1^* S_k, \quad \forall i \neq k\end{aligned} \tag{11}$$

To realize the channel coding rate effect under wireless Rayleigh fading channel with AWGN noise conditions, we have performed the experiment for 2×2 system antenna structure with three convolutional coding rates: 2/5, 1/2 and 2/3, respectively. The resulted system performance is shown in Figure 7. The system performance is improved with lower channel coding rate in the experiment. It can be found from Fig. 7, rate 2/3 convolutional coded system is with the worst bit error rate (BER) performance, where rate 2/5 convolutional coded system shown the best BER performance at the same SNR conditions. On the other side, system with lower channel coding rate (2/5 in this case) resulted in slower overall transmission rate. Therefore, if we may alternate the source coding rate corresponding to the channel coding rate, we are able to remain a consistent transmission rate which achieves channel capacity with considerable system BER performance.

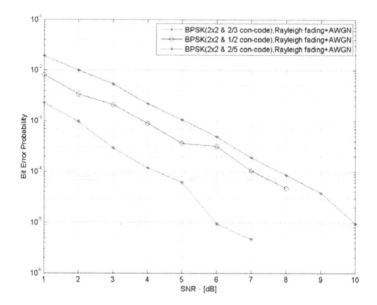

Fig. 7. Bit error rate (BER) performance of three concolutional channel coding rates under Rayleigh fading channel with AWGN noise in a 2×2 MIMO system.

2.3 Performance Control Unit (PCU)

Rates assigned to MPEG2 source coding and convolutional channel coding schemes as well as STBC space diversity selection are based on the feedback information from Performance Control Unit (PCU) under system channel capacity limitation, which ensures the given system achieved the best performance compared to conventional systems. PCU is the key components in the adaptive system design, where we have assigned three PCU states to report the changeable overall transmission status as shown in Table 3.

PCU state	BER after CTS state feedback	Convolutional code rate	MPEG2 code rate	No. of receiver antenna
State A: $H = 0$	BER = 0 %	2/3	0.6659 bpp	2
State B: $H = 1$	BER ≤ 20%	1/2	0.4994 bpp	2
State C: $H = -1$	BER > 20%	2/5	0.3986 bpp	1

Table 3. System state assignment of PCU

We adopt first-order Markov chain to describe the system states transfer (Daut & Ma, 1998). The present state is associated with the one-step adjacent state as shown in Figure 8. We have set-up three states to collaborate with the variable Rayleigh fading channel conditions. The three states is arranged to form a circular situation where the state transition is made according to Table 3, the system state assignment of PCU. On Fig. 8, H is the output status index of the PCU. We have assigned that, $H = 0$ is the "state A" index, system with good channel condition and a fast channel coding rate ($n = 2/3$) is assigned; $H = 1$ is the "state B" index, the channel is in an "OK" condition and the transmission data need more protection (channel coding rate $n = 1/2$); $H = -1$ is the "state C" index, channel condition has degraded and the channel code with good protection has to be utilized ($n = 2/5$).

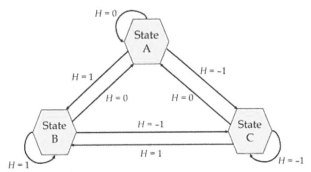

Fig. 8. System state transition diagram

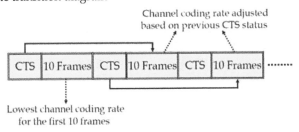

Fig. 9. Transmission rate adjustable for MPEG2 video frames

In the simulation experiment, we first send Command Testing Sequence (CTS), consisting of 10 bits stream of "1", which is attached in front of the transmitted data stream as shown in

Fig. 9. After receiver been channel decoded the received data sequence, the BER information of the CTS is fed-back to the transmitter site as a status index H to adjust the next transmission status as shown in Table 3.

3. System performance analysis

Under the channel capacity constraint, which we assumed in the simulation experiment is 1 bit/transmission; we have proposed an adaptive MPEG2 video transmission over wireless MIMO system. Based upon the feedback information index from Performance Control Unit, we adjust the compression rate of MPEG-2 video coder jointly with associated convolutional channel code rate to reach the 1-bit channel capacity limitation. We have also utilized the space diversity with 2×2, 2×1 or 1×2 antenna configurations to obtain an accessible system performance. We have adopted three types of rate assignment as shown in Table 1. According to the feedback error rate information from test sequence as shown in Table 3, we can choose adequate joint code rate assignment (system state, Fig. 8) with suitable space diversity STBC to achieve the best system performance.

3.1 Experiment procedure

System transmission simulation is based on the system block diagram shown in Fig. 2. The experiment procedures are provided as follows, (1) capture video image streams from video camera and applied MPEG2 video coding scheme to produce a better data compression ratio and then stored as an MPEG file (*.mpg); (2) the MPEG2 coded video file is fed into a convolutional encoder, a random interleaver (size = 1024), M-PSK modulation and STBC encoder, consecutively; (3) the resulted data streams are transmitted through wireless Rayleigh fading channel with AWGN noises. For the proposed adaptive video transmission system, we have assigned three combinations of the joint source-channel code transmission rate adjusted to be nearly but not greater than 1 bit/transmission ($r \approx 1$ and $r \leq 1$) associated with proper M-PSK modulation scheme (as listed in Table 1).

The system simulation transmitted a total of 30 video frames, each transmission (10 video frames) will be added up a 10 bits Command Testing Sequence before transmitted over wireless channel consisting of Rayleigh fading and AWGN noises. With appropriate selection of receiver antenna numbers (as shown in Table 3), we have gained space diversity to improve system performance. At the receiver end, de-modulation, de-interleaving, and de-coding procedures are provided to reconstructed MPEG video. After received the feedback error rate information of the CTS sequence, a status index H of the PCU is fed-back to the transmitter site to adjust the next 10 video frames transmission status as shown in Table 3.

3.2 Simulation results

The bit error rate (BER) performance versus SNR for different space diversity schemes over Rayleigh fading and AWGN channel is shown in Figure 10. It is assumed that the amplitudes of fading noise from each transmitter antenna to each receiver antenna are mutually uncorrelated Rayleigh distributed and that the average signal power at each receiver antenna from each transmitter antenna is the same. Furthermore, we assumed that the receiver has perfect knowledge of the channel conditions. The simulation results of two transmitter antennas and two receiver antennas (2×2) STBC coded system shows the best

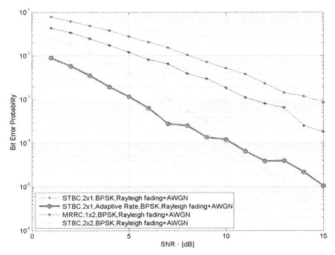

Fig. 10. The BER performance comparison of STBC systems (2/3 convolutional coded) and the proposed adaptive system (with 2×1 antennas structure) over Rayleigh fading channel.

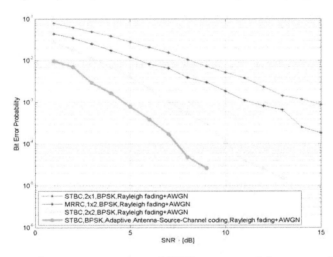

Fig. 11. The BER performance comparison of STBC systems and the proposed adaptive system over Rayleigh fading channel (the number of receiver antenna is adaptive).

BER performance at higher SNR values (> 10dB), while the worst performance goes to the 2x1 STBC coded system. The proposed adaptive coding system with 2x1 (in this case, number of antenna is fixed) space diversity can improve the system performance especially in lower SNR (< 10dB) situation, and with close performance as the 2x2 STBC coded system in SNR > 10 dB environment. The BER system performance can be improved more with adaptive receiver antenna numbers (as given in Table 2) of the proposed scheme as shown in Figure 11. It is about 2.5 dB SNR gain at the same BER condition for the proposed system. We have extended the total transmitted video frames to 100 for the experiment, each transmission (10 video frames) is added up a 10 bits CTS before transmitted over wireless

Rayleigh fading channel. From Figure 12, we have noticed that the proposed adaptive coding system with 2x2 (fixed antenna numbers) space diversity is outperformed the conventional systems: 2x2 STBC coded scheme, 2x1 STBC coded scheme, and 1x2 maximal ratio receive combining (MRRC) scheme. Figure 13 shows the reconstructed video frames of the proposed PCU controlled adaptive system (in Fig. 10, SNR = 9 dB, BER ≈ 7x10^{-4}).

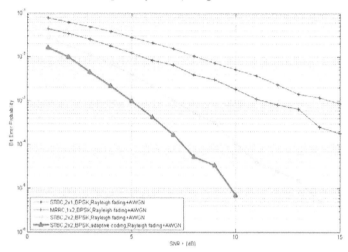

Fig. 12. The BER performance comparison of STBC systems (2/3 convolutional coded) and the proposed adaptive system (with 2×2 antennas structure) over Rayleigh fading channel. (100 video frames transmitted)

4. Conclusions

Video transmission over MIMO systems offers numerous new research opportunities. Lots of new researches are originated from the fundamental change in data transmission from single link to multiple simultaneous links in the MIMO systems. In this study, we applied joint source-channel coding with modulation scheme to design an adaptive video transmission over wireless MIMO system. The bit rates of MPEG2 video can be adaptive to associate with the convolutional channel codes and space-time block code (STBC) under the channel capacity constraint consideration. In order to be consistent with the channel capacity constraint (which is set to be 1 bit/transmission), there are three rate combination types of the joint source-channel coding algorithm as shown in Table 1. From the simulation results, we found that the space diversity and the channel code rate both are important factors influenced reconstructed video quality. The simulation results shows that two transmitter antennas and two receiver antennas (2×2) STBC coded system demonstrates the best BER performance, while the worst performance goes to the 2×1 STBC coded system. The system performance is also improved with lower channel coding rate in the experiment. It can be found from the simulation, rate 2/3 convolutional coded system is with the worst bit error rate performance, where rate 2/5 convolutional coded system shown the best BER performance at the same SNR conditions.

In this study, the proposed adaptive system can choose an adequate transmission rate and the number of receiver antennas based on the channel condition. With the feedback BER

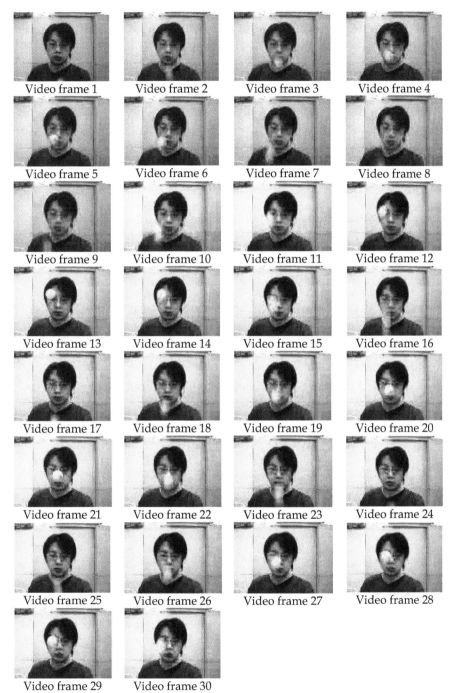

Fig. 13. The reconstructed video frames of the proposed PCU controlled adaptive system.

information provided by the performance control unit (PCU), the proposed system is able to choose an appropriate source-channel rate to transmit video. Therefore, the transmitted video quality may keep at an almost uniform level over a Rayleigh fading channel condition. The study has ensured the proposed system achieved a better BER performance compared to conventional systems.

5. References

Alamouti, S. (1998). A Simple Transmit Diversity Technique for Wireless Communications, *IEEE Journal Selected Areas on Communications*, Vol. 16, 1451–1458

Burr, A. (2003). Capacity Bounds and Estimates for the Finite Scatterers MIMO Wireless Channel, *IEEE Journal on Selected Areas in Communications*, Vol. 21, 812–818

Chen, C. & He, Z. (2006). Signal Processing Challenges in Next Generation Multimedia Communications, *China Communications*, Vol. 4 (5), 20-29

Daut, D. & Ma, W. (1998). Integrated Design of Digital Communication Systems for Fixed Channel Conditions, *Proceedings of International Telecommunication Symposium*, Vol. I, 10-15

Daut, D. & Modestino, J. (1983). Two-Dimensional DPCM Image Transmission over Fading Channel, *IEEE Transactions on Communications*, Vol. 31 (3), 315-328

Driessen, P. & Foschini, G. (1999). On the Capacity Formula for Multiple Input-Multiple Output Wireless Channels: a Geometric Interpretation, *IEEE Transaction on. Communications*, Vol. 47 (2), 173–176

Foschini, G. & Gans, M. (1998). On the Limits of Wireless Communications in a Fading Environment when using Multiple Antenna, *Wireless Personal Communications*, Vol. 6 (3), 311–335

Proakis, J. (2001). *Digital Communications*, Fourth Edition. ISBN 0-07-232111-3, McGraw-Hill, New York, USA.

Sikora, T. (1997). MPEG Digital Video-Coding Standards, *IEEE Signal Processing Magazine*, Vol. 14, 82-100

Song, D. & Chen, C. (2008). Maximum-Throughput Delivery of SVC-based Video over MIMO Systems with Time-Varying Channel Capacity, *Journal of Visual Communication and Image Representation*, Vol. 19, 520-528

Song, D. & Chen, C. (2007). Scalable H.264/AVC Video Transmission over MIMO Wireless Systems with Adaptive Channel Selection Based on Partial Channel Information, *IEEE Transactions on Circuits and Systems for Video Technology*, Vol. 17 (9), 1218-1226

Tarokh, V.; Jafarkhani, H. & Calderbank, A. (1999). Space-Time Block Codes from Orthogonal Designs. *IEEE Transactions on Information Theory*, Vol. 45 (5), 1456–1467

Wolniansky, P. ; Foschini, G.; Golden, G. & Valenzuela, R. (1998). V-BLAST: An Architecture for Realizing Very High Data Rates over the Rich-Scattering Wireless Channel, *Proceedings of IEEE International Symposium on Signals, Systems and Electronics*, 295-300

Yin, L., Chen; W., Lu, J. & Chen, C. (2004). Joint Source Channel Decoding for MPEG-2 Video Transmission, *Proceedings of SPIE Conference on Multimedia Systems and Applications*, Vol. 5600, 128-136

Zeng, X. & Ghrayeb, A. (2006). Performance Bounds for Combined Channel Coding and Space-Time Block Coding with Receive Antenna Selection, *IEEE Transactions on Vehicular Technology*, Vol. 55 (4), 1441-1446

5

Video Editing Based on Situation Awareness from Voice Information and Face Emotion

Tetsuya Takiguchi, Jun Adachi and Yasuo Ariki
Kobe University Japan

1. Introduction

Video camera systems are becoming popular in home environments, and they are often used in our daily lives to record family growth, small home parties, and so on. In home environments, the video contents, however, are greatly subjected to restrictions due to the fact that there is no production staff, such as a cameraman, editor, switcher, and so on, as with broadcasting or television stations.

When we watch a broadcast or television video, the camera work helps us to not lose interest in or to understand its contents easily owing to the panning and zooming of the camera work. This means that the camera work is strongly associated with the events on video, and the most appropriate camera work is chosen according to the events. Through the camera work in combination with event recognition, more interesting and intelligible video content can be produced (Ariki et al., 2006).

Audio has a key index in the digital videos that can provide useful information for video retrieval. In (Sundaram et al, 2000), audio features are used for video scene segmentation, in (Aizawa, 2005) (Amin et al, 2004), they are used for video retrieval, and in (Asano et al, 2006), multiple microphones are used for detection and separation of audio in meeting recordings. In (Rui et al, 2004), they describe an automation system to capture and broadcast lectures to online audience, where a two-channel microphone is used for locating talking audience members in a lecture room. Also, there are many approaches possible for the content production system, such as generating highlights, summaries, and so on (Ozeke et al, 2005) (Hua et al, 2004) (Adams et al, 2005) (Wu, 2004) for home video content.

Also, there are some studies that focused on a facial direction and facial expression for a viewer's behavior analysis. (Yamamoto, et al, 2006) proposed a system for automatically estimating the time intervals during which TV viewers have a positive interest in what they are watching based on temporal patterns in facial changes using the Hidden Markov Model. In this chapter, we are studying about home video editing based on audio and face emotion. In home environments, since it may be difficult for one person to record video continuously (especially for small home parties: just two persons), it will require the video content to be automatically recorded without a cameraman. However, it may result in a large volume of video content. Therefore, this will require digital camera work which uses virtual panning and zooming by clipping frames from hi-resolution images and controlling the frame size and position (Ariki et al, 2006).

In this chapter, our system can automatically capture only conversations using a voice/non-voice detection algorithm based on AdaBoost. In addition, this system can clip and zoom in on a talking person only by using the sound source direction estimated by CSP, where a two-channel (stereo) microphone is used. Additionally, we extract facial feature points by EBGM (Elastic Bunch Graph Matching) (Wiskott et al, 1997) to estimate atmosphere class by SVM (Support Vector Machine).

One of the advantages of the digital shooting is that the camera work, such as panning and zooming, is adjusted to user preferences. This means that the user can watch his/her own video produced by his/her own virtual editor, cameraman, and switcher based on the user's personal preferences. The main point of this chapter is that home video events can be recognized using techniques based on audio and face emotion and then used as the key indices to retrieve the events and also to summarize the whole home video.

The organization of this chapter is as follows. In Section 2, the overview of the video editing system based on audio and face emotion is presented. Section 3 describes voice detection with AdaBoost in order to capture conversation scenes only. Section 4 describes the estimation of the talker's direction with CSP in order to zoom in on the talking person by clipping frames from the conversation scene videos. Section 5 describes facial emotion recognition. Section 6 describes the digital camera work.

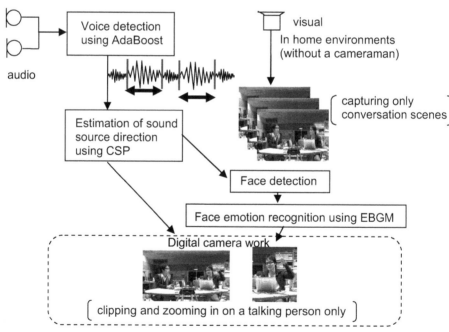

Fig. 1. Video editing system using digital camera work based on audio and face emotion

2. Overview of the system

Figure 1 shows the overview of the video editing system using digital camera work based on audio and face emotion. The first step is voice detection with AdaBoost, where the system identifies whether the audio signal is a voice or not in order to capture conversation scenes only. When the captured video is a conversation scene, the system performs the second step. The second step is estimation of the sound source direction using the CSP (Crosspower-Spectrum Phase) method, where a two-channel microphone is used. Using the sound source direction, the system can clip and zoom in on a talking person only. The third step is face emotion recognition. Using the emotion result, the system can zoom out on persons who have positive expressions (happiness, laughter, etc).

3. Voice detection with AdaBoost

In automatic production of home videos, a speech detection algorithm plays an especially important role in capture of conversation scenes only. In this section, a speech/non-speech detection algorithm using AdaBoost, which can achieve extremely high detection rates, is described.

"Boosting" is a technique in which a set of weak classifiers is combined to form one highperformance prediction rule, and AdaBoost (Freund et al, 1999) serves as an adaptive boosting algorithm in which the rule for combining the weak classifiers adapts to the problem and is able to yield extremely efficient classifiers.

Figure 2 shows the overview of the voice detection system based on AdaBoost. The audio waveform is split into a small segment by a window function. Each segment is converted to the linear spectral domain by applying the discrete Fourier transform (DFT). Then the logarithm is applied to the linear power spectrum, and the feature vector is obtained. The AdaBoost algorithm uses a set of training data,

$$\{(X(1),Y(1)),...,(X(N),Y(N))\} \tag{1}$$

where $X(n)$ is the n-th feature vector of the observed signal and Y is a set of possible labels. For the speech detection, we consider just two possible labels, $Y = \{-1, 1\}$, where the label, 1, means voice, and the label, -1, means noise. Next, the initial weight for the n-th training data is set to

$$w_1(n) = \begin{cases} \dfrac{1}{2m}, & Y(n)=1 \quad (voice) \\ \dfrac{1}{2l}, & Y(n)=-1 \quad (noise) \end{cases} \tag{2}$$

where m is the total voice frame number, and l is the total noise frame number.

As shown in Figure 2, the weak learner generates a hypothesis $h_t : X \rightarrow \{-1,1\}$ that has a small error. In this chapter, single-level decision trees (also known as decision stumps) are used as the base classifiers. After training the weak learner on t-th iteration, the error of ht is calculated by

$$e_t = \sum_{n:h_t(X(n))\neq Y(n)} w_t(n). \tag{3}$$

Next, AdaBoost sets a parameter α_t. Intuitively, α_t measures the importance that is assigned to ht. Then the weight wt is updated.

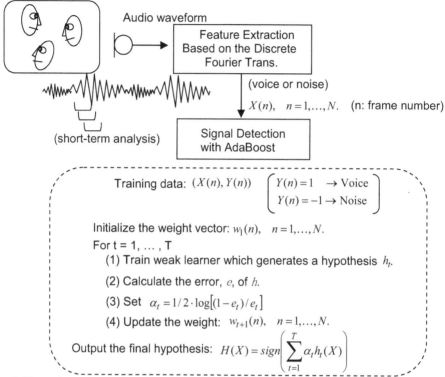

Fig. 2. Voice detection with AdaBoost

$$w_{t+1}(n) = \frac{w_t(n)\exp\{-\alpha_t \cdot Y(n) \cdot h_t(X(n))\}}{\sum\limits_{n=1} w_t(n)\exp\{-\alpha_t \cdot Y(n) \cdot h_t(X(n))\}} \qquad (4)$$

The equation (4) leads to the increase of the weight for the data misclassified by ht. Therefore, the weight tends to concentrate on "hard" data. After T-th iteration, the final hypothesis, $H(X)$, combines the outputs of the T weak hypotheses using a weighted majority vote.

In home video environments, speech signals may be severely corrupted by noise because the person speaks far from the microphone. In such situations, the speech signal captured by the microphone will have a low SNR (signal-to-noise ratio) which leads to "hard" data. As the AdaBoost trains the weight, focusing on "hard" data, we can expect that it will achieve extremely high detection rates in low SNR situations. For example, in (Takiguchi et al, 2006), the proposed method has been evaluated on car environments, and the experimental results show an improved voice detection rate, compared to that of conventional detectors based on the GMM (Gaussian Mixture Model) in a car moving at highway speed (an SNR of 2 dB)

4. Estimation of sound source direction with CSP

The video editing system is requested to detect a person who is talking from among a group of persons. This section describes the estimation of the person's direction (horizontal localization) from the voice. As the home video system may require a small computation resource due to its limitations in computing capability, the CSP (Crosspower-Spectrum Phase)-based technique (Omologo et al, 1996) has been implemented on the video-editing system for a real-time location system.

The crosspower-spectum is computed through the short-term Fourier transform applied to windowed segments of the signal $x_i[t]$ received by the i-th microphone at time t

$$CS(n;\omega) = X_i(n;\omega)X_j^*(n;\omega) \tag{5}$$

where $*$ denotes the complex conjugate, n is the frame number, and ω is the spectral frequency. Then the normalized crosspower-spectrum is computed by

$$\phi(n;\omega) = \frac{X_i(n;\omega)X_j^*(n;\omega)}{|X_i(n;\omega)||X_j^*(n;\omega)|} \tag{6}$$

that preserves only information about phase differences between x_i and x_j. Finally, the inverse Fourier transform is computed to obtain the time lag (delay) corresponding to the source direction.

$$C(n;l) = InverseDFT(\phi(n;\omega)) \tag{7}$$

Given the above representation, the source direction can be derived. If the sound source is non-moving, $C(n; l)$ should consist of a dominant straight line at the theoretical delay. In this chapter, the source direction has been estimated averaging angles corresponding to these delays. Therefore, a lag is given as follows:

$$\hat{l} = \arg\max_l \left\{ \sum_{n=1}^{N} C(n;l) \right\} \tag{8}$$

where N is the total frame in a voice interval which is estimated by AdaBoost. Figure 3 shows the overview of the sound source direction by CSP.

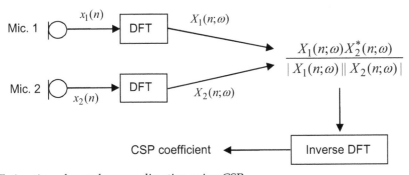

Fig. 3. Estimation of sound source direction using CSP

Figure 4 shows the CSP coefficients. The left is the result for a speaker direction of 60 degrees, and the right is that for two speakers' talking. As shown in Figure 4, the peak of the CSP coefficient (in the left figure) is about 60 degrees, where the speaker is located at 60 degrees.

When only one speaker is talking in a voice interval, the shape peak is obtained. However, plural speakers are talking in a voice interval, a sharp peak is not obtained as shown in the bottom figure. Therefore, we set a threshold, and the peak above the threshold is selected as the sound source direction. In the experiments, the threshold was set to 0.08. When the peak is below the threshold, a wide shot is taken.

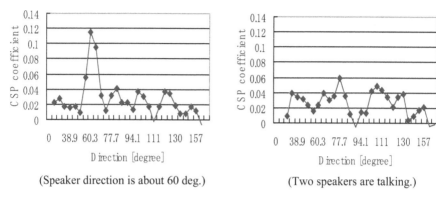

(Speaker direction is about 60 deg.)   (Two speakers are talking.)

Fig. 4. CSP coefficients

5. Facial feature point extraction using EBGM

To classify facial expressions correctly, facial feature points must be extracted precisely. From this viewpoint, Elastic Bunch Graph Matching (EBGM) (Wiskott et al, 1997) is employed in the system. EBGM was proposed by Laurenz Wiskott and proved to be useful in facial feature point extraction and face recognition.

5.1 Gabor wavelets
Since Gabor wavelets are fundamental to EBGM, it is described here. Gabor wavelets can extract global and local features by changing spatial frequency, and can extract features related to a wavelet's orientation.

Eq. (9) shows a Gabor Kernel used in Gabor wavelets. This function contains a Gaussian function for smoothing as well as a wave vector $\vec{k}_j$ that indicates simple wave frequencies and orientations.

$$\varphi_j(\vec{x}) = \frac{\vec{k}_j^2}{\sigma^2} \exp\left(-\frac{\vec{k}_j^2 \vec{x}^2}{2\sigma^2}\right)\left[\exp(i\vec{k}_j \vec{x}) - \exp(-\frac{\sigma^2}{2})\right] \tag{9}$$

$$\vec{k}_j = \begin{pmatrix} k_{jx} \\ k_{jy} \end{pmatrix} = \begin{pmatrix} k_v \cos\varphi_\mu \\ k_v \sin\varphi_\mu \end{pmatrix} \tag{10}$$

Here, $k_v = 2^{-\frac{v+2}{2}\pi}$, $\varphi_\mu = \mu\frac{\pi}{8}$. We employ a discrete set of 5 different frequencies, index $v = 0, ..., 4$, and 8 orientations, index $\mu = 0, ..., 7$.

5.2 Jet

A jet is a set of convolution coefficients obtained by applying Gabor kernels with different frequencies and orientations to a point in an image. To estimate the positions of facial feature points in an input image, jets in an input image are compared with jets in a facial model.

A jet is composed of 40 complex coefficients (5 frequencies * 8 orientations) and expressed as follows:

$$J_j = a_j \exp(i\phi_j) \quad j = 0,...,39 \tag{11}$$

where $\vec{x} = (x,y), a_j(\vec{x})$ and ϕ_j are the facial feature point coordinate, magnitude of complex coefficient, and phase of complex coefficient, which rotates the wavelet at its center, respectively.

5.3 Jet similarity

For the comparison of facial feature points between the facial model and the input image, the similarity is computed between jet set $\{J\}$ and $\{J'\}$. Locations of two jets are represented as $\vec{x}$ and $\vec{x}'$. The difference between vector $\vec{x}$ and vector $\vec{x}'$ is given in Eq. (12).

$$\vec{d} = \vec{x} - \vec{x}' = \begin{pmatrix} dx \\ dy \end{pmatrix} \tag{12}$$

Here, let's consider the similarity of two jets in terms of the magnitude and phase of the jets as follows:

$$S_D(J,J') = \frac{\sum_j a_j a'_j \cos(\phi_j - \phi'_j)}{\sqrt{\sum_j a_j^2 \sum_j a'^2_j}} \tag{13}$$

where the phase difference $(\phi_j - \phi'_j)$ is qualitatively expressed as follows:

$$\phi_j - \phi'_j = \vec{k}_j \vec{x} - \vec{k}_j \vec{x}' = \vec{k}_j(\vec{x} - \vec{x}') = \vec{k}_j \vec{d} \tag{14}$$

To find the best similarity between $\{J\}$ and $\{J'\}$ using Eq. (13) and Eq. (14), phase difference is modified as $\phi_j - (\phi'_j + \vec{k}_j \vec{d})$ and Eq. (13) is rewritten as

$$S_D(J,J') = \frac{\sum_j a_j a'_j \cos(\phi_j - (\phi'_j + \vec{k}_j \vec{d}))}{\sqrt{\sum_j a_j^2 \sum_j a'^2_j}} \tag{15}$$

In order to find the optimal jet J' that is most similar to jet J, the best $\vec{d}$ is estimated that will maximize similarity based not only upon phase but magnitude as well.

5.4 Displacement estimation

In Eq. (15), the best $\vec{d}$ is estimated in this way. First, the similarity at zero displacement (dx = dy = 0) is estimated. Then the similarity of its North, East, South, and West neighbors is estimated. The neighboring location with the highest similarity is chosen as the new center of the search. This process is iterated until none of the neighbors offers an improvement over the current location. The iteration is limited to 50 times at one facial feature point.

5.5 Facial feature points and face graph
In this chapter, facial feature points are defined as the 34 points shown in Fig. 5. A set of jets extracted at all facial feature points is called a face graph. Fig. 5 shows an example of a face graph.

Fig. 5. Jet extracted from facial feature points

5.6 Bunch graph
A set of jets extracted from many people at one facial feature point is called a bunch. A graph constructed using bunches at all the facial feature points is called a bunch graph. In searching out the location of facial feature points, the similarity described in Eq. (15) is computed between the jets in the bunch graph and a jet at a point in an input image. The jet with the highest similarity, achieved by moving $\vec{d}$ as described in Section 5.4, is chosen as the target facial feature point in the input image. In this way, using a bunch graph, the locations of the facial feature points can be searched allowing various variations. For example, a chin bunch may include jets from non-bearded chins as well as bearded chins, to cover the local changes. Therefore, it is necessary to train data using the facial data of various people in order to construct the bunch graph. The training data required for construction of bunch graph was manually collected.

5.7 Elastic bunch graph matching
Fig. 6 shows an elastic bunch graph matching flow. First, after a facial image is input into the system, a bunch graph is pasted to the image, and then a local search for the input face commences using the method described in Section 5.4. A set of jets extracted from many people at one facial feature point is called a bunch. Finally, the face graph is extracted after all the locations of the feature points are matched.

Input Image   Pasted   Local Search   Face Graph

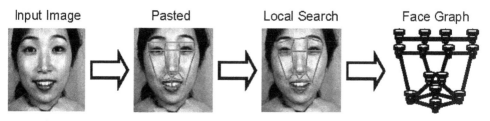

Fig. 6. Elastic Bunch Graph Matching procedure

6. Facial expression recognition using SVM

In this study, three facial expression classes are defined; "Neutral," "Positive" and "Rejective". Table 1 shows the class types and the meanings.

Classes	Meanings
Neutral	Expressionless
Positive	Happiness, Laughter, Pleasure, etc.
Rejective	Watching other direction, Occluding part of face, Tilting the face, etc.

Table 1. Facial expression classes

The users of our system register their neutral images as well as the personal facial expression classifier in advance. The differences between the viewer's facial feature points extracted by EBGM and the viewer's neutral facial feature points are computed as a feature vector for SVM. In our experiments, Radial Basis Function (RBF) is employed as a kernel function of SVM.

7. Camera work module

In the camera work module, the only one digital panning or zooming is controlled in a voice interval. The digital panning is performed on the HD image by moving the coordinates of the clipping window, and the digital zooming is performed by changing the size of the clipping window.

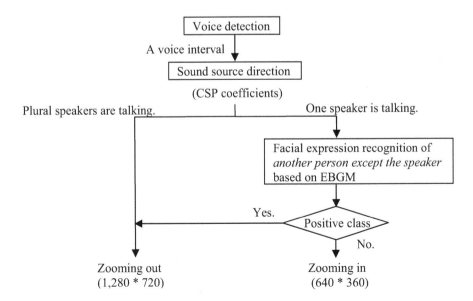

Fig. 7. Processing flow of digital zooming in and out

7.1 Zooming

Figure 7 shows the processing flow of the digital camera work (zooming in and out). After capturing a voice interval by AdaBoost, the sound source direction is estimated by CSP in order to zoom in on the talking person by clipping frames from videos.

As described in Section 4, we can estimate that one speaker is talking or plural speakers are talking in a voice interval. In the camera work, when plural speakers are talking, a wide shot (1280*720) is taken. On the other hand, when one speaker is talking in a voice interval, the system estimates the atmosphere of another person. When the atmosphere of another person is "positive" class, a wide shot (1280*720) is taken. When the atmosphere of another person except the speaker is not "positive" class, the digital camera work zooms in the speaker. In our experiments, the size of the clipping window (zooming in) is fixed to 640*360.

7.2 Clipping position (Panning)

The centroid of the clipping window is selected according to the face region estimated by using the OpenCV library. If the centroid of the clipping window is changing frequently in a voice interval, the video becomes not intelligible so that the centroid of the clipping window is fixed in a voice interval.

The face regions are detected within the 200 pixels of the sound source direction in a voice interval as shown in Figure 8. Then the average centroid is calculated in order to decide that of the clipping window.

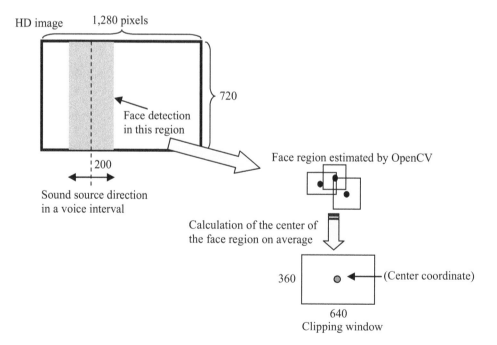

Fig. 8. Clipping window for zooming in

8. Experiments

8.1 Voice detection and sound source direction

Preliminary experiments were performed to test the voice detection algorithm and the CSP method in a room. Figure 9 shows the room used for the experiments, where a two-person conversation is recorded. The total recording time is about 303 seconds.

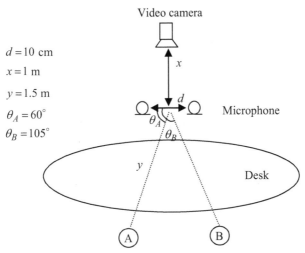

Fig. 9. Room used for the experiments. A two-person conversation is recorded.

In the experiments, we used a Victor GR-HD1 Hi-vision camera (1280*720). The focal length is 5.2 mm. The image format size is 2.735 mm (height), 4.864 mm (width) and 5.580 mm (diagonal). From these parameters, we can calculate the position of a pixel number corresponding to the sound source direction in order to clip frames from high-resolution images. (In the proposed method, we can calculate the horizontal localization only.)

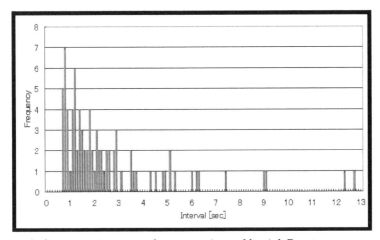

Fig. 10. Interval of conversation scene that was estimated by AdaBoost

Figure 10 shows the interval of the conversation scene that was estimated by AdaBoost. The max interval is 12.77 sec., and the minimum is 0.71 sec. The total number of conversation scenes detected by AdaBoost is 84 (223.9 sec), and the detection accuracy is 98.4%.

After capturing conversation scenes only, the sound source direction is estimated by CSP in order to zoom in on the talking person by clipping frames from videos. The clipping accuracy is 72.6% in this experiment. Some conversation scenes cause a decrease in the accuracy of clipping. This is because two speakers are talking in one voice (conversation) interval estimated by AdaBoost, and it is difficult to set the threshold of the CSP coefficient. Figure 11 shows an example of time sequence for zooming in and out.

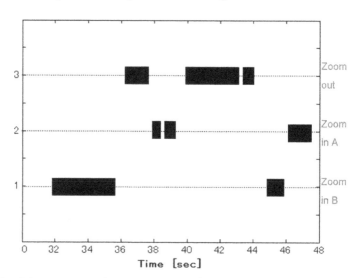

Fig. 11. Example of time sequence for zooming in and out

8.2 Facial expression recognition

	Neutral	Positive	Rejective	Total
Subject A	3,823	2,517	153	6,493
Subject B	3,588	2,637	268	6,493

Table 2. Tagged results (frames)

Next, we tagged the video with three labels, "Neutral," "Positive," and "Rejective." Tagged results for all conversational frames in the experimental videos are shown in Table 2.

Facial regions were extracted using AdaBoost based on Haar-like features (Viola et al, 2001) in all frames of conversation scenes except Reject frames. Extracted frames were checked manually to confirm whether they were false regions or not. The experimental results are shown in Table 3 and Table 4. The extraction rate of the facial region for subject B was not good, compared with that for subject A. The reason for the worse false extraction rate for subject B is attributed to his face in profile, where he often looks toward subject A.

	Neutral	Positive
False extraction	13	16
Total frames	3,823	2,517
Error rate [%]	0.34	0.64

Table 3. Experimental results of facial region extraction for subject A

	Neutral	Positive
False extraction	1,410	1,270
Total frames	3,588	3,719
Error rate [%]	39.3	48.2

Table 4. Experimental results of facial region extraction for subject B

For every frame in the conversation scene, facial expression was recognized by Support Vector Machines. The 100 frames for each subject were used for training data, and the rest for testing data. The experiment results were shown in Table 5 and Table 6.

	Neutral	Positive	Rejective	Sum.	Recall [%]
Neutral	3,028	431	364	3,823	79.2
Positive	230	2,023	264	2,517	80.4
Rejective	32	10	121	153	79.1
Sum.	3,280	2,464	749	6,493	-
Precision [%]	92.3	82.1	16.2	-	-

Table 5. Confusion matrix of facial expression recognition for subject A

	Neutral	Positive	Rejective	Sum.	Recall [%]
Neutral	1,543	214	1,831	3,588	43.0
Positive	194	1,040	1,403	2,637	39.4
Rejective	34	24	210	264	78.4
Sum.	1,771	1,278	3,444	6,493	-
Precision [%]	87.1	81.4	6.1	-	-

Table 6. Confusion matrix of facial expression recognition for subject B

The averaged recall rates for subject A and B were 79.57% and 53.6%, respectively, and the averaged precision rates for subject A and B were 63.53% and 58.2%, respectively. The result of the facial expression for subject B was lower than that for subject A because of the worse false extraction rate of the facial region. Moreover, when the subjects had an intermediate facial expression, the system often made a mistake because one expression class was only assumed in a frame.

Figure 12 and Figure 13 show an example of the digital shooting (zooming in) and an example of zoom out, respectively. In this experiment, the clipping size is fixed to 640*360. In the future, we need to automatically select the size of the clipping window according to each situation, and subjective evaluation of video production will be described.

9. Conclusion

In this chapter, we investigated about home video editing based on audio with a two-channel (stereo) microphone and facial expression, where the video content is automatically recorded without a cameraman. In order to capture a talking person only, a novel voice/non-voice detection algorithm using AdaBoost, which can achieve extremely high detection rates in noisy environments, is used. In addition, the sound source direction is estimated by the CSP (Crosspower-Spectrum Phase) method in order to zoom in on the talking person by clipping frames from videos, where a two-channel (stereo) microphone is used to obtain information about time differences between the microphones. Also, we extract facial feature points by EBGM (Elastic Bunch Graph Matching) to estimate atmosphere class by SVM (Support Vector Machine). When the atmosphere of the other person except the speaker is not "positive" class, the digital camera work zooms in only the speaker. When the atmosphere of the other person is "positive" class, a wide shot is taken. Our proposed system can not only produce the video content but also retrieve the scene in the video content by utilizing the detected voice interval or information of a talking person as indices. To make the system more advanced, we will develop the sound source estimation and emotion recognition in future, and we will evaluate the proposed method on more test data.

Fig. 12. Example of camera work (zooming in)

Fig. 13. Example of camera work (zoom out)

10. References

Y. Ariki, S. Kubota, & M. Kumano (2006). Automatic production system of soccer sports video by digital camera work based on situation recognition, *Eight IEEE International Symposium on Multimedia (ISM)*, pp. 851-858, 2006.

H. Sundaram & S.-F. Chang (2000). Video scene segmentation using audio and video features, *Proc. ICME*, pp. 1145-1148, 2000.

K. Aizawa. Digitizing personal experiences: Capture and retrieval of life log, *Proc. Multimedia Modelling Conf.*, pp. 10-15, 2005.

T. Amin, M. Zeytinoglu, L. Guan, & Q. Zhang. Interactive video retrieval using embedded audio content, *Proc. ICASSP*, pp. 449-452, 2004..

F. Asano & J. Ogata. Detection and separation of speech events in meeting recordings, *Proc. Interspeech*, pp. 2586-2589, 2006.

Y. Freund & R. E. Schapire. A short introduction to boosting, *Journal of Japanese Society for Artificial Intelligence*, 14(5), pp. 771-780, 1999.

Y. Rui, A. Gupta, J. Grudin, & L. He. Automating lecture capture and broadcast: technology and videography, *ACM Multimedia Systems Journal*, pp. 3-15, 2004.

M. Ozeke, Y. Nakamura, & Y. Ohta. Automated camerawork for capturing desktop presentations, *IEEProc.-Vis. Image Signal Process.*, 152(4), pp. 437-447, 2005.

X.-S. Hua, L. Lu, & H.-J. Zhang. Optimization-based automated home video editing system, IEEE Transactions on circuits and systems for video technology, 14(5), pp.572-583, 2004.

B. Adams & S. Venkatesh. Dynamic shot suggestion filtering for home video based on user performance, *ACM Int. Conf. on Multimedia*, pp. 363-366, 2005.

P. Wu. A semi-automatic approach to detect highlights for home video annotation, *Proc. ICASSP*, pp. 957-960, 2004.

M. Yamamoto, N. Nitta, N. Babaguchi, Estimating Intervals of Interest During TV Viewing for Automatic Personal Preference Acquisition. *Proceedings of The 7th IEEE Pacific-Rim Conference on Multimedia*, pp. 615-623, 2006.

L. Wiskott, J.-M. Fellous, N. Kruger, & C. von der Malsburg, Face Recognition by Elastic Bunch Graph Matching, *IEEE Transactions on Pattern Analysis and Machine Intelligence* 19(7), pp. 775-779, 1997.

T. Takiguchi, H. Matsuda, & Y. Ariki. Speech detection using real AdaBoost in car environments, *Fourth Joint Meeting ASA and ASJ*, page 1pSC20, 2006.

M. Omologo & P. Svaizer. Acoustic source location in noisy and reverberant environment using CSP analysis, *Proc. ICASSP*, pp. 921-924, 1996.

P. Viola & M. Jones, Rapid object detection using a boosted cascade of simple features, *Proc. IEEE conf. on Computer Vision and Pattern Recognition*, pp. 1-9, 2001.

6

Passive Radar using COFDM (DAB or DVB-T) Broadcasters as Opportunistic Illuminators

Poullin Dominique
ONERA
France

1. Introduction

This chapter is not dedicated to improve DVB-T (Digital Video Broadcasters-Terrestrial) reception in critical broadcasting conditions. Our purpose is to explain and illustrate the potential benefits related to the COFDM (Coded Orthogonal Frequency Division Multiplex) waveform for passive radar application. As we'll describe, most of the benefits related to COFDM modulation (with guard interval) for communication purpose, could be derived as advantages for passive radar application. The radar situation considered is the following: the receiver is a fixed terrestrial one using COFDM civilian transmitters as illuminators of opportunity for detecting and tracking flying targets. The opportunity COFDM broadcasters could be either DAB as well as DVB-T ones even in SFN (Single Frequency Network) mode for which all the broadcasters are transmitting exactly the same signal. Such application is known in the literature as PCL (Passive Coherent Location) application [Howland et al 2005], [Baker & Griffiths 2005].

This chapter will be divided into three main parts. The first ones have to be considered as simple and short overviews on COFDM modulation and on radar basis. These paragraphs will introduce our notations and should be sufficient in order to fully understand this chapter. If not, it is still possible to consider a „classical" radar book as well as some articles on COFDM like [Alard et al 1987]. More specifically, the COFDM description will outline the properties that will be used in radar detection processing and the radar basis will schematically illustrate the compulsory rejection of the „zero-Doppler" paths received directly from the transmitter or after some reflection on the ground.

Then the most important part will detail and compare two cancellation filters adapted to COFDM waveform. These two filters could be applied against multipaths (reflection on ground elements) as well as against multiple transmitters in SFN mode. In this document, no difference will be done between SFN transmitters contributions and reflections on fixed obstacles : all these zero-Doppler paths will be considered as clutter or propagation channel. Obviously, these filters will be efficient also in a simple MFN (Multiple Frequency Network) configuration. Most of the results presented below concerns experimental data, nevertheless some simulations will also be used for dealing with some specific parameters.

2. Principle of COFDM modulation

As mentioned in the introduction, the purpose of this paragraph is just to briefly describe the principle and the main characteristics of the COFDM modulation in order to explain its advantages even for radar application. For further details, it's better to analyse the reference [Alard et al 1987], however for radar understanding this short description should be sufficient.

2.1 Basis principle

In a COFDM system of transmission, the information is carried by a large number of equally spaced sinusoids, all these sub-carriers (sinusoids) being transmitted simultaneously.
These equidistant sub-carriers constitute a "white" spectrum with a frequency step inversely proportional to the symbol duration.
By considering these sub-carriers:

$$f_k = f_0 + \frac{k}{T_s} \tag{1}$$

with T_s corresponding to symbol duration.
It becomes easy to define a basis of elementary signals taking into account the transmission of these sinusoids over distinct finite duration intervals T_s:

$$\psi_{j,k}(t) = g_k(t - jTs) \text{ with } \begin{cases} 0 \leq t < T_s & : & g_k(t) = e^{2i\pi f_k t} \\ elsewhere & : & g_k(t) = 0 \end{cases} \tag{2}$$

All these signals are verifying the orthogonality conditions:

$$j \neq j' \text{ or } k \neq k' : \int_{-\infty}^{+\infty} \psi_{j,k}(t)\psi_{j',k'}^*(t)dt = 0 \qquad and \qquad \int_{-\infty}^{+\infty} \left\| \psi_{j,k} \right\|^2 dt = T_s \tag{3}$$

By considering the complex elements $\{C_{j,k}\}$ belonging to a finite alphabet (QPSK, 16 QAM,...) and representing the transmitted data signal, the corresponding signal can be written:

$$x(t) = \sum_{j=-\infty}^{+\infty} \sum_{k=0}^{N-1} C_{j,k}\psi_{j,k}(t) \tag{4}$$

So the decoding rule of these elements is given by:

$$C_{j,k} = \frac{1}{T_s} \int_{-\infty}^{+\infty} x(t)\psi_{j,k}^*(t)dt \tag{5}$$

Remark:
From a practical point of view this decomposition of the received signal on the basis of the elementary signals $\psi_{j,k}(t)$ could be easily achieved using the Fourier Transform over appropriate time duration T_s.

2.2 Guard interval use

In an environment congested with multipaths (reflections between transmitter and receiver), the orthogonality properties of the received signals $\psi_{j,k}(t)$ are no longer satisfied.

In order to avoid this limitation, the solution currently used, especially for DAB and DVB, consists in the transmission of elementary signals $\psi_{j,k}'(t)$ over a duration T_s' longer than T_s. The difference between these durations is called guard interval. The purpose of this guard interval is to absorb the troubles related to the inter-symbols interferences caused by the propagation channel. This absorption property needs the use of a guard interval longer than the propagation channel length. Then, we just have to "wait for" all the contributions of the different reflectors in order to study and decode the signal on a duration restricted to useful duration T_s.

The transmitted signal could be written:

$$x(t) = \sum_{j=-\infty}^{+\infty} \sum_{k=0}^{N-1} C_{j,k} \psi_{j,k}'(t) \tag{6}$$

$$\text{with } \psi_{j,k}'(t) = g_k'(t - jT_s') \text{ with } \begin{cases} -\Delta \le t < T_s & : \quad g_k'(t) = e^{2i\pi f_k t} \\ elsewhere & : \quad g_k'(t) = 0 \end{cases} \tag{7}$$

Nevertheless the decoding rule of these elements is still given by:

$$C_{j,k} = \frac{1}{T_s} \int_{-\infty}^{+\infty} x(t) \psi_{j,k}^*(t) dt \tag{8}$$

with $\psi_{j,k}(t)$ always defined on useful duration T_s while signal is now specified (and transmitted) using elementary signals $\psi_{j,k}'(t)$ defined on symbol duration $T_s' = T_s + \Delta$.

This decoding rule means that even when signals are transmitted over a duration $T_s' = T_s + \Delta$, the duration used, in reception for decoding will be restricted to T_s. Such a "cut" leads to losses equal to $10\log T_s' / T_s$ but allows easy decoding without critical hypothesis concerning the propagation channel. In practice, this truncation doesn't lead to losses higher than 1 dB (the maximum guard interval Δ is generally equal to a quarter of the useful duration Ts).

The guard interval principle could be illustrated by the figure 1.

The previous figure illustrates the main advantage of guard interval truncation: by "waiting" for all the fixed contributors, it's easy to avoid signal analysis over transitory (and unstationary) time durations.

Considering the parts of signal used for decoding (so after synchronisation on the end of the guard interval related to the first path received), the received signal in an environment containing clutter reflectors could be written as:

$$jT_s' \le t < jT_s' + T_s \quad : \quad y(t) = \sum_{k=0}^{N-1} H_{j,k} C_{j,k} \psi_{j,k}(t) \tag{9}$$

The propagation channel for the symbol j after the guard interval could be "summarized" with only one complex coefficient per transmitted frequency ($H_{j,k}$) as, during this portion of studied time, all the reflectors were illuminated by the signal $C_{j,k} \psi_{j,k}'(t)$ alone.

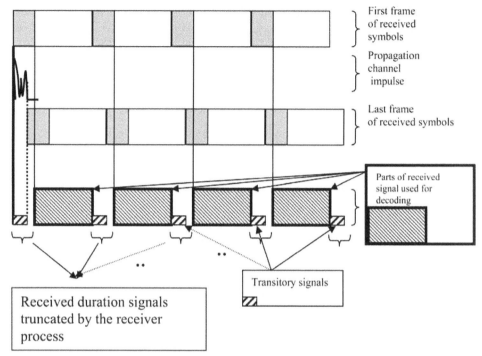

Fig. 1. Guard interval principle

Remark:
COFDM Waveform (with guard interval principle) can support superposition of different paths "without troubles". Such a property also allows a particular mode in a multiple transmitters configuration: all the transmitters can use simultaneously the same code and the same carrier frequency. This specific mode is called SFN (Single Frequency Network). In the rest of this chapter, there will be no difference considered between a multipath or a SFN transmitter. Furthermore, the propagation channel considered will include all the coherent paths, that means multipath on ground clutter as well as SFN transmitters.

2.3 Demodulation

The purpose of this paragraph is not to explain the demodulation principle well described in the DVB norm or in articles [Alard et al 1987 for example] for differential decoding when phase modulation is used.
Whatever considering optimal demodulation or differential one for phase codes, the decoding principle is based on estimating the transmitted codes using the received signal:

$$Y_{j,k} = H_{j,k}C_{j,k} + N_{j,k} \qquad (10)$$

where $N_{j,k}$ represents a gaussian noise:
The knowledge of the channel impulse response $H_{j,k}$ and of the noise standard deviation $\sigma_{j,k}^2$ can be used for the coherent demodulation. This optimal demodulation consists in maximising over the $C_{j,k}$ the following relation:

$$\sum_{j}\sum_{k} \mathrm{Re}\left(Y_{j,k}H_{j,k}^{*}C_{j,k}^{*} / \sigma_{j,k}^{2}\right) \tag{11}$$

In order to simplify this demodulation, it's possible to perform differential demodulation instead of coherent demodulation for QPSK codes. This differential demodulation assumes propagation channel stationarity and consists in estimating the channel response from the previous symbol:

$$H_{j,k} \cong \frac{Y_{j-1,k}}{C_{j-1,k}} \tag{12}$$

This differential demodulation is particularly interesting for its simplicity. The 3 dB losses due to this assumption have to be compared to the practical difficulties encountered for the coherent demodulation implementation.

As a small comment, the differential demodulation doesn't estimate directly the elements of code $C_{j,k}$ but only the transitions between $C_{j-1,k}$ and $C_{j,k}$. However, for phase codes, like BPSK (or QPSK) the transition codes remains phase codes with two (or four) states of phase. In practice, such a differential demodulation just consists in Fourier transforms and some differential phase estimations (according to four possible states).

The most important conclusion dealing with these two possible demodulation principles is the following: using the received signal, it is possible to obtain and reconstruct an ideal vision of the transmitted one. In communication domain, this ideal signal is used for estimating the information broadcasted while for radar application this ideal signal will be used as a reference for correlation and could be also used for some cancellation process. For these radar applications, it is important to notice that this reference is a signal based on an ideal model. Furthermore, the decision achieved during the demodulation process has eliminated any target (mobile) contribution in this reference signal.

2.4 Synthesis

The COFDM signal has interesting properties for radar application such as:

- it is used for DAB and DVB European standard providing powerful transmitters of opportunity.
- the spectrum is a white spectrum of 1.5MHz bandwidth (1536 orthogonal sub-carriers of 1kHz bandwidth each) for DAB and 7.5 MHz for DVB-T
- the transmitted signal is easy to decode and reconstruct
- this modulation has interesting properties in presence of clutter : it is easy to consider and analyze only some parts of received signal without any transitory response due to multipaths effects.

3. Radar detection principle

3.1 Introduction

The principle of radar detection using DAB or DVB-T opportunistic transmitters will be classically based on the correlation of the received signals with a reference (match filter).

In the case of a transmitter using COFDM modulation, the estimation of the transmitted signal (reference) is easy to implement in order to ensure capabilities of range separation and estimation.

However, as the transmitted signal is continuous, we have to take a particular care of the ambiguity function side lobes for such a modulation. Firstly, we'll just verify that these side lobes related to the direct path (path between the transmitter and the receiver) are too high in order to allow efficient target detection and then we'll describe an adaptive filter whose purpose is to cancel all the main zero-Doppler path contributions and ensure efficient detection for mobile targets.

For limiting some specific correlation side lobes observable with the DVB-T signals, it is possible to consider the following article [Saini & Cherniakov 2005]: their analysis lead to a strong influence of the boosted pilot sub-carriers. The main suggestion of this article is to limit this influence by weighting these specific sub-carriers proportionally to the inverse of the „boosted level" of 4 over 3.

3.2 Radar equation example

In a first approach, that means excepting the specific boosted sub-carriers mentioned above for DVB-T, the COFDM modulation ambiguity side lobes can be considered as quite uniform (in range-Doppler domain) with a level, below the level of direct path, given by the following figure:

$$-10\log_{10}(MN) \tag{13}$$

where M designs the number of symbols (considered for correlation) and N the number of sinusoids broadcasted.

The next figure presents the exact ambiguity function (left part of the figure) for a COFDM signal with 100 symbols and 150 sinusoids per symbol, we can observe that the secondary lobes are roughly - 42 dB below the main path (except for low Doppler and range lower than the guard interval: here 75 kilometres). Under some assumptions (right part of the figure: Doppler rotation neglected inside one symbol)), we can consider, in some restricted range-Doppler domain (especially for range lower than the guard interval), a lower level of side-lobes. However, this improvement, related to an "optimal" use of the sub-carriers orthogonality, remains not enough efficient in an "operational" context so we'll don't discuss such considerations in this paper.

We'll just end this COFDM ambiguity function considerations by the following expression ($\phi(\tau,v)$ represents the (range, Doppler) ambiguity function).

$$\phi_{left}(\tau,v) = \int_{T_{integration}} s_{received}(t) s^*_{reference}(t-\tau)e^{-i2\pi vt}dt \tag{14}$$

$$\phi_{right}(\tau,v) = \sum_{j=0}^{J-1} e^{-i2\pi v\left(j+\frac{1}{2}\right)T_s'} \int_{jT_s'+\Delta}^{(j+1)T_s'} s_{received}(t) s^*_{reference}(t-\tau)dt \tag{15}$$

where the coherent integration time $T_{integration}$ is equal to $T_{integration} = J\left(T_s'\right) = J(T_s + \Delta)$
The signal of reference is obtained using differential decoding principle.

The two previous expressions illustrate that the "right" correlation is equal to the "left" one under the assumption that Doppler influence is negligible inside each symbol duration. Furthermore, equation (15) illustrates that range correlations are just estimated over useful signal durations for which all the sub-carriers are orthogonal until the effective temporal support (function of the delay) remains exactly equal to useful duration T_S.

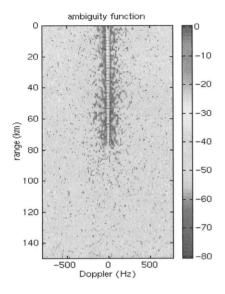
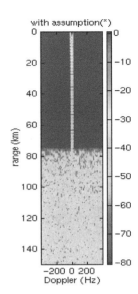

Fig. 2. COFDM ambiguity side lobes

(*) The Doppler rotation inside one symbol is neglected (right figure)

This property implies the lower level of side-lobes (visible on previous figure) for delays lower than guard interval length as using expression (15) there are no sub-carriers interferences in this range domain.

As our main purpose is to focus on the adaptive filter and not on radar equation parameters (coherent integration time, antenna gain and diagram,...), we'll don't discuss more in details on these radar equation parameters. We'll just consider: " as DAB or DVB-T waveforms are continuous, the received level of main path is always high and the isolation provided by side-lobes is not sufficient in order to allow detection."

As the side-lobes isolation (eq 13) is equal to the correlation gain (product between bandwidth and coherent integration time): when we receive a direct path with a positive signal to noise ratio (in the bandwidth of the signal), such a received signal allows reference estimation but its side-lobes will hide targets as these side lobes will have the same positive signal to noise ratio after compression (whatever coherent integration time we consider).

This phenomenon is schematically represented on next figure. Finally, observing this schematic radar equation, it's obvious that an efficient zero-Doppler cancellation filter is required as the targets are generally hidden by zero-Doppler paths side lobes.

3.3 Synthesis

This short description on radar principle had the only objective to prove the compulsory cancellation of the zero-Doppler paths in order to allow mobile target detection.

Only short overview on the correlation hypothesis and adjustments (for example for the boosted DVB-T pilots carriers) were given in order to be able to focus on the cancellation filter in the next part.

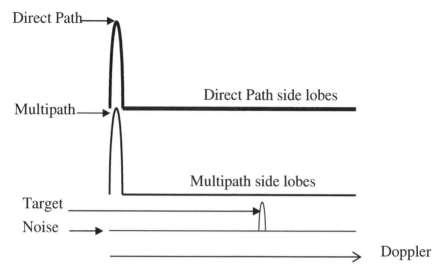

Fig. 3. Schematic radar equation (target hidden by side-lobes).

4. Detection principle

The purpose here is to present two approaches for the adaptive cancellation filter after a schematic description of the whole detection process.

The detection principle is divided into four main tasks described below:

- the first part consists in the transmitter parameters analysis (like carrier frequency, sampling frequency) and a "truncation" of the received signal in order to process only on stationary data
- the second part consists in estimating (by decoding) the reference signal that will be used for correlation
- the third part is more a diagnostic branch in order to allow a finest synchronisation for the direct path and consequently for the target echoes delays. This branch is also used for the propagation channel characterisation.
- The fourth part is related to the target detection and parameters estimation (Bistatic Doppler, bistatic range and azimuth).

This part dedicated to the target detection will be described in details in the following paragraphs.

5. Adaptive filter

5.1 Introduction

Before analyzing the filter itself, it seems important to remind the following elements.

- COFDM waveform allows the specific mode called SFN for which all the transmitters in a given area are broadcasting the same signal.
- From a global point of view, the level of COFDM side lobes is lower than the main path from the product (Bandwidth x integration time). As this product is also equal to the coherent gain over the integration time, a path with a positive signal to noise ratio in the

bandwidth of the signal (so typically most of the SFN transmitters direct paths) will have side lobes with the same positive signal to noise ratio after coherent integration. Such considerations imply that the adaptive filter has to cancel efficiently all zero-Doppler contributors and not only the direct path. The two following filters considered here are fully adapted to the COFDM modulation and requires only a small array elements for the receiving system despite some other solutions sometimes developed [Coleman & Yardley 2008]. Furthermore, all the antennas (and related receivers) are used for the target analysis and detection: no additional hardware complexity and cost is added due to the zero-Doppler cancellation filters.

5.2 Adaptive filter principles
5.2.1 Cancellation filter using a receiving array

This first cancellation filter considers a small receiving array constituted by a set of typically four or eight receiving antennas: all these antennas will be used for the target analysis [Poullin 2001a]

Considering the signals over the different antennas of the receiver system, the zero-Doppler received signals for antenna i and symbol j (index k corresponds to the frequency) can be expressed as follows:

$$S_j^i = \sum_k H_{j,k}^i C_k^j \exp(j\, 2\pi k \frac{t_j}{T_s}) + N_{j,k}^i \tag{16}$$

$$\text{for } t_j \in \left[jT_s' + T_O + L, (j+1)T_s' + T_O \right]$$

with: $H_{j,k}^i$: complex coefficient characterizing the propagation channel for symbol j, antenna i and frequency k. We'll see an explicit expression of such a coefficient some lines below, this expression will consider a specific simple configuration.

T'_s: is the transmitted duration (per symbol)

T_o: corresponds to the first path time of arrival

L: designs the propagation channel length (delay between first path and last significant one including multipaths (echoes on the ground) as well as SFN paths).

$N_{j,k}^i$ designs the contribution of the noise (symbol j, antenna i and frequency k)

If the propagation channel length is lower than the guard interval, the previous expression will be valid for a duration longer than the useful one $T_s = T_s' - \Delta$. So it will be possible to consider this expression over durations T_s for which all sub-carriers are orthogonal between each other.

Generally, we could consider stationary propagation channel over the whole duration of analysis (coherent integration time for radar) and so replace expression $H_{j,k}^i$ by H_k^i

Finally considering the received signals over:

- the appropriate signal durations: for each transmitted symbol over T'_s, we just keep signal over useful duration T_s. (defined by the first path received and the guard interval).
- the appropriate frequencies: over that specific durations, the composite received signals always verify the sub-carrier orthogonality conditions even in multipath (and SFN) configuration.
- the receiver antenna array.

It's possible to synthesise the propagation channel response over the receiver array with a set of vectors

$$\left\{ (H_k^1,...H_k^i,...H_k^N)\,/\,k = 1,...,K : \text{frequency} , i = 1,...,\text{N: number of antennas} \right\} \qquad (17)$$

where N is the number of elements in the receiver system.
So for each frequency k, it is possible to cancel the "directional vector" $\mathbf{H}_k = (H_k^1,...H_k^i,...H_k^N)^t$ using classical adaptive angular method based on covariance matrix as it can be seen below:
Considering for each frequency k the covariance matrix (with size related to the number of antenna) given by

$$R_k = E\left(\mathbf{H}_k \mathbf{H}_k^H C_k^j C_k^{j*} + \sigma_k^{j2}I \right) \qquad (18)$$

$$\text{So } R_k = \mathbf{H}_k \mathbf{H}_k^H + \sigma_k^2 I \qquad (19)$$

Consequently, when we'll apply the weightings related to the inverse of Rk for each frequency k, it appears weighting coefficients related to:

$$R_k^{-1} \approx \frac{1}{\sigma_k^2}\left(I - \frac{\mathbf{H}_k \mathbf{H}_k^H}{\mathbf{H}_k^H \mathbf{H}_k} \right) \qquad (20)$$

which is the orthogonal projector to $\mathbf{H}_k = (H_k^1,...H_k^i,...H_k^N)^t$: propagation channel response vector at the sub-carrier k.
Remark:
This remark is just to give an explicit expression of a typical propagation channel response H_k^i (k: frequency, i antenna) in the particular case of two receiver antennas with a main path in the normal direction and a multipath characterized by its angle of arrival (θ). The normal path received on the first antenna is considered as reference. Under these hypothesis, the propagation channel responses could be written as:

$$H_k^1 = (1 + \alpha \exp(j\phi)\exp(-2\pi\, jf_k\,\tau))$$
$$H_k^2 = (1 + \alpha \exp(j\phi)\exp(-2\pi\, jf_k\,\tau)\exp(j\,2\pi\, d_{12}\,\sin(\theta)/\lambda)) \qquad (21)$$

where d$_{12}$ designs the distance between the two antennas and λ is the wavelength
$\alpha \exp(j\phi)$ represents the difference of reflectivity between main and multi-path (and τ is the delay between main path and multipath referred to antenna 1).
It is quite clear that H_k^1 and H_k^2 will quickly fluctuate according to frequency k due to the term $\exp(-j2\pi f_k\tau)$. Furthermore, for a given frequency the term $j2\pi d_{12}\sin(\theta)/\lambda$ implies different combinations of the two paths for the antenna.

5.2.1.1 Example of cancellation efficiency on experimental data

The filter implemented in order to cancel the zero-Doppler contributions was using four real antennas and the adaptive angular cancellation for each transmitted frequency as described previously. The transmitter was a DAB one and the correlation outputs in range-

Doppler already illustrate the cancellation capabilities that could be read on the cut along the Doppler axis for which the zero level reference corresponds to the receiver noise.

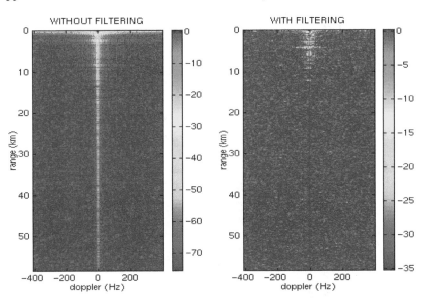

Fig. 4. Correlation output without cancellation filter (left) and with cancellation filter (right)

On the next figure, it could be seen that the level of the main path before cancellation had a signal to noise ratio (in the bandwidth of 10 Hz (related to the 100 milliseconds of integration) of 110 dB and the corresponding side lobes (for range lower than the guard interval which is equal to 75 kilometres) were still 35 dB above the noise level. After cancellation this residual spurious was only 7 dB above noise level. So the residual level of spurious could be considered as -103 dB below the main path

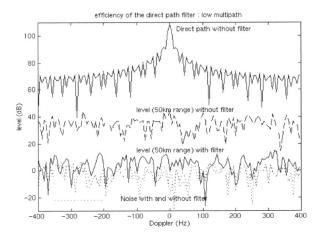

Fig. 5. Comparison of correlation outputs with and without cancellation filter .

5.2.1.2 *Specific case of filter efficiency*

The next figure corresponds to a target crossing the zero-Doppler axis. The trial configuration corresponds to the VHF-DAB transmitter analyzed just previously and six "snapshots" delayed from 1.5 seconds each are presented

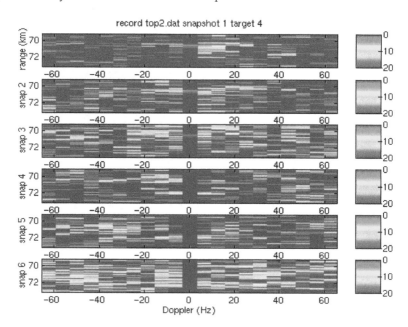

Fig. 6. Example of Results

This example of detection clearly shows the efficiency of the filter against multipath (reflector with null Doppler): when the target crosses the zero Doppler axis it is considered as an element of the clutter, so such a target is (during that time) fully coherent with clutter and main path and its contribution is integrated into the filter coefficients estimation, so such "mixed" coefficients reject both clutter and zero-Doppler target.

Such a result implies that even low multipath (clutter element whose signal to noise ratio is much lower than zero (dB) for the filter coefficient learning phase) could be filtered using such adaptive technique as "they are carried by the main path". From a schematic point of view, the filter detects a level of interference related to $(A + \Delta A)^2$ even if ΔA^2 is negligible with respect to the noise level (A correspond to the main path level and ΔA to the multipath).

5.2.1.3 *Example of target detections after filtering in SFN mode*

The first figure represents the output of the correlation filter (match filter) without zero-Doppler cancellation filter. Such a process allows the analysis of the main fixed echoes generally corresponding to the main transmitters in a SFN configuration.

The different transmitters are identified using "a priori" knowledge of the multi-static configuration while the multipath was located and identified using several receiver locations and triangulation. During that experiment, receiver noise level was high: the receiving system used was an existing "generic" one and not a specific receiver defined for passive DAB application. The figure 9 is normalised according to this high receiver noise. These results were obtained in a DAB-SFN configuration with numerous broadcasters and a two receiver antennas.

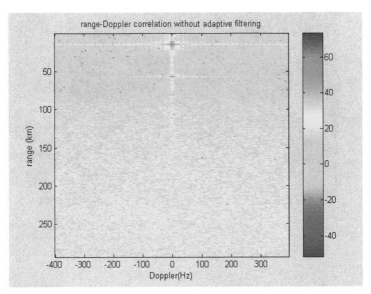

Fig. 7. Range Doppler correlation without zero-Doppler cancellation filter

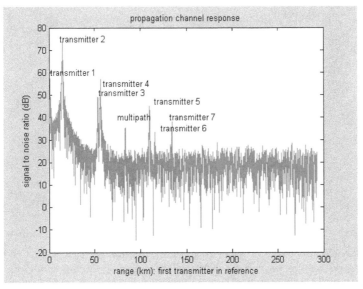

Fig. 8. Propagation channel response (analysis of correlation at zero Doppler: no filtering)

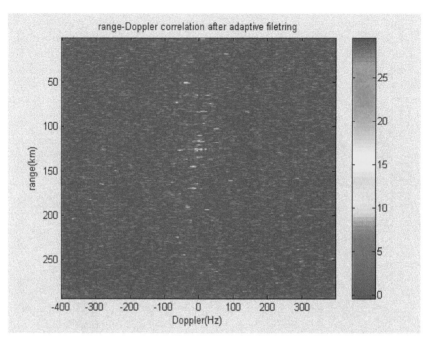

Fig. 9. Examples of mobile (non zero Dopplers) target detections after clutter cancellation

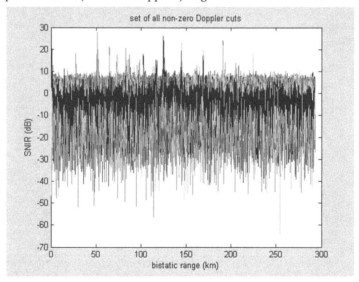

Fig. 10. Non-zero-Doppler cuts (of the range-Doppler correlation) after adaptive filtering

This figure corresponds to the previous multistatic situation with at least seven transmitters clearly identified on the propagation channel response. It becomes obvious that many mobile targets could be detected after zero-Doppler cancellation adapted to the COFDM-SFN configuration even using only two receiving antenna.

The superposition of all non-zero Doppler cuts is represented in order to give a "clear idea" of the detected targets (2-D images like the upper one with high number of pixels aren't always suitable for such a purpose). Furthermore, these cuts illustrate that after adaptive filtering the floor level corresponds to the (high) level of receiver noise.

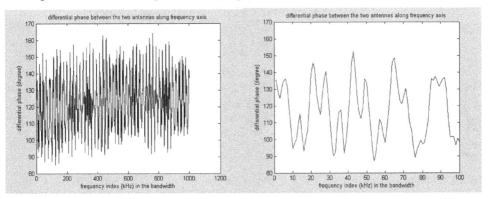

Fig. 11. Differential phase fluctuation between the two antennas along frequency axis.

Between the two distinct antenna, the important differential phase fluctuation along frequency axis in SFN mode (or high multipath configuration) is clearly illustrated on the previous figure.

These results show that, with COFDM modulation, it is possible to filter many SFN transmitters (or multipaths) with a small antenna array receiver. Nevertheless, the following principle: "bigger is your array, better are your results in terms of stability and narrow corrupted domain" remains true.

5.2.1.4 *Synthesis:*

In order to filter the clutter contributions (or the SFN transmitters), it is possible to consider the following algorithm described above involving time, frequency and angular domains:

• time domain: (cut of received guard intervals)
  this truncation ensure stationary durations for signal analysis with no time codes superposition

• frequency domain (analysis over the transmitted sub-carriers)
  The Fourier transform over the selected useful durations ensure signal analysis over stationary frequencies: no frequency codes superposition.

• "angular" domain: (adaptive beamforming for each frequency)
  the adaptive filter (for each transmitted sub-carrier) ensures clutter rejection. On that specific durations and frequencies, as all the clutter contributors are fully coherent, only one degree of freedom is necessary for adaptive cancellation of all the fixed echoes.

This filter has been successfully tested on real DAB signals and is currently tested using DVB-T broadcasters for which preliminary results seem encouraging.

This "angular" filtering applied for each transmitted sub-carrier will:

• lower all the zero-Doppler contributors as the set of H_k coefficients summarises all the clutter contributions.

• Be theoretically able to lower multiple transmitters using two antennas as only one degree of freedom is required for cancelling the zero-Doppler paths as long as the propagation channel length remains lower than the guard interval.

- Orthogonalise the received signals to a composite vector that doesn't correspond to a particular direction (see explicit expressions of H_k coefficient in equation (21)). This phenomenon is due to the full coherency of all the clutter contributors over that selected time durations and that frequency sub-carriers. This particularity also implies that only one degree of freedom (per frequency) is used for all clutter cancellation.
- Have to be applied for each transmitted frequency as the composite propagation channel vector fluctuates quickly in frequency domain. This fluctuation could be deduced from the explicit expression of H_k (equation 21) coefficient. Furthermore, this fluctuation was illustrated on an experimental example on figure 11.

The next paragraph will present another cancellation filter that will be less efficient in most of the situations. Nevertheless, its interest relies in the following capabilities: it requires only one real antenna in order to lower the different SFN contributions and it could be more efficient than the previous filter when the target is close to the composite directional vector of the zero-Doppler contributors.

5.2.2 Cancellation using a single antenna

This other zero-Doppler path cancellation filter could be obtained according two different approaches:

- An "angular" approach derived from the previous method but with the following adaptation: the cancellation is no longer achieved between several real antenna of the receiving array but between each real antenna and a sort of fictive one receiving the signal of reference obtained after decoding.
- A "temporal approach" using the classical Wiener Filter adapted to COFDM waveform.

We'll detail simply the "temporal" approach

Considering the decoded signal and a signal received on a real antenna it is possible to consider the Wiener filter:

$$z(t) = s_{received}(t) - \sum_{\tau=1}^{L} W(\tau)ref(t - \tau) \tag{22}$$

$$\text{with } \min_{w}\left(\left|s_{reçu}(t) - \sum_{\tau} w(\tau)ref(t - \tau)\right|^2\right)$$

Under that formulation, there is no specifity due to COFDM waveform and the similarity with the previous cancellation filter is not obvious.

So let us consider the spectral domain and the assumption that the length of the propagation channel and the corresponding Wiener filter length (here L) are lower than the guard interval.

So under that assumption, it is possible to consider the following expression

$$\sum_{\tau} W(\tau)ref(t - \tau) = \sum_{k=1}^{K} G_k C_k e^{j2\pi\frac{k}{T_u}t} \quad \text{with} \quad L_{channel} < \Delta \tag{23}$$

And as the signal received on one of the real antenna is:

$$S_{antenna\,1}(t_j) = \sum_{k=1}^{K} H_k^{antenna\,1} C_k^j e^{j2\pi \frac{k}{T_u} t_j} + \text{target}(t) + b(t) \qquad (24)$$

It becomes clear that these two signals could be used to cancel the zero-Doppler paths using the same kind of algorithm than previously but with the important following modification:

- The previous adaptive angular filter was using only real antenna. All these antenna were containing the moving targets contribution as well as some "common" imperfections on the received signal.
- The new suggested filter is involving one real antenna with the target contributions and the signal of reference which is an ideal one. Furthermore, this ideal signal doesn't contain the targets contributions.

5.2.3 Comparison of the two filters

5.2.3.1 *Introduction*

The previous comments dealing with the main differences in the signals used at the input of the two zero-Doppler cancellation filters allow us to have the following observations:

- The filter involving only real antenna:
  - Requires several receiving antenna to cancel the zero-Doppler paths. Nevertheless a few antenna system could be sufficient as only one degree of freedom is required for cancelling all the zero-Doppler paths below the guard interval.
  - will be more robust to the imperfections as all the antennas suffer from that nuisances and the cancellation filter will be able (at least in a first order) to deal with most of these troubles
  - will have potential influence (and losses) on the targets contributions.
- The filter involving each real antenna and the signal of reference
  - Could be implemented using only one real receiving antenna
  - Will be more sensitive to all the defaults affecting the received signal according to the ideal model used for estimating the reference
  - Will have no influence on the targets contributions as these targets are no longer in the signal of reference obtained after decoding the received one.

In other words, the limitation of these two filters are not identical and it is quite obvious, that the filter involving only real antenna will be more efficient in terms of zero-Doppler cancellation. It is also evident that the consequences on some targets will be higher than with the filter involving real antenna mixed with the reference signal.

5.2.3.2 *Example of comparison on experimental data*

On the left figure, the adaptive filter was able to cancel efficiently the zero-Doppler paths but the losses on the target were too high due to the vicinity between the target directional vector and the one characterizing the zero-Doppler paths.

On the right figure, the adaptive filter involving one real antenna and the reference signal was also able to cancel efficiently the zero-Doppler path without destructive effect on the target. The small image of the target called ghost (fantôme) was due to a required correction in order to adapt the reference signal model to some imperfections occurring in the receiver system.

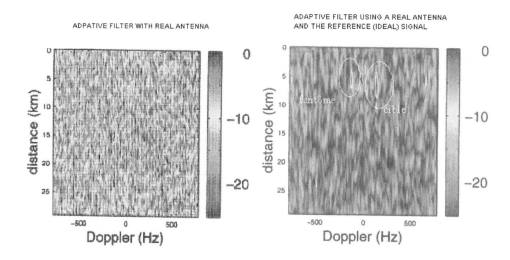

Fig. 12. Example for which the losses on the targets were too high with the adaptive filter involving only real antennas

Nevertheless, generally the method using the reference signal could not be as efficient (in terms of cancellation) as the one involving only real antenna.

5.2.3.3 *Example of limitations due to carrier frequency errors.*

This short paragraph is just to illustrate the higher sensitivity of the cancellation filter involving the ideal reference signal to one of the possible misfits between the received signal and this "ideal reference". This illustration will consider a non-corrected error of frequency between the receiver and the transmitter which corresponds to an error between the received signal and the ideal reconstructed reference.

In such a situation, it is possible to consider that this frequency error will lead, for the filter using the reference signal, to an additional interference due to the superposition of the different sinus cardinal functions:

The other filter, involving only real antenna, is less sensitive to such an error as it is the same error on all the antenna used for cancellation.

$$RSI_j = \frac{\left(H_j C_j\right)^2}{\left(\sum_{\substack{k=1 \\ k \neq j}}^{K}\left(H_k C_k \frac{\sin((k-j)\pi + \pi\Delta vT)}{(k-j)\pi + \pi\Delta vT}\right)e^{j\left(\pi(k-j)+\pi\Delta vT\right)}\right)^2} \tag{25}$$

If we consider small errors on this frequency carrier, the expression above could be simplified using:

$$I_j = \left(\sum_{\substack{k=1 \\ k \neq j}}^{K} \left(H_k C_k \frac{\sin((k-j)\pi + \pi \Delta vT)}{(k-j)\pi + \pi \Delta vT} \right) e^{j(\pi(k-j)+\pi \Delta vT)} \right)^2$$

(26)

$$I_j \approx H^2 \left(\sum_{\substack{k=1 \\ k \neq j}}^{K} \left(C_k \frac{(-1)^{k-j} \Delta vT}{(k-j)} \right) \right)^2$$

considering the average power of that perturbation:

$$H^2 C^2 \Delta v^2 T^2 \frac{\pi^2}{6} \leq E\left[I_j \right] \leq 2H^2 C^2 \Delta v^2 T^2 \frac{\pi^2}{6}$$

(27)

Finally

$$\frac{1}{2\Delta v^2 T^2 \frac{\pi^2}{6}} \leq RSI_j \leq \frac{1}{\Delta v^2 T^2 \frac{\pi^2}{6}}$$

(28)

The following figure illustrates the influence of an error of 80 Hertz on simulated data. According to the level of the main path (80 dB including the gain of 50 dB for coherent integration time) considered and the useful duration time of 1 millisecond, the troubles due to a misfit between the transmitter frequency and the receiver one become to occur at 20 Hz.

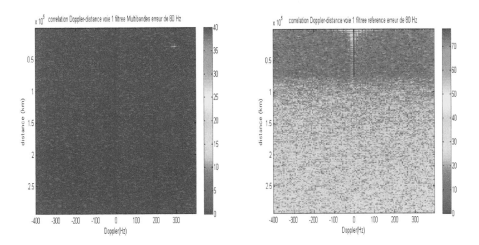

Fig. 13. Correlation output for the two cancellation filter described considered a 80 Hz error between transmitter and receiver (filter with real antenna only: left, filter with real antenna and ideal signal: right)

As illustrated on the following figures, the influence of such an error becomes to occur (according to our simulation parameters) at 20 Hz

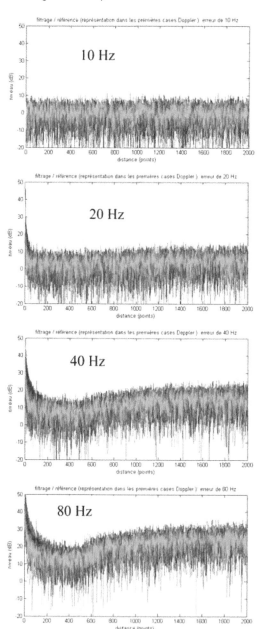

Fig. 14. Analysis of the frequency errors over correlation cut for the cancellation filter involving real antenna and ideal signal.

Of course, it is still possible to define and correct such an error, this example was just an illustration of the higher sensitivity of the second filter to the misfits. Nevertheless, this higher sensitivity will remain even for other kind of interferences that couldn't be corrected as easily as the frequency error...

6. Acknowledgement

We'd like to thanks French MoD (former DGA / DRET and DGA/UM AERO) for his financial support and interest with special thanks to Michel Granger who initiated these works.

7. Conclusion

The COFDM waveform has a great robustness against propagation effects as according to some basic operations (synchronisation and truncation), under the hypothesis of a propagation channel length lower than the guard interval, it is still possible to analyse the received signals over the orthogonal basis of the transmitted sub-carriers even in an environment with numerous reflections.

Using such COFDM civilian broadcasters like DAB or DVB-T as opportunity transmitters for radar application leads to implement a compulsory efficient cancellation filter in order to remove all the main fixed (zero-Doppler) contributors and their corresponding multipaths. Such application is known as Passive Coherent Location: PCL.

Two specific cancellation filters were described in this chapter and illustrated on real data. Their main characteristics are the following:

- The two filters are using the properties of the COFDM modulation in order to "optimise" their efficiencies
- Under the assumption of a propagation channel length lower than the guard interval, only few antenna are necessary in order to lower all the fixed contributors as only one degree of freedom is required for such a cancellation.
- The first method requires a small receiving array (typically 4 or 8 antenna) while the second method could be applied even with one antenna but it implies a higher sensitivity to errors and misfits between the receiving signal and the ideal reconstructed reference
- In practice, these two methods can be complementary as the first one is more efficient for cancelling zero-Doppler paths but it could lower also the targets while the second one is less efficient (due to its higher sensitivity) from the cancellation consideration but it has no destructive effects on the targets.

8. References

Paul E.Howland, D Maksimiuk and G Reitsma 'FM radio based bistatic radar' IEE Proceedings Radar Sonar and Navigation. Special issue: Passive Radar system Volume 152 Number 3 june 2005 pages 107-115.

CJ Baker, H D Griffiths and I. Papoutsis 'Passive coherent location radar systems: Part 2: Waveform properties' IEE Proceedings Radar Sonar and Navigation. Special issue: Passive Radar system Volume 152 Number 3 june 2005 pages 160-169.

M.Alard, R.Halbert, R.Lassalle: Principles of modulation and channel coding for digital
    broadcasting for mobile receivers. EBU review N° 224, August 1987, pp3-25
R Saini, M.Cherniakov 'DTV signal ambiguity function analysis for radar application'
    Proceedings Radar Sonar and Navigation. Special issue: Passive Radar system
    Volume 152 Number 3 june 2005 pages 133-142.
C Coleman, H Yardley ' Passive bistatic radar based on taregt illuminations by digital audio
    broadcasting' IET Radar Sonar and Navigation Volume 2 issue 5 october 2008,
    pages 366-375
D Poullin Patent 2 834 072 'Réjection de fouillis dans un récepeteur radar passif de signaux
    OFDM a réseau d'antennes' 26/12/2001
D Poullin Patent 2 820 507 'Réjection de fouillis dans un récepeteur radar passif de signaux
    OFDM' 07/02/2001

7

The Deployment of Intelligent Transport Services by using DVB-Based Mobile Video Technologies

Vandenberghe, Leroux, De Turck, Moerman and Demeester
Ghent University
Belgium

1. Introduction

ITS systems combine (wired and wireless) communication systems, innovative applications, integrated electronics and numerous other technologies in a single platform. This platform enables a large number of applications with an important social relevance, both on the level of the environment, mobility and traffic safety. ITS systems make it possible to warn drivers in time to avoid collisions (e.g. when approaching the tail of a traffic jam or when a ghost driver is detected) and to inform them about hazardous road conditions. Navigation systems can take detailed real-time traffic info into account when calculating their routes. In case of an accident, the emergency services can be automatically informed about the nature and the exact location of the accident, saving very valuable time in the first golden hour. In case of traffic distortions, traffic can be immediately diverted. These are just a few of the many applications that are made possible because of ITS systems, but it is very obvious that these systems can make a significant positive contribution to traffic safety. In literature it is estimated that the decrease of accidents with injuries of fatalities will be between 20% and 50% (Bayle et al., 2007).

Attracted by the high potential of ITS systems, the academic world, the standardization bodies and the industry are all very actively involved in research and development of ITS solutions. The pillars of these systems are the communication facilities connecting the vehicles, the roadside infrastructure and the centralized safety and comfort services. Several wireless technologies can be considered when designing ITS architectures, and they can be divided into three categories: Dedicated Short Range Communication (DSRC) of which IEEE 802.11p WAVE, ISO CALM-M5 and the ISO CALM-IR standard are typical examples, wireless Wide Area Networks (WAN) such as GPRS, WiMAx and UMTS and finally digital broadcast technologies like RDS, DAB and the DVB specifications (DVB-T, DVB-S, DVB-H, etc.).

Since so many suitable technologies exist or are in development today, it is very hard to decide on which technologies future ITS architectures should be based. This problem is the starting point of several major ITS research projects, where much attention is given to solutions based on DSRC and wireless WAN networks. In the CVIS project, the implementation focuses on CALM-M5, CALM-IR, GPRS and UMTS technology (Eriksen et al., 2006). The Car2Car Communication Consortium aims to create and establish an open European industry standard for car2car communication systems based on the WAVE standard (Baldessari et al., 2007). The COOPERS project evaluates the GPRS, CALM IR and DAB communication media (Frötscher, 2008). Although broadcast technologies are not neglected by the research community, it is harder to find examples focused on this category. As already mentioned, the COOPERS project has some attention for DAB, and in Korea a trial implementation of a TPEG based traffic information service system was deployed on their T-DMB network (Cho et al., 2006).

In this book chapter, we focus on the usage of DVB-H and DVB-SH for ITS systems. This approach is driven by the lower cost for the end user compared to wireless WAN solutions, by the lack of scalability issues and by the high provided bandwidth. Section 2 introduces the mobile broadcast technologies that are used in our architecture, and explains what the advantages are of using them in ITS systems. Section 3 describes how heterogeneous communication in mobile environments can be realized by means of the ISO TC204/WG16 CALM standard. This standard enables the seamless combination of DVB-H/SH with other wireless communication technologies such as IEEE 802.11p WAVE or an UMTS internet connection. In section 4 the functional description of our architecture is elaborated, the service architecture is described and a more in depth explanation of the implementation details is given. In section 5, the conclusions are drawn and section 6 finishes with the acknowledgment of the enablers of our research.

2. Mobile broadcast technologies

In this section we will elaborate on the broadcast specifications on which our architecture is based upon. We will first shortly introduce each specification and then explain why these technologies are used in our architecture and what the advantage is of using them instead of other communication standards.

2.1 Broadcasting to Handhelds (DVB-H)

DVB-H (Digital Video Broadcasting – Handheld) is a technical specification (ETSI, 2004) for bringing broadcast services to handheld receivers. It adapts the successful DVB-T (Terrestrial) system for digital terrestrial television to the specific requirements of handheld, battery-powered receivers. The conceptual structure of a DVB-H receiver is depicted in Fig. 1. It includes a DVB-H demodulator and a DVB-H terminal. The DVB-H demodulator includes a DVB-T demodulator, a time-slicing module and a MPE-FEC module.

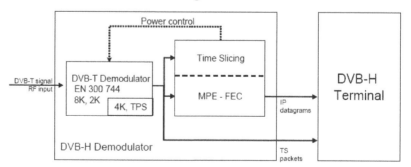

Fig. 1. Conceptual structure of a DVB-H receiver.

The DVB-T demodulator recovers the MPEG-2 Transport Stream packets from the received DVB-T RF signal. It offers three transmission modes 8K, 4K and 2K with the corresponding

Transmitter Parameter Signaling (TPS). Note that the 4K mode, the in-depth interleavers and the DVB-H signaling have been defined while elaborating the DVB-H standard. It aims to offer an additional trade-off between single frequency network (SFN) cell size and mobile reception performance, providing an additional degree of flexibility for network planning.

The time-slicing module, provided by DVB-H aims to save receiver power consumption while enabling to perform smooth and seamless frequency handover. Power savings of up to 90% are accomplished as DVB-H services are transmitted in bursts (using a high instantaneous bit rate), allowing the receiver to be switched off in inactive periods. The same inactive receiver can be used to monitor neighboring cells for seamless handovers. Time-slicing is mandatory for DVB-H.

The objective of Multi-Protocol Encapsulation - Forward Error Correction (MPE-FEC) is to improve the mobile channel tolerance to impulse interference and Doppler effect. This is accomplished through the introduction of an additional level of error correction at the MPE layer. By adding parity information calculated from the datagrams and sending this parity data in separate MPE-FEC sections, error-free datagrams can be output (after MPE-FEC decoding) even under bad reception conditions.

DVB-H is designed to be used as a bearer in conjunction with the set of DVB-IPDC (see Section 2.3) systems layer specifications. DVB-H has broad support across the industry. Currently, more than fifty DVB-H technical and commercial trials have taken place all over the world and further commercial launches are expected. In March 2008 the European Commission endorsed DVB-H as the recommended standard for mobile TV in Europe, instructing EU member states to encourage its implementation.

2.2 Satellite Services to Handhelds (DVB-SH)

DVB-H is primarily targeted for use in the UHF bands (but may also be used in the VHF- and L-band), currently occupied in most countries by analogue and digital terrestrial television services. DVB-SH (ETSI, 2007a; ETSI, 2008) seeks to exploit opportunities in the higher frequency S-band, where there is less congestion than in UHF. The key feature of DVB-SH is the fact that it is a hybrid satellite/terrestrial system that will allow the use of a satellite to achieve coverage of large regions or even a whole country. This is shown in Fig. 2. TR(a) are broadcast infrastructure transmitters which complement reception in areas where satellite reception is difficult, especially in urban areas; they may be collocated with mobile cell site or standalone. Local content insertion at that level is possible, relying on adequate radio frequency planning and/or waveform optimizations.

TR(b) are personal gap-fillers of limited coverage providing local on-frequency re-transmission and/or frequency conversion; typical application is indoor enhancement under satellite coverage; no local content insertion is possible.

TR(c) are mobile broadcast infrastructure transmitters creating a "moving complementary infrastructure". Depending on waveform configuration and radio frequency planning, local content insertion may be possible.

DVB-SH's major enhancements when compared to its sister specification DVB-H are:

- The availability of more alternative coding rates.
- The inclusion of support for 1.7 MHz bandwidth.
- FEC using Turbo coding.
- Improved time interleaving.

As mentioned above, DVB-H systems have already been widely deployed, mostly on a trial basis so far. DVB-SH will be a complement to DVB-H and could potentially be used as such

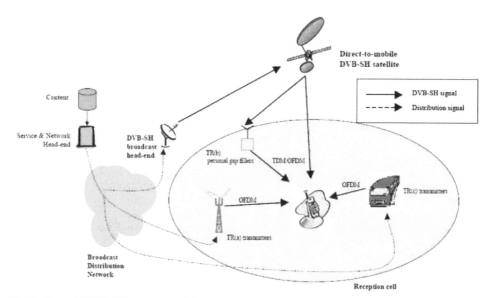

Fig. 2. Overall DVB-SH system architecture.

in a number of ways. Nationwide coverage could be achieved with the satellite footprint. Terminals that are in development will be dual mode, receiving DVB-SH in S-Band and DVB-H at UHF, and the over-lapping use of the DVB-IPDC specifications ensures that the two systems will be complementary.

2.3 Internet Protocol Datacast (DVB-IPDC)
Many commercial mobile TV networks are likely to be hybrid networks combining a uni-directional broadcast network, typically involving a wide transmission area and high data throughput, with a bi-directional mobile telecommunications network, involving much smaller transmission areas (cells). The set of DVB specifications for IP Datacasting (DVB-IPDC) (ETSI, 2007b) are the glue that bind these two networks together so that they can co-operate effectively in offering a seamless service to the consumer.

DVB-IPDC is originally designed for use with the DVB-H physical layer, but can ultimately be used as a higher layer for all DVB mobile TV systems. Currently, work is ongoing to make the necessary additions and adaptations to the DVB-IPDC specifications to allow interfacing with the DVB-SH standard. This work already resulted in the recent document "DVB Document A112-2r1: IP Datacast over DVB-SH". DVB-IPDC consists of a number of individual specifications that, taken together, form the overall system. The way the different elements fit together is defined in a reference architecture of the IPDC system whilst a further specification sets out the various use cases that are allowed for within the system.

The protocolstack of an IP Datacast over DVB-H system is shown in Fig. 3. The integration of an IP layer in the broadcaststack is one of the key concepts of an IPDC system. These IP datagrams are encapsulated inside the MPEG Transport Stream (TS) using MPE and MPE-FEC to improve mobile performance. For the delivery of streaming media, IP Datacast specifies the use of the Real-time Transport Protocol (RTP) and file delivery is performed by using File Delivery over unidirectional Transport (FLUTE) (IETF, 2004). FLUTE is a protocol for unidirectional delivery of files over the Internet. In Section 3.3 we elaborate on the DVB-IPDC specifications as we point out how ITS services are incorporated into our architecture.

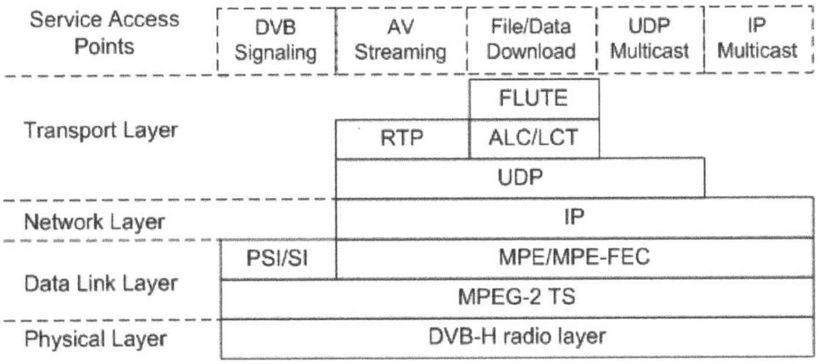

Service Access Points	DVB Signaling	AV Streaming	File/Data Download	UDP Multicast	IP Multicast
			FLUTE		
Transport Layer		RTP	ALC/LCT		
			UDP		
Network Layer			IP		
Data Link Layer	PSI/SI		MPE/MPE-FEC		
			MPEG-2 TS		
Physical Layer			DVB-H radio layer		

Fig. 3. The DVB-IPDC protocol stack.

2.4 Advantages of using DVB-H/SH as bearer technology

The goal of this section is to point out why DVB-H/SH technology is a very well suited candidate for the implementation of ITS systems. First, the advantages of using a digital broadcast technology are described. Second, we compare DVB-H and DVB-SH with other (mobile) broadcast technologies.

As already mentioned in the introduction, several wireless technologies can be considered when designing ITS architectures. There are roughly three categories of wireless systems that may be used: DSRC, wireless WAN and digital broadcast technologies. DSRC systems typically have a limited range of a few up to a few hundred meters. They were originally designed for direct link communications such as toll collect, but newer technologies support multi-hop communications. Examples are the IEEE 802.11p WAVE standard, or the ISO CALM-M5 standard. Wireless WAN technologies have a much larger range, and typically provide internet connectivity to mobile devices. Examples are GPRS, UMTS and WiMAX. Digital broadcast technologies can also cover large areas, but they do not offer two-way communications, only broadcast services. Examples technologies are RDS, DAB and the on DVB based technologies such as DVB-T or DVB-S.

When selecting a technology for the implementation of ITS systems, it is important to know that using broadcast technologies instead of wireless WAN solutions has some important advantages:

Scalability – Using a broadcast medium offers independence of the number of users that are connected to the system and thus the number of users that is able to receive ITS services. Antennas of non-broadcast systems could become overloaded when e.g. there is a traffic jam and all the car terminals would retrieve the same traffic info from the same antenna that covers the traffic jam's region.

Low cost – high user adoption – Recent large-scale motorist surveys have revealed that although users find ITS systems very useful, they are not very willing to pay for these services (RACC Automobile Club, 2007). This means that the cost of wireless WAN solutions could be a major stumbling block in the adoption of ITS systems by motorists. As broadcast media may provide free-to-air services, the cost to end users is kept much lower. When ITS systems use e.g. UMTS as the bearer technology then even if the service itself is free, the user (or the terminal manufacturer) still has to pay for the UMTS data connection.

Another cost-lowering property of broadcast technology is the fact that it enables travellers to enjoy ITS services abroad without having to pay expensive roaming fees.

Within the group of broadcast technologies, the usage of DVB-H and DVB-SH provides some additional advantages compared with its competitors:

Mobility – As DVB-H and DVB-SH are specifically developed for the delivery of data to handheld terminals, they provide a lot of error correction mechanisms for terminals that are moving at high speed. This is a major advantage over e.g. DVB-T.

High Bandwidth – As DVB-H and DVB-SH are initially developed for the delivery of mobile TV services, they provide a much bigger bandwidth (8 to 15 mbit per second for DVB-H) in comparison to other standards such as DAB (120 kbit per second) and RDS (1.1 kbit per second) (Chevul et al., 2005).

Industry adoption – As already mentioned in the previous sections, DVB-H has become the European standard for mobile television thus giving DVB-H a lead to other mobile television technologies such as T-DMB. This advantage is of course dependant on the region where the ITS service will be deployed but note that the deployment of DVB-H (and in the near future DVB-SH) is definitely not restricted to only Europe.

User adoption – When using DVB-H and DVB-SH technology for ITS services, user can also receive DVB-H/SH digital television broadcasts on their on-board equipment. This extra comfort service could be an important feature to attract new users, and could prove to be the catalyst that accelerates the adoption of on-board ITS equipment. The consumer interest in on-board television can already be observed today: portable DVD-players have become common consumer products, and some of the newest personal navigation devices can already receive DVB television broadcasts (e.g. Garmin nüvi).

Return channel integration – As DVB-IPDC is specifically designed for the convergence of DVB-H and DVB-SH with a bidirectional channel such as UMTS (through the integration of an IP layer), mobile terminals can still make use of a return channel. Since only the client uplink data will be transported over this return channel, the data cost will be much lower than when only using a unicast channel. This combination of technologies heavily relieves the bidirectional channel, having a positive influence on the scalability issues of wireless WAN solutions.

All the above makes it obvious that an ITS system based on IP Datacast over DVB-H/SH theoretically has many advantages, but as with all new technologies the question remains if the technology will be able to live up to the expectations in practice. Based on our experience within the IBBT MADUF project (MADUF, 2008), which was a trial DVB-H rollout in the city of Ghent, we are convinced that this will indeed be the case. In this trial we implemented our own middleware framework for the delivery of interactive services through DVB-H (Leroux et al., 2007). Measurements were also done concerning the performance of DVB-H for in-car usage (Plets et al., 2007). This trial made clear that DVB-IPDC is very suitable for the delivery of non-video data and that DVB-H has a good performance, even when using in a car at high speed.

3. Heterogeneous communication in mobile environments

In this section, we elaborate on the ISO TC204/WG16 CALM standard (Williams, 2004). This standard is the ISO approved framework for heterogeneous packet-switched communication in mobile environments, and supports user transparent continuous communications across various interfaces and communication media. It is, together with the DVB-H/SH broadcast technology, one of the key components of the ITS architecture presented in this book chapter.

The CALM architecture is depicted in Fig. 4. The two main elements are the CALM router, which provides the seamless connectivity, and the CALM host which runs the ITS applications with varying communication requirements. On both the CALM router and the host, different subcomponents can be distinguished:

- **CALM communication interface:** the CALM Communication Interface (CI) consists of a communication module and the necessary service access point for interfacing with the CALM networking layer (C-SAP)
- **CALM networking layer:** the CALM networking layer routes packets to the appropriate functional unit or program addressed. It also isolates the upper OSI layers from the different technologies that are making the connections. CALM supports multiple optional and complementary network protocols running independent of each other. Example protocols are standard IPv6 routing; CALM FAST, which is a non-IP protocol required for user applications with severe timing constraints and low-latency requirements (e.g. time-critical safety related applications); and geographic-aware routing, with or without map information. The CALM networking layer also provides a service access point for interaction with the CALM User Services / Applications (the T-SAP)
- **CALM management:** The CALM communications and station management comprises global functionality, and functionality grouped into three groups: Interface Management Entity (IME), Network Management Entity (NME) and CALM Management Entity (CME). Disregard of this grouping, the CALM management is one entity, and there are no observable or testable interfaces between IME, NME and CME. The role of the IME is to directly control the communication interfaces, and to allow access to a communication interface for the purpose of receiving and transmitting management data packets. The role of the NME is to directly control the network and transport layer protocols. The CME provides the decision-making process to the CALM mechanism. The CME collects the specification of the communication parameters enabled by each of the desired communications mechanisms and the requirements from each of the applications from the initialization process. It monitors the availability of lower level communications mechanisms and issues. Based on this information and on policies a decision on how to route data packets is made.
- **CALM service layer:** The CALM service layer shall provide an application programmer interface (API) to user applications, and it shall provide an A-SAP to the CME. Using the API, applications can easily define how their data should be exchanged with other CALM nodes (local broadcast, n-hop broadcast, directional communication, unicast to known address, ...), the level of importance of the data (for QoS classification), the delay constraints, etc.
- **CALM applications:** three kinds of applications can run on the CALM host: CALM FAST applications, CALM IP-based applications, and non-CALM aware applications. The first category has the ability to control the interaction with the CALM environment. Such applications can respond to CALM management entity requests for registration information or are able to request registration upon initialization. They get real-time access to pre-selected parameters of specific CALM communication interfaces in line with applicable regulations, and to the CALM networking layer in order to control the real-time behaviour of the communication link. This control functionality includes e.g. power settings, channel settings, beam pointing. These applications typically use the CALM FAST or Geo-routing networking protocols. CALM IP-based applications are

similar to CALM FAST applications, but they typically have less stringent timing constraints, and are more session oriented. Therefore they generally use the IPv6 networking protocol. Non-CALM aware applications operate with the assumption of the programmer that a normal UDP or TCP connection is being established for communication. Such applications operate without the ability to control any interaction with the CALM environment. The CALM management entity must hide al CALM environment peculiarities from these applications.

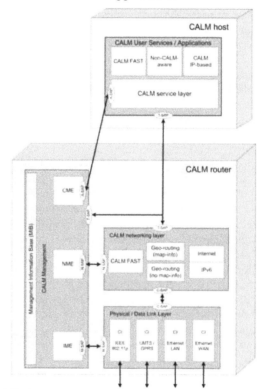

Fig. 4. The CALM architecture

4. Architecture

In this section, we present our ITS architecture based on IP Datacast over DVB-H/SH. First, the functional description of the architecture and its global communication aspects are described. Then the service architecture is detailed, and finally some implementation details of the architecture will be given.

4.1 Functional description
The core idea of the communication architecture (Fig. 5) is to use DVB technology to broadcast data to the vehicles. When DVB-H coverage is already available, this infrastructure can be reused, minimizing necessary investments. If this is not the case, rural areas can be covered by a single DVB-SH satellite, and DVB-SH repeater antennas can be

installed in urban areas to guarantee coverage. Communication between vehicles is provided by the IEEE 802.11p WAVE technology. Since the combination of DVB and WAVE technologies provides both communication from the central infrastructure to the vehicles, and between vehicles, most ITS applications are supported by this base architecture (collision avoidance, hazardous road warnings, traffic situation-aware navigation, etc.). If the user requires interactive applications (notification of emergency services, sending info to the traffic control centre, etc.) the base architecture can be expanded with a return channel, e.g. by using existing UMTS infrastructure.

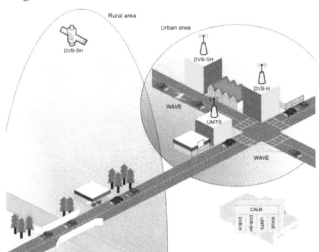

Fig. 5. Communication architecture

In this communication architecture, it is necessary to equip every vehicle with at least a WAVE module and a DVB-H or DVB-SH receiver. Optionally, an UMTS module can also be installed. To coordinate the collaboration of these different wireless interfaces, we rely on the ISO TC204/WG16 CALM standard (Williams, 2004) described in section 3. This standard is the ISO approved framework for heterogeneous packet-switched communication in mobile environments, and supports user transparent continuous communications across various interfaces and communication media. It already supports WAVE and UMTS technology, and due to its modular design, it can easily be expanded to support DVB-S/H media. The CALM standard is, together with the WAVE standard, one of the most important upcoming communication standards within the ITS domain. Since both technologies are incorporated in the architecture, it is compliant with current and future ITS trends and activities.

Since the proposed communication architecture is based on the usage of DVB-H/SH, it inherits the advantages of this technology (see section 2.4): the cost to end users is kept low, scalability issues do not arise, and users can enjoy extra comfort services such as mobile digital television.

4.2 Service architecture
The service architecture of the proposed ITS solution is depicted in Fig. 7. An important concept within this service architecture is the use of the Transport Protocol Expert Group

(TPEG) standards. TPEG is a bearer and language independent Traffic and Travel Information (TTI) service protocol which has a unidirectional and byte oriented asynchronous framing structure (Cho et al., 2006). It is defined in two standards: TPEG binary, originally developed for digital radio, and tpegML, developed for internet bearers and message generation using XML. Integrating them into our service architecture makes the architecture compliant with current and future ITS trends and activities.

```
<?xml version="1.0" encoding="ISO-8859-1" ?>
<!DOCTYPE tpeg_document (View Source for full doctype...)>
- <tpeg_document generation_time="2009-07-13T13:58:09+0">
  - <tpeg_message>
      <originator country="UK" originator_name="BBC Travel News" />
      <summary xml:lang="en">M25 Surrey - Two lanes closed and queueing traffic anticlockwise due to overturned lorry between
        J8, Reigate and J7 M23</summary>
    - <road_traffic_message message_id="3147219" message_generation_time="2009-07-13T13:37:52+0" version_number="7"
        start_time="2009-07-13T13:26:03+0" stop_time="2009-07-13T14:37:37+0" severity_factor="very severe">
      - <obstructions number_of="1">
        - <vehicles number_of="1">
            <vehicle_problem vehicle_problem="overturned" />
            <vehicle_info vehicle_type="lorry" />
          </vehicles>
        </obstructions>
      - <network_conditions>
          <position position="driving lane 1" />
          <restriction restriction="restriction" />
        </network_conditions>
      - <network_performance>
          <performance network_performance="queuing traffic" />
        </network_performance>
      - <location_container language="English">
        - <location_coordinates location_type="route">
            <WGS84 latitude="51.258436" longitude="-0.198008" />
            <location_descriptor descriptor_type="road number" descriptor="M25;" />
            <location_descriptor descriptor_type="town name" descriptor="Surrey" />
            <location_descriptor descriptor_type="intersection name" descriptor="Reigate" />
            <location_descriptor descriptor_type="junction name" descriptor="M25; 8" />
            <location_descriptor descriptor_type="Junction with" descriptor="A217;" />
            <WGS84 latitude="51.263682" longitude="-0.127723" />
            <location_descriptor descriptor_type="road number" descriptor="M25;" />
            <location_descriptor descriptor_type="town name" descriptor="Surrey" />
```

Fig. 6. TpegML example

In our architecture, the tpegML variant will be used for broadcasting traffic information. The advantage of this XML based flavour is that tpegML can be decoded by end-users with any XML enabled browser, tpegML messages are human understandable and machine readable, and tpegML messages are usable with and without navigation systems (European Broadcasting Union, 2009). An example tpegML message is shown in Fig. 6 (BBC, 2009).

As shown in Fig. 7, the service architecture contains the several entities involved, and how they relate to each other. Together, they provide all the mechanisms needed by ITS systems, from content generation to end user applications. The Traffic Control Centre is responsible for generating road traffic information, and forwarding it to the TPEG service provider. The information is produced using several sources such as cameras and counter loops in the road. It can include various kind of information, e.g. real time average travel time on road segments, incident reports and speed limit alterations.

The Public Transport Services are the different public transport operators (e.g. bus, rail or air operator). They posses information regarding their operations, and are responsible for sending this information (such as schedules, delays, etc.) to the TPEG service provider.

The Touristic Info Services can be any entity involved in touristic activities, and they can send metadata information that that links to their web servers to the TPEG service provider. The real data on the web servers is available on demand through the return channel.

Optionally, very popular information may also be sent to the Broadcast Network Provider for transmission on a dedicated broadcast channel.

The TPEG service provider is responsible for gathering all kinds of ITS relevant data from different sources and generating TPEG message from this content. It is also responsible for

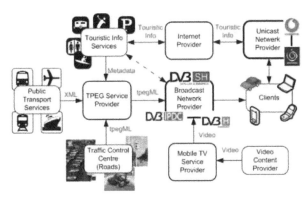

Fig. 7. Service architecture

providing these messages to the end user. Therefore, it will deliver the generated tpegML messages to the broadcast network provider. From the end users perspective, the TPEG service provider is the contact point for ITS information.

The Video Content Providers produces digital television programs and delivers them to the Mobile TV Service Provider. The Mobile TV Service Provider collects content from different Video Content Providers, and is responsible for providing this content to the clients. From the end user point of view, the Mobile TV Service Provider is the contact point for mobile digital television.

The Broadcast Network Provider is responsible for the DVB-H or DVB-SH network. It broadcasts digital television and ITS information to the end devices. It receives this content from the TPEG service provider and the Mobile TV Service Provider.

The clients are all the devices that can receive DVB-S/H broadcasts. The most obvious example is the in-vehicle infotainment system, but this can also be a PDA, a personal navigation device or a mobile phone.

The Unicast Network Provider is responsible for the wireless network that provides the (optional) two-way communication necessary for interactive applications. The Internet Provider is responsible for the internet access for clients connected to the unicast network. In most cases, the Internet Provider and the Unicast Network Provider will be the same company, both from a logical and service provider point of view they are two separate entities.

4.3 Implementation details

This subsection provides a more in depth explanation of how the required services can be provided over DVB-H/SH. Attention is given to the question how TPEG services can be integrated into the IPDC headend, and how the tpegML files can be delivered through FLUTE.

4.3.1 Integrating TPEG services in the IPDC headend

Fig. 8 details how the ITS services are integrated into a typical DVB-IPDC headend. In our setup, the Video Content Provider streams its multimedia data over SDI (Serial Digital Interface) to the encoders. These H.264 encoders also encapsulate all the data into RTP packets. Following the protocol stack as defined by DVB-IPDC, these RTP-streams are sent over UDP and then multicasted into the Multicast IP Network. At the TPEG Service Provider, a file server sends all the tpegML data to the Flute Server of the headend.

Both the encoders (through Session Description Protocol (SDP) (IETF, 1998) files) and the TPEG Service Provider (not standardized) sent metadata to the ESG server in order to make

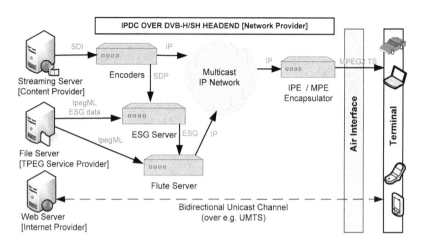

Fig. 8. Coupling of the TPEG Service Provider with the IPDC over DVB-H/SH headend

sure that the TPEG middleware and the decoders are able to find and correctly interpret all the broadcasted data. All the ESG data is then sent to the Flute server which will multicast all the data into the Multicast IP Network.

The IPE/MPE Encapsulator encapsulates all the multicasted IP packets into an MPEG2 TS (transport stream). This MPEG2 TS is then sent to the satellite or antennas, where the stream is finally modulated and sent over the air to the user's terminal. As a return channel, a bidirectional unicast channel such as e.g. UMTS may be used to acquire more information (such as local touristic information) through the Internet Provider. Note that for single frequency networks (SFN) an additional component, a so-called SFN adapter, should be placed after the IP/MPE encapsulators.

4.3.2 Delivery of tpegML through FLUTE

DVB-IPDC not only defines protocols for the delivery of audio and video streams, but it also specifies how binary files should be incorporated into the MPEG data streams and sent to the end users. This IPDC file delivery mechanism is based on the FLUTE protocol (IETF, 2004). FLUTE (File delivery over Unidirectional Transport) is a fully-specified protocol to transport files (any kind of discrete binary object), and uses special purpose objects – the File Delivery Table (FDT) Instances - to provide a running index of files and their essential reception parameters in-band of a FLUTE session. FLUTE is built on top of the Asynchronous Layered Coding (ALC) protocol instantiation (IETF, 2002) which provides reliable asynchronous delivery of content to an unlimited number of concurrent receivers from a single sender. FLUTE is carried over UDP/IP, and is independent of the IP version and the underlying link layers used.

There are 5 types of file delivery sessions that are specified on the basis of FLUTE. We will only detail the most advanced session type, more specifically the Dynamic file delivery carousel as this is the required method in our architecture for the delivery of ITS related data to all the users. A dynamic file delivery carousel is a possibly time-unbounded file delivery session in which a changing set of possibly changed, added or deleted files is delivered. The use of a carousel mechanism (of which teletext is a typical example) is necessary as in a broadcast scenario you don't know exactly when a user tunes in. As a carousel mechanism continuously repeats or updates the traffic info, users who just started their car will still be able to receive all relevant traffic info, even if they missed the initial message.

The time that a random user has to wait for its traffic info will be dependent on the size of the carousel. As we want to support an unlimited number of TPEG services in our architecture, encompassing all these services into the same data carousel would invoke a round trip time of the data carousel that is much too high. Secondly, the use of one big carousel would ensue that the antenna has to be turned on for longer periods which in turn partly undoes one of the main advantages of DVB-H/SH, namely the reduced power consumption. Therefore we use one main FLUTE data carousel which continuously repeats all road related traffic info. After each such road related traffic block, exactly one other object is placed. This second object will be one of the public transport services or the touristic metadata. As already explained in section III.B, the touristic metadata only informs the user's terminal where to find specific information, related to the current location of the terminal.

Our FLUTE data carousel is illustrated in Fig. 9. Object 1 always contains the road-related data. As shown in Fig. 9, object 1 is continuously repeated while changes in this object (object 1') and the fact that the second object is continuously alternating are indicated by the File Delivery Table (object 0).

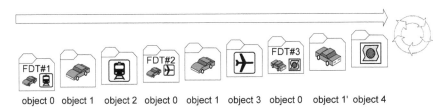

Fig. 9. Delivering ITS services via a dynamic FLUTE carousel

Note that DVB-IPDC only specifies that one FLUTE channel should be supported but that the use of several concurrent FLUTE channels may be supported by the terminals. For terminals that do not support multiple channels, it should be possible for them to receive enough data from the first channel named base FLUTE channel in order to declare the channel as complete. In our architecture the base FLUTE channel contains all the information that comes from the Traffic Control Centre and the changes in Bus, Rail and Air operator services. As such, all DVB-H terminals shall automatically be able to receive all the traffic related info. If the manufacturer finds it relevant to also support other services than the manufacturer may still incorporate the support of multiple FLUTE sessions into its devices. Terminals that do not support multiple channels shall ignore all but the base FLUTE channel.

5. Conclusion

In this paper we presented an ITS architecture that was based on the usage of the mobile broadcast technologies DVB-H and DVB-SH. It was explained why these technologies are very well suited for the delivery of ITS services and what the advantages are of using these technologies. The proposed architecture is complimentary with the available set of DVB-IPDC specifications and details were provided of how exactly ITS services should be integrated into a DVB-IPDC system.

6. Acknowledgment

The authors would like to thank the Flemish Interdisciplinary institute for Broadband technology (IBBT) for defining the MADUF and NextGenITS projects.

7. References

Baldessari, R.; Bödekker, B.; Brakemeier, A. et al (2007). *CAR 2 CAR Communication Consortium Manifesto*, deliverable of C2C-CC project

Bayly, M.; Fildes, B.; Regan, M. & Young K. (2007). Review of crash effectiveness of Intelligent Transport Systems, *Deliverable D4.1.1-D6.2*, TRACE project

BBC (2009). *BBC Travel News – TPEG*, accessed online at http://www.bbc.co.uk /travelnews/xml/ on July 13th 2009

Chevul; Karlsson; Isaksson et al (2005). Measurements of Application-Perceived Throughput in DAB, GPRS, UMTS and WLAN Environments, *Proceedings of RVK'05*, Linköping, Sweden

Cho, S.; Geon, K.; Jeong, Y.; Ah,n C.; Lee, S.I. & Lee, H. (2006). Real Time Traffic Information Service Using Terrestrial Digital Multimedia Broadcasting System. *IEEE transactions on broadcasting*, vol. 52, no 4, 2006

Eriksen, A.; Olsen, E.; Evensen K. et al (2006). Reference Architecture, *Deliverable D.CVIS.3.1*, CVIS project

European Broadcasting Union (2009). *TPEG- What is it all about?*, accessed online at http://tech.ebu.ch/docs/other/TPEG-what-is-it.pdf on June 25th 2009

ETSI (2004). *EN 302304 v1.1.1:Digital Video Broadcasting (DVB), Transmission System for Handheld Terminals (DVB-H)*

ETSI (2007a). *TS 102 585 V1.1.1:System Specifications for Satellite services to Handheld devices (SH) below 3 GHz - TS 102 585*

ETSI(2007b). *TS 102 468 V1.1.1: Digital Video Broadcasting (DVB); IP Datacast over DVB-H: Set of Specifications for Phase 1*

ETSI (2008). *EN 302 583 V1.1.0:Framing Structure, channel coding and modulation for Satellite Services to Handheld devices (SH) below 3 GHz*

DVB Document A112-2r1. Digital Video Broadcasting (DVB); IP Datacast: Electronic Service Guide (ESG) Implementation Guidelines Part 2: IP Datacast over DVB-SH.

Frötscher, A. (2008). *Co-operative Systems for Intelligent Road Safety*, presentation of COOPERs project, available on http://www.coopers-op.eu/uploads/media/ COOPERS_Presentation TRA_Ljubljana_2008.pdf

IETF (1998). *RFC 2327: SDP, Session Description Protocol*

IETF (2002). *RFC 3450: Asynchronous Layered Coding (ALC) Protocol Instantiation*

IETF *RFC 3926: FLUTE- File Delivery over Unidirectional Transport*, 2004.

Leroux, P.; Verstraete, V.; De Turck, F. & Demeester, P. (2007). Synchronized Interactive Services for Mobile Devices over IPDC/DVB-H and UMTS, *Proceedings of IEEE Broadband Convergence Networks*, Munchen

MADUF, https://projects.ibbt.be/maduf, 2008.

Plets, D.; Joseph, W.; Martens, L.; Deventer, E. & Gauderis, H. (2007). Evaluation and validation of the performance of a DVB-H network, *2007 IEEE International Symposium on Broadband Multimedia Systems and Broadcasting*, Orlando, Florida, USA

RACC Automobile Club (2007). Stakeholder utility, data privacy and usability analysis and recommendations for operational guarantees and system safeguards: Europe, *Deliverable D.DEPN.4.1*, CVIS project

Williams, C.C. B. (2004). *The CALM handbook*, available on http://www.tc204wg16.de /Public/The%20CALM%20Handbookv2-060215.pdf

8

Video Content Description using Fuzzy Spatio-Temporal Relations

Archana M. Rajurkar[1], R.C. Joshi[2],
Santanu Chaudhary[3] and Ramchandra Manthalkar[4]

[1]Dept. of Computer Sc. and Engg. M.G.M.'s College of Engineering, Nanded – 431 605,
[2]Dept. of Electronics and Computer Engg. Indian Institute of Technology Roorkee,
Roorkee - 247 667,

[3]Dept. of Electrical Engg., Indian Institute of Technology, Delhi, New Delhi,
[4]Dept. of Electronics and Telecommunication Engg. S.G.G.S. Institute of Engineering,
and Technology Nanded – 431 605, India

1. Introduction

There has been an explosive growth in multimedia data such as images, video and audio in the past few years. The rapid proliferation of the Web made a large amount of video data publicly available. This necessitates a system that provides the ability to store and retrieve video in a way that allows flexible and efficient search based on semantic content.

Most of the existing video retrieval techniques search video based on visual features such as color, texture and shape (Zhang et al., 1997; Chang et al.,1998; Hampapur et al., 1997). A video sequence is first segmented into shots, each shot is then represented in terms of a number of key frames and then the visual features are used for retrieval (Zhang et al., 1993; Zhang et al., 1995; Mottaleb et al., 1996). Key frame based methods do not always consider events occurring in the video that involves various objects and choosing the key-frames is a challenging problem. Furthermore, in these approaches the temporal nature of video is neglected. A few systems have addressed the issue of object-based video retrieval (Deng & Manjunath, 1998; Courtney, 1997) and spatial modeling of video data that involve temporal information (Bimbo et al., 1995; Little & Ghafoor, 1993; Dagtas & Ghafoor, 1999; Vazirgiannis et al., 1998).

The semantic modeling of video content is a difficult problem. One simple way to model the video content is by using textual annotation (Oomoto & Tanaka, 1993) or visual features (Zhang et al., 1997; Chang et al., 1998), but the annotation is tedious and time consuming and simple visual features are not always sufficient to represent the rich semantics of digital video. Another way to model the video content is by using spatio-temporal concepts or events that describe the dynamic spatio-temporal behavior and interaction of video objects. As humans think in terms of events and remember different events and objects after watching a video, these high-level concepts are the most important cues in content-based retrieval (Petkovik & Jonker, 2001). For example, in a football game, we usually remember goals, interesting actions etc. Therefore there is a great need for development of robust tools for modeling and extraction of spatio-temporal relations among objects visible in a video sequence.

Some approaches have been suggested in the literature for modeling the spatial and temporal relations of video objects. In most of the approaches, spatial relationships are based on projecting objects on a two or three-dimensional coordinate systems (Dagtas & Ghafoor, 1999), while temporal relations are based on Allen's temporal interval algebra (Allen, 1983). Some models, which use temporal relations for video retrieval, are proposed in (Oomoto & Tanaka, 1993; Little & Ghafoor, 1993). Very few efforts integrate both spatial and temporal aspects (Dagtas, 1998, Vazirgiannis et al., 1998; Nepal & Srinivasan, 2002; Pissiou et al., 2001). A Spatio-Temporal Logic (STL) language is presented in (Bimbo et al., 1995), which is used to describe the contents of an image sequence. A prototype image retrieval system supporting visual querying by example image sequences is discussed in this but; the problem of modeling higher-level concepts of spatio-temporal events is not addressed. A framework for semantic modeling of video data using generalized n-ary operators is presented in (Day et al., 1995). A graph-based model, called Video Semantic Directed graph (VSDG) is proposed in (Dagtas, 1998) for unbiased representation of video data using directed graph model. It also suggests the use of Allen's temporal interval algebra to model relations among objects. A model for complete declarative representation of spatio-temporal composition is presented in (Vazirgiannis et al., 1998). Nepal and Srinivasan (2002) presented a binary representation-based framework for modeling and querying video content using video object relationships at a semantic level that supports conceptual spatio-temporal queries. A topological-directional model for spatio-temporal composition of objects in video sequences is presented in (Rajurkar and Joshi, 2001). It describes the spatio-temporal relationships among objects for each frame and models temporal composition of an object.

Most of the previous spatio-temporal models do not deal with extraction of spatio- temporal relations rather they use handcrafted precise definitions of spatial relations (Egenhofer & Fanzosa, 1991) and temporal relations (Allen, 1983). It is not always possible to precisely characterize spatial and temporal relations between objects in the video sequence because of the inherent dynamic nature of the media. Further, spatial relations such as LEFT, ABOVE and others defy precise definitions, and seem to be best modeled by fuzzy sets (Matsakis & Wendling, 1999). Furthermore, errors may occur in shot segmentation and object detection due to non-robustness of the image/video processing operations leading to erroneous inference of crisp spatio-temporal relations between objects. By using fuzzy definitions of spatio-temporal relations, we can take care of these errors and ambiguities. Consequently, this approach facilitates video modeling as well as query processing based upon spatio-temporal relations extracted automatically from the actual video data without manual intervention.

Motivated by the above observation, we present a new approach for video content description. A fuzzy spatio-temporal model that is based on fuzzy directional and topological relations and fuzzy temporal relations between video objects is proposed. We use the linguistic definitions of spatial relations using *histogram of forces* presented in our earlier work (Rajurkar & Joshi, 2001). Fuzzy definitions and membership functions of temporal relations are presented and the second order fuzzy temporal relations have been proposed. A video representation scheme is presented using the proposed fuzzy spatio-temporal model. We have illustrated query processing with our fuzzy spatio-temporal model.

The rest of the chapter is organized as follows. Section 2 describes the method used for object detection using motion segmentation. The proposed fuzzy spatio-temporal model is presented in section 3. Query processing and retrieval results are given in section 4 and conclusions are presented in section 5.

2. Object detection using motion based segmentation

In our approach, a video sequence is modeled in terms of fuzzy spatio-temporal relations between objects visible in the video sequence. For sake of simplicity it is assumed that the objects of importance in a video sequence are in motion and simple motion based segmentation scheme for identification/detection of the objects is used in this work. A simple approach for motion-based segmentation using difference picture has been described here. More sophisticated approaches can improve the system performance.

In the proposed model, moving objects in every frame are detected in the video sequence using motion segmentation method described in (Courtney, 1997). For each frame F_n in the video sequence, the motion segmentation stage computes segmented image C_n as

$$C_n = T_h \bullet k$$

Where T_h is a binary image resulting from the absolute difference of images I_n and I_0 at threshold h. $T_h \bullet k$ is the morphological close operation on T_h with structuring element k. The image T_h is defined for all pixels (i,j) in T_h as

$$T_h(i, j) = \begin{cases} 1 & \text{if } |I_n(i,j) - I_0(i,j)| \geq h \\ 0 & \text{otherwise} \end{cases}$$

Connected component analysis is then performed on the segmented image C_n resulting in a unique label for each connected region. Each connected component is further recognized and identified manually for constructing the offline video model.

An example of motion segmentation process explained above is shown in Fig. 1. The reference image and the image to be segmented are shown in Fig.1 (a) and (b) respectively. Absolute difference and thresholded image is shown in Fig. 1(c) that detect motion region in the image. Fig. 1(d) shows the morphological close operation that joins small regions together into smoothly shaped objects. The result of connected component analysis that assigns each detected object a unique label is shown in Fig. 1(e). The output of the motion segmentation stage is C_n after discarding components, which are smaller than a given threshold. Fuzzy spatio-temporal relations between these objects are then defined.

Such a motion segmentation technique is best suited for video sequences containing object motion within an otherwise static scene, such as in surveillance and scene monitoring applications (Courtney, 1997).

3. Fuzzy spatio-temporal model

Spatio-temporal relations of the salient objects play a crucial role in characterization of the "content" of video. The spatial characteristics are referred to as spatial relationship between any two objects in a sampled frame, whereas the temporal characteristics are referred as the dynamics of the spatial relationships between every two objects over the frames in a video sequence.

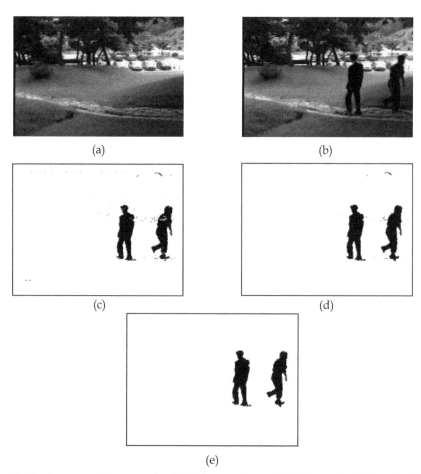

Fig. 1. Motion Segmentation example: (a) Reference Image I_0 (b) Image I_n (c) Thresholded Image T_h (d) Result of Morphological Close Operation (e) Result of Connected Component Analysis

In the proposed model the description of a scene is expressed by the mutual spatial relationships between every two objects and the temporal change in their relationships. Frame intervals specify the period for which a particular spatial relationship holds. For each object $O_i t$ in a frame t, its fuzzy spatial and temporal relationships, $O_{ST_{ij}} t$, with every other object, $O_j t$, in the same frame are recorded in a vector of size $n(n-1)$, where n is the number of objects in the frame t. The fuzzy spatio-temporal relationship between the two objects is defined as the function:

$$O_{ST_{ij}} t \ (O_i t, O_j t) = (S_{ij} t, T_{ij} t) \tag{1}$$

where $S_{ij} t$ and $T_{ij} t$ are the spatial and temporal relationships, respectively, between the objects $O_i t$ and $O_j t$ in the frame t.

3.1 Spatial relationships

The relative positions between two objects O_i and O_j can be captured as a fuzzy spatial relation using *histogram of forces* (F-Histogram) (Matsakis & Wendling, 1999). The spatio-temporal models presented earlier in (Dagtas & Ghafoor, 1999; Nepal and Srinivasan, 2002; Pissiou et al., 2001) use precise definitions of spatial relations using either angle measurements or minimum bounding rectangles (*MBR*). Spatial relations such as *left of*, *above* and others defy precise definitions, and seem to be best modeled by fuzzy sets (Matsakis & Wendling, 1999). Miyajima and Ralescu (1994) developed the idea of representing the relative position between two objects by *histogram of angles*. Matsakis and Wending (1999) introduced the notation of the F-histogram, which generalizes and supersedes that of the histogram of angles is discussed in the following section.

3.2 F-histograms

The F-histogram represents the relative position of a 2D object A with regard to another object B by a function FAB from **R** in to **R+**. For any direction θ, the value FAB(θ) is the total weight of the arguments that can be found in order to support the proposition "A is in direction θ of B". Object A is the argument and object B is the referent. The directional spatial relations between objects are defined from a fuzzy subset of **R**. Its membership function μ is continuous, with a period 2π that decreasing on [0, π], and takes the value 1 at 0 and the value 0 at π/2 shown in Fig. 2(a). It can be employed to define a family of fuzzy directional relations between points (Rajurkar & Joshi, 2001). We used the typical triangular function graphed in Fig. 2(a). Let α and β be two reals and A and B be two distinct points. If β is an angle measure, then (Fig. 2(b)): $R_\alpha(A, B) = \mu(\beta-\alpha)$. In our earlier work (Rajurkar & Joshi, 2001) we have presented definitions of fuzzy directional spatial relations and topological relations using F-histogram. We make use of these definitions of fuzzy spatial relations as perceived by humans for capturing relative position of a 2D object O_it with regards to another object O_jt. Each pair of objects in every frame in the video sequence is represented by relative position histograms and then the degree of truth of a proposition "*A is in direction θ of B*" is computed. The degree of truth is a real number generated greater than or equal to 0 (proposition completely false) and less than or equal to 1 (proposition completely true).

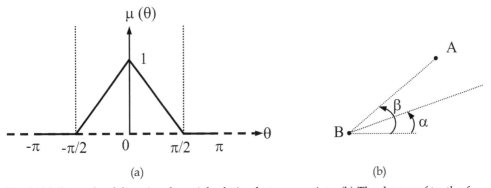

(a) (b)

Fig. 2. (a) Example of directional spatial relation between points. (b) The degree of truth of the proposition "A is in direction α of B" is $\mu(\beta-\alpha)$

The spatial relationships, $S_{ij}t$, between two objects are defined as follows:

$$S_{ij}t = (R_{ij}t, O_it, O_jt) \qquad (2)$$

The $R_{ij}t$ represents the degree of truth of a proposition "*A is in direction θ of B*" computed as described in (Rajurkar & Joshi, 2001).

3.3 Temporal relationships

Allen (1983) introduced temporal interval algebra for representing and reasoning about temporal relations between events represented as intervals. The elements of the algebra are sets of seven basic relations that can hold between two intervals. The relations are not reflective except equals and a set of inverse relations exists for the other six relations. A list and graphical illustrations of the binary interval relations is provided in Fig. 3. A qualitative description of relative position of objects (*MBRs*) when their projections on X and Y-axes are considered as interval operands to the relations are provided by interval relations.

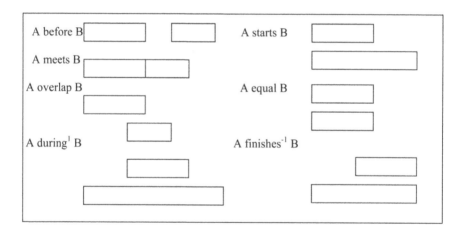

Fig. 3. Binary Interval Relations

Crisp description of temporal relations may not be suited for defining spatio-temporal models of video because of errors in segmentation, event and object detection due to noise and processing errors. We present some examples to illustrate this point. Figure 4 shows an example of error occurred in segmentation. Original image is shown in Fig. 4(a). Thresholded absolute difference image is shown in Fig. 4(b), and the results of motion segmentation after morphological close operation and connected component analysis is shown in Fig. 4(c). It is observed that though the objects *Person 1* and *Person 2* are disjoint after the segmentation they appear to be meet. Further it is also shown that how errors can occur in event detection and segmentation of noisy images. Fig. 5(a) shows an example of noisy image. The thresholded absolute difference image is shown in Fig. 5(b), and results of segmentation are given in Fig 5(c). It can be seen that though the objects *Person 1* and *Person*

2 are disjoint they appear to be meet after segmentation. Fig. 6 shows an example of error occurred in object detection. Fig. 6(a) shows the original image and the results of segmentation are presented in Fig. 6(b). It can be observed that half of the part of *Person2* is missing in the result, which may lead to wrong event and object detection. We present fuzzy definitions of temporal relations in this section that can take care of these errors in event-detection, segmentation and object detection and allows flexible description of video scene (see Table 1). Relations defined in Table 1 are applicable between objects, in particular for the intervals for which two objects are visible. For example, *A before B* with a membership function "mu" means that the *object A* is not visible, in general, in the scene when *B* appears. The temporal relation T_{ij} between the spatial relationships, $S_{ij}t$, of objects $O_i t$ and $O_j t$ can be described at two levels. In the first level, the temporal interval Δf for which a fuzzy spatial relationship between the two objects is valid is determined. In the second level, the second order fuzzy temporal relationships between the two spatial relations are described. The advantage of the second order fuzzy temporal relations is that they are more informative and provide global description of a sequence. The proposed second order fuzzy temporal relations using fuzzy spatial relations are shown in the Table 2. Graphical illustration of two second order fuzzy temporal relations are presented in Fig. 7.

The temporal relationship, T_{ij}, between the temporal intervals of two spatial relationships, $S_{ij}t$ and $S_{ij}t'$ is defined as follows:

$$T_{ij}^{1} = (S_{ij}t_{\Delta f})$$

$$T_{ij}^{2} = (S_{ij}t_{\Delta f} \langle FTOP \rangle S_{ij}t'_{\Delta f}) \tag{4}$$

where $\langle FTOP \rangle$ is one of the temporal operators representing the fuzzy temporal relationship between two intervals and Δf is temporal interval for which fuzzy spatial relationship S_{ij} is valid.

(a)　　　　　　　　(b)　　　　　　　　(c)

Fig. 4. Error Occurred in Segmentation (a) Original Image (b) Thresholded Absolute Difference Image (c) Results of Segmentation

(a)   (b)   (c)

Fig. 5. Error Occurred in Segmentation (a) Noisy Image (b) Thresholded Absolute Difference Image (c) Results of Segmentation

(a)   (b)

Fig. 6. Error Occurred in Event and Object Detection (a) Original Image (b) Results of Segmentation

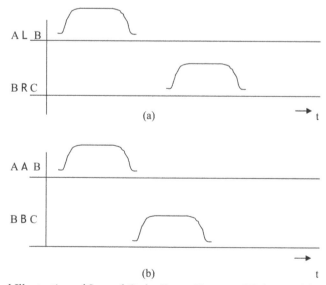

Fig. 7. Graphical Illustration of Second Order Fuzzy Temporal Relations (a) Relation A L B μ_{before} B R C (b) Relation A A B μ_{meets} B B C

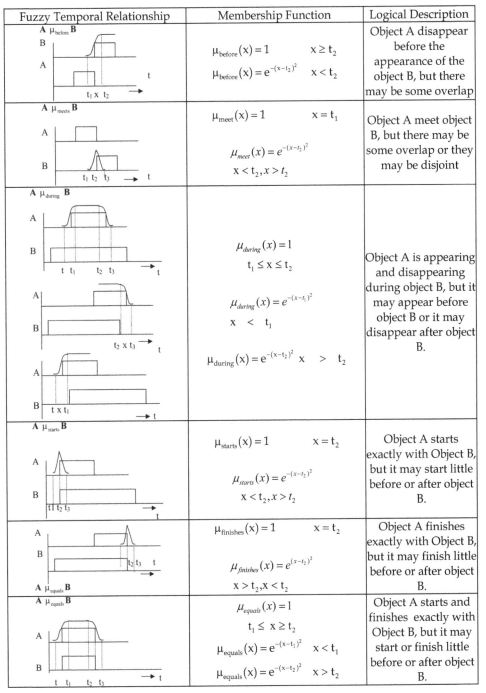

Fuzzy Temporal Relationship	Membership Function	Logical Description
A μ_{before} B	$\mu_{before}(x) = 1 \qquad x \geq t_2$ $\mu_{before}(x) = e^{-(x-t_2)^2} \qquad x < t_2$	Object A disappear before the appearance of the object B, but there may be some overlap
A μ_{meets} B	$\mu_{meet}(x) = 1 \qquad x = t_1$ $\mu_{meet}(x) = e^{-(x-t_2)^2}$ $x < t_2, x > t_2$	Object A meet object B, but there may be some overlap or they may be disjoint
A μ_{during} B	$\mu_{during}(x) = 1$ $t_1 \leq x \leq t_2$ $\mu_{during}(x) = e^{-(x-t_1)^2}$ $x < t_1$ $\mu_{during}(x) = e^{-(x-t_2)^2} \quad x > t_2$	Object A is appearing and disappearing during object B, but it may appear before object B or it may disappear after object B.
A μ_{starts} B	$\mu_{starts}(x) = 1 \qquad x = t_2$ $\mu_{starts}(x) = e^{-(x-t_2)^2}$ $x < t_2, x > t_2$	Object A starts exactly with Object B, but it may start little before or after object B.
A	$\mu_{finishes}(x) = 1 \qquad x = t_2$ $\mu_{finishes}(x) = e^{(x-t_2)^2}$ $x > t_2, x < t_2$	Object A finishes exactly with Object B, but it may finish little before or after object B.
A μ_{equals} B	$\mu_{equals}(x) = 1$ $t_1 \leq x \geq t_2$ $\mu_{equals}(x) = e^{-(x-t_1)^2} \quad x < t_1$ $\mu_{equals}(x) = e^{-(x-t_2)^2} \quad x > t_2$	Object A starts and finishes exactly with Object B, but it may start or finish little before or after object B.

Table 1. Fuzzy Temporal Relationships and Corresponding Logical Descriptions

3.4 Representation of video sequence using fuzzy spatio-temporal model

This section presents the representation of a video sequence using the proposed fuzzy spatio-temporal model. The video database V_{db} contains video sequences $S_1, S_2 \ldots S_n$ as follows:

$$V_{db} = \langle S_1 \rangle \; \langle S_2 \rangle \; \langle S_3 \rangle \ldots\ldots\ldots\ldots\ldots \langle S_n \rangle \tag{5}$$

A video sequence S is an ordered set of n frames (t), denoted $S = \{t_0, t_1, t_3, \ldots t_n\}$, where t_n is the nth frame in the sequence. For each frame t in the video sequence S the moving objects are detected and labeled using motion segmentation method outlined in Section 2. Then the attributes of labeled objects are derived.

Spatial Relation 1	Temporal Relation	Spatial Relation 2	Definition of Second Order Fuzzy Temporal Relations
A *left of* B	Before	B *right of* C	A L B μ_{before} B R C
A *above* B	Before	B *below* C	A A B μ_{before} B B C
A *left of* B	Meets	B *left of* C	A L B μ_{meets} B L C
A *above* B	Meets	B *below* C	A A B μ_{meets} B B C
A *left of* B	Overlap	B *right of* C	A L B $\mu_{overlaps}$ B R C
A *above* B	Overlap	B *below* C	A A B $\mu_{overlaps}$ B B C
A *left of* B	During	B *right of* C	A L B μ_{during} B R C
A *above* B	During	B *below* C	A A B μ_{during} B B C
A *left of* B	Starts	B *right of* C	A L B μ_{starts} B R C
A *above* B	Starts	B *below* C	A A B μ_{starts} B B C
A *left of* B	Finishes	B *right of* C	A L B $\mu_{finishes}$ B R C
A *above* C	Finishes	B *below* C	A A C $\mu_{finishes}$ B B C
A *left of* B	Equals	B *right of* C	A L B μ_{equals} B R C
A *above* B	Equals	B *below* C	A A B μ_{equals} B B C

Note: Set of inverse relations exists for all above relations except *equals*. The symbols used for spatial relations are L – *left of*, R – *right of*, A – *above*, B – *below*.

Table 2. Second Order Fuzzy Temporal Relations

For each object $O_i t$ of a frame t, its fuzzy spatial and temporal relationship $O_{ST_{ij}} t$, with every other object, $O_j t$, is represented using the proposed fuzzy spatio-temporal model as discussed in Section 3.

$$O_{ST_{ij}} t \left(O_i t, O_j t \right) = \left(S_{ij} t, T_{ij} t \right) \tag{6}$$

where $S_{ij}t$ and $T_{ij}t$ are defined by Eq. (2) and (3) respectively.

For each frame t fuzzy spatio-temporal relationship between all object pairs (*e.g.* suppose there are four objects in the frame t) is represented as follows:

$$O_{ST}t = (O_{ST_{12}}, O_{ST_{13}}, O_{ST_{14}}, O_{ST_{23}}, O_{ST_{24}}, O_{ST_{34}}) \qquad (7)$$

To capture the dynamic change in the fuzzy spatial relationship of two objects $O_i t$ and $O_j t$ over the video scene, interval of l frames in which the corresponding spatial relation is valid is determined. The temporal interval of a spatial relationship is found from the frame t of the initial appearing of a particular spatial relationship, which represent the beginning of the temporal interval in which that spatial relationship is valid. Then the frame t' of the initial appearance of the first different relationship is determined. Thus the duration of the temporal interval in which a particular spatial relation is valid is $t'- t$. Based on these durations, fuzzy spatio-temporal relations are computed for describing the video sequences. The detailed algorithm for representing video sequences in a video database using the proposed fuzzy spatio-temporal model is presented in Fig. 8.

Algorithm *Represent video*_{fstm}

Input: V_{db}(video database)
Output: Representation of video database sequences.
Procedure:
For every video sequences in the video database do the following
1. Motion segmentation
   For each frame t in the database video sequence, the motion segmentation stage computes segmented image C_n. as $C_n = T_h \bullet k$. Connected component analysis is then performed on the segmented image C_n and objects are identified, labeled and their attributes are derived.
2. Compute fuzzy spatio-temporal relations
   For every frame in the video sequence S, for each object pair ($O_i t$, $O_j t$)
   Compute fuzzy spatial relations $S_{ij}t = (R_{ij}t, O_i t, O_j t)$
   Compute the temporal interval Δt for which the spatial relationship $S_{ij}t$ is valid

$$T_{ij}^{1} = (S_{ij} t_{\Delta f})$$

3. Compute the second order fuzzy temporal relations between every two different spatial relations.

$$T_{ij}^{2} = (S_{ij} t_{\Delta f} < FTOP > S_{ij} t'_{\Delta f})$$

Fig. 8. Algorithm *Represent_video*_{fstm}

We used *MPEG-7* video content *ETRI_od_A.mpg* to illustrate the proposed video sequence representation scheme. Fig. 9 shows few frames in the video sequence *ETRI_od_A.mpg*. Moving objects in the sequence are detected and labeled as *Person1*, *Person2*, *Person3* and *Person4* using the motion segmentation method described earlier in section 2 and their attributes are derived. Initial appearing of two objects *Person1* and *Person 2* is detected in frame 173 and their spatial relation is *"Person1 in white shirt is left of Person2 in black shirt "* shown in Fig.9. The temporal interval in which this spatial relationship is valid starts from frame 173 and ends at frame 290. The same spatial relationship holds for another temporal intervals from frame 2316 to frame 2343 and from the frame 2792 to frame 2900. The fuzzy spatio-temporal relationship is given by

$$O_{ST_{12}}t(O_1 173, O_2 173) = (S_{12} 173, T_{12} 173) \qquad (8)$$

$$S_{12} 173 = (\textit{left of}, \text{Person1}, \text{Person2})$$

$$T_{12}^l = 354$$

Similarly initial appearing of the different spatial relationships between objects *Person1* and *Person2* is detected in frame 636 and its temporal interval is computed as described above. The procedure is repeated for the initial appearing of the other object pairs in the video sequence and their fuzzy spatio-temporal relationships are computed.

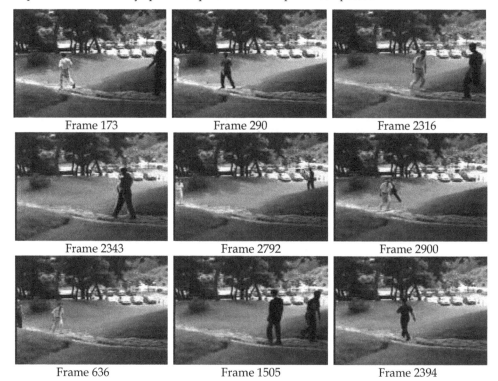

Fig. 9. Few Sample Frames in Video ETRI_od_A.mpg

The second level temporal relationship is determined by computing the second order fuzzy temporal relationships between the two different spatial relationships. In the video sequence *ETRI_od_A.mpg* the first two spatial relations are detected in frame 173 and 636 and their first level temporal intervals are 116 and 187. The second level temporal relationship is given by:

$$T_{12}^2 = (S_{12_{116}} \, 173 \left\langle \mu_{before} \right\rangle S_{12_{187}} \, 636)$$ (9)

$$S_{12} \, 173 = (\textit{left of, Person1, Person2})$$

$$S_{12} \, 636 = (\textit{right of, Person1, Person2})$$

The second level temporal relationships between all the different spatial relationships found in the video sequence are determined as described above. In this way all the video sequences in the database are represented by the fuzzy spatio-temporal relationships among the objects in the sequence.

4. Querying and retrieval

Formulation of meaningful and clear query is very important for searching and retrieving video. Content-based retrieval of video is rather difficult than that of the image due to the temporal information in the video. The issue of efficient handling queries related to the spatio-temporal relationships among objects is discussed here. We perform the ranking of the database sequences that are similar to the query using the relevance membership function (RMF). The temporal intervals for all spatial relations between two objects over a sequence are computed to decide the maximum number of frames for which a particular spatial relationship between two objects is valid. Depending on the query, the relevance membership function, which is the ratio of total number of frames in the sequence to the maximum number of frames for which the spatial relationship in the query is valid for every sequence in the database, is computed. The detailed algorithm *Search_Video*$_{fstm}$ for searching and ranking the video sequences in the database similar to the query V_{qr} is presented in Fig. 10.

In the following, we present some examples of queries using the spatio-temporal properties.

Query1: Find a video sequence in which a *Person P1* approaches *Person P2* from the left.

    Select   S
    From   sequences S_n
    Where   S contains P1 and P2 and P1 L P2

Query 2: Find a video sequence in which a *Car* is moving to the right reaches to a *House*

    Select   S
    From   sequences S_n
    Where   S contains a Car and a House and Car R House

Query 3: Find a video sequence in which *Car A* is in the left of *Car B* before *Car C* is in the right of *Car D* in the race.

    Select   S
    From   sequences S_n
    Where   S contains Car A, Car B, Car C and Car D and Car A L Car B μ_{before} Car C R
    Car D

Query 4: Find a video sequence in which *Flowers* are right to the *Lake* and a *Jeep* is passing besides the *Lake*.

Select S
From   sequences S_n
Where S contains *Flowers, Lake* and *Jeep* and *Flowers* R *Lake* μ_{overlaps} *Jeep*.

We used *MPEG-7* video content to evaluate the effectiveness of our query processing scheme. Video sequences in the database are represented using the proposed fuzzy spatio-temporal model as described in section 3.4.

Algorithm Search_Video$_{\text{fstm}}$

Input: V_{qr}
Output: Ranking of video sequences that are similar to the query V_{qr}
Procedure:
1. For every video sequences in the video database compute the relevance membership function (RMF)

$$RMF = \frac{\text{Number of frames in the database video sequence } S}{\text{Maximum number of frames for which the spatial relation in the query } V_{qr} \text{ is valid}}$$

2. Rank the video sequences in the database in the increasing order of the value of RMF

Fig. 10. Algorithm Search_Video$_{\text{fstm}}$

Now, consider a query *"Find video sequences in which Person1 in white shirt is left of Person2 in black shirt"*. The query results are shown in Table 3. The temporal intervals representing the number of frames for which a spatial relationship *left of* is valid for every sequence and the RMF values are given in the Table 3. Low value of *RMF* function corresponds to the more number of frames while higher value of *RMF* corresponds to the less number of frames that satisfy the spatial relationship *left* in the sequence. The sequences in the database are then ranked depending on the value of *RMF*. The video sequences having low *RMF* values are retrieved as similar to that of the spatio-temporal relation described in the query. For the query in question the most similar sequence in the video database is ETRI_od_A.mpg, which has maximum number of frames *i.e.* 273 for which spatial relationship *Person1 in white shirt is left of Person 2 in black shirt* is valid. The database video sequences are ranked as 1, 3, 2 depending on the *RMF* value for the query in question.

Consider a query *"Find video sequences in which a blue car is going towards North"*. Table 4 shows the results for this query. The temporal intervals representing the number of frames for which a spatial relationship *blue car is going towards north* is valid for every sequence and the *RMF* values are given in the Table 4. The video sequences in the database are ranked depending on the *RMF* values. For the above query the most similar video sequence is *speedwa2.mpg*, which has the maximum number of frames *i.e.* 1132 that satisfy the spatial relationship mentioned in the query. The ranking of the database video sequences for this query is 2, 3, 4, 1.

Consider another query *"Find video sequences in which red car is standing right side of the road"*. The results for this query are shown in Table 5. The most similar video sequence for this query in the database is *speedwa5.mpg* and the ranking obtained for the database video sequences is 5, 4, and 3.

5. Conclusions

We have presented a fuzzy spatio-temporal model for video content description that supports spatio-temporal queries. The proposed model is based on fuzzy directional and topological relations and fuzzy temporal relation. The problems associated with the use of crisp spatio-temporal relations were highlighted. It is shown that errors may occur in segmentation, event detection and object detection due to noisy video data and use of precise spatial relations. In order to minimize these errors fuzzy definitions of temporal relations are proposed. In addition, the second order temporal relations are presented that are more informative and provide global information about the sequence. The proposed model provides a mechanism that represents the fuzzy spatio-temporal relationships among the objects in video sequences in the database and ranks the database sequences based on the query for effective content-based retrieval. We reported the results of our experiment on a sample video from *MPEG-7* data set.

Video Sequence	Spatial Relation *Person 1 in white shirt is left of Person 2*	Relevance Membership Function (*RMF*) *
1 (ETRI_od_A.mpg)	273	3086/273 = 11.3040
2 (ETRI_od_B.mpg)	0	3455/0 = Positive Infinity
3 (ETRI_od_C.mpg)	219	8910/219 = 40.6849

* RMF value 1 indicate maximum relevance and positive infity indicate minimum relevance

Table 3. Temporal Intervals and Relevance Membership Function (*RMF*) Values for the Query "*Find The VideoSequences in Which Person1 in White Shirt is Left of Person 2 in Black Shirt*" for the Video Sequences in *MPEG-7* Video Content Set

Video Sequence	Spatial Relation *Blue car is going towards north*	Relevance Membership Function (*RMF*)
1 (speedwa1.mpg)	87	1420/87 = 16.32
2 (speedwa2.mpg)	1132	13185/1132 = 11.64
3 (speedwa3.mpg)	388	14019/388=36.13
4 (spedwa4.mpg)	100	7496/100=74.96
5 speedwa5.mpg)	0	7497/0=Positive Infinity

Table 4. Temporal Intervals and Relevance Membership Function (*RMF*) Values for the Query "*Find the Video Sequences in which Blue Car is Going Towards North*" for the Video Sequences in the *MPEG-7* Video Content Set

Video Sequence	Spatial Relation *Red car is standing right side of the road*	Relevance Membership Function (*RMF*)
1 (speedwa1.mpg)	0	1420/0 = Positive Infinity
2 (speedwa2.mpg)	0	13185/0 = Positive Infinity
3 (speedwa3.mpg)	452	14019/452=31.01
4 (spedwa4.mpg)	1506	7496/1506=4.97
5 speedwa5.mpg)	1834	7497/1834=4.08

Table 5. Temporal Intervals and Relevance Membership Function (*RMF*) Values for the Query *"Find the VideoSequences in which Red Car is Standing Right Side of the Road "* for the Video Sequences in the *MPEG-7*Video Content Set

6. References

Allen J.F., (1983). Maintaining knowledge about temporal intervals. Communications of ACM 26 (11), pp. 832-843.

Bimbo A.D., Vicario E., Zingoni D., (1995). Symbolic description and visual querying of image sequences using spatio-temporal logic. IEEE Trans. Knowledge and Data Engineering 7 (4), pp. 609-621.

Chang S. F., Chen W., Meng H., Sundaram H., Zhong D., (1998). A fully automated content-based video search engine supporting spatiotemporal queries. IEEE Trans. on Circuits and Systems for Video Technology 8 (5),pp. 602-615.

Courtney J.D., 1997. Automatic video indexing via object motion analysis. Pattern Recognition 30 (4), pp. 607-625.

S. Dagtas, A. Ghafoor, (1999). Indexing and retrieval of video based on spatial relation sequences, Proc. ACM International Multimedia Conf. (part 2) Oriando, FL, USA, , pp. 119-121.

Dagtas S., (1998). Spatio-Temporal Content-Characterization and Retrieval in Multimedia Databases, Ph.D. Thesis, Purdue University.

Deng Y., Manjunath B.S., (1998). NeTra-V: Toward an object-Based video representation. IEEE Trans. Circuits and Systems for Video technology 8 (5), pp. 616-627.

Day Y.F., Dagtas S., Lino M., Khokhar A., and Ghafoor A., 1995. Object-oriented conceptual modeling of video data. Proc. Eleventh Int. Conf. on Data Engineering, Taipei, Taiwan, pp.401-408,.

Egenhofer M.J., Fanzosa R., (1991). Point-set topological spatial relations. International Journal on Geographic Information Systems 5 (2), pp.161-174.

El-Kwae E., Kabuka M. R., (1999). A robust framework for content-based retrieval by spatial similarity in image databases. ACM Trans. on Information Systems 17(2), pp.174-198.

Gudivada V., Raghvan V., (1995). Design and evaluation of algorithms for image retrieval by spatial similarity. ACM Trans. on Information Systems 13 (2), pp.115-144.

Hampapur A., Gupta A., Horowitz B., Shu C.F., Fuller C., Bach J., Gorkani M., Jain R., (1997). Virage Video Engine. Proc. SPIE Storage and retrieval for Image and Video Databases V, San Jose, pp.188-197.

Little T.D.C., Ghafoor A., (1993). Interval-based conceptual models for time dependent multimedia data. IEEE Trans. Knowledge and Data Engineering 5 (4), pp.551-563.

Li J. Z., Ozsu M. T., Szafron D., (1997). Modeling of video spatial relationships in an object database management system. Proc. IS & T/ SPIE Int'l Symposium on Electronic Imaging: Multimedia Computing and Networking, San Jose, USA, pp.81-90.

Li J. Z., Ozsu M. T., Szafron D., Oria V., (1997). MOQL: A multimedia object query language. Proc. Third International Workshop on Multimedia Information Systems, Italy, pp. 19-28.

Mottaleb M.A., Dimitrova N., Desai R., Martino J., (1996). CONIVAS: COntent-based image and video access system. Proc. ACM Multimedia Conf., Bostan, MA USA, pp. 427-428.

Matsakis P., Wendling L., (1999). A new way to represent the relative position between areal objects. IEEE Transactions on Pattern Analysis and Machine Intelligence 21 (7), pp. 634-643.

Miyajima K., Ralescu A., (1994). Spatial organization in 2D segmented images: representation and recognition of primitive spatial relations. Fuzzy Sets and Systems 65, pp. 225-236.

Nabil M., Ngu A., Shepherd J., (1996). Picture similarity retrieval using the 2D projection interval representation. IEEE Trans. on Knowledge and Data Engineering 8 (4), pp. 533-539.

Nepal S., Srinivasan U., (2002). Spatio-temporal modeling and querying video databases using high level concepts. Proc. Sixth Working Conference on Visual Database System (VDB 6), 29-31 May, Brisbane, Australia .

Oomoto E., Tanaka K., (1993). OVID: Design and implementation of a video-object database system. IEEE Trans. on Knowledge and Data Engineering 5 (4), pp. 629-643.

Petkovik M., Jonker W., (2001). Content-based video retrieval by integrating spatio-temporal and stochastic recognition of events. Proc. IEEE workshop on Detection and Recognition of Events in Video, Vancouver, Canada.

Pissiou N., Radev I., Makki K., Campbell W.J.,(2001). Spatio-temporal composition of video objects: representation and querying in video database systems. IEEE Trans. on Knowledge and Data Engineering 13 (6), pp. 1033-1040.

Rajurkar A. M., Joshi R.C., (2001). Content-Based Image Retrieval: A fuzzy spatial similarity approach. Proc. of the International Symposium on Artificial Intelligence, ISAI'2001, Fort Panhala (Kolhapur), INDIA, Dec pp. 18-20.

Vazirgiannis M., Theodoridis Y., Sellis T., (1998). Spatio-temporal composition and indexing for large multimedia a pplications. Multimedia Systems 6, pp. 284-298.

Zhang H.J., Wu J., Zhong D., Smoliar S.W., (1997). An integrated system for content-based video retrieval and browsing, Pattern Recognition 30 (4), pp. 643-658.

Zhang H.J., Kankanhalli A., Smoliar S.W., (1993). Automatic partitioning of full-motion video. Multimedia Systems 1 (1), pp. 10-28.

Zhang H.J., Low C.Y., Smoliar S.W., Wu J.H., (1995). Video parsing, retrieval and browsing: an integrated and content-based solution. Proc. of the ACM Multimedia Conf., San Francisco, CA, November 5-9, pp. 15-24.

9

Video Quality Metrics

Mylène C. Q. Farias
*Department of Computer
Science University of Brasília
(UnB) Brazil*

1. Introduction

Digital video communication has evolved into an important field in the past few years. There have been significant advances in compression and transmission techniques, which have made possible to deliver high quality video to the end user. In particular, the advent of new technologies has allowed the creation of many new telecommunication services (e.g., direct broadcast satellite, digital television, high definition TV, video teleconferencing, Internet video). To quantify the performance of a digital video communication system, it is important to have a measure of video quality changes at each of the communication system stages. Since in the majority of these applications the transformed or processed video is destined for human consumption, humans will ultimately decide if the operation was successful or not. Therefore, human perception should be taken into account when trying to establish the degree to which a video can be compressed, deciding if the video transmission was successful, or deciding whether visual enhancements have provided an actual benefit.

Measuring the quality of a video implies a direct or indirect comparison of the test video with the original video. The most accurate way to determine the quality of a video is by measuring it using psychophysical experiments with human subjects (ITU-R, 1998). Unfortunately, psychophysical experiments are very expensive, time-consuming and hard to incorporate into a design process or an automatic quality of service control. Therefore, the ability to measure video quality accurately and efficiently, without using human observers, is highly desirable in practical applications. Good video quality metrics can be employed to monitor video quality, compare the performance of video processing systems and algorithms, and to optimize the algorithms and parameter settings for a video processing system.

With this in mind, fast algorithms that give a physical measure (objective metric) of the video quality are used to obtain an estimate of the quality of a video when being transmitted, received or displayed. Customarily, quality measurements have been largely limited to a few objective measures, such as the mean absolute error (MAE), the mean square error (MSE), and the peak signal-to-noise ratio (PSNR), supplemented by limited subjective evaluation. Although the use of such metrics is fairly standard in published literature, it suffers from one major weakness. The outputs of these measures do not always correspond well with human judgements of quality.

In the past few years, a big effort in the scientific community has been devoted to the development of better video quality metrics that correlate well with the human perception of quality (Daly, 1993; Lubin, 1993; Watson et al., 2001; Wolf et al., 1991). Although much has been done in the last ten years, there are still a lot of challenges to be solved since most of the achievements have been in the development of full-reference video quality metrics that evaluate compression artifacts. Much remains to be done, for example, in the area of no-reference and reduced-reference quality metrics. Also, given the growing popularity of video delivery services over IP networks (e.g. internet streaming and IPTV) or wireless channel (e.g. mobile TV), there is a great need for metrics that estimate the quality of the video in these applications.

In this chapter, we introduce several aspects of video quality. We give a brief description of the Human Visual System (HVS), discuss its anatomy and a number of phenomena of visual perception that are of particular relevance to video quality. We also describe the main characteristics of modern digital video systems, focusing on how visible errors (artifacts) are perceived in digital videos. The chapter gives a description of a representative set of video quality metrics. We also discuss recent developments in the area of video quality, including the work of the Video Quality Experts Group (VQEG).

2. The Human Visual System (HVS)

In the past century, the knowledge about the human visual system (HVS) has increased tremendously. Although much more needs to be learned before we can claim to understand it, the current state of the art of visual information-processing mechanisms is sufficient to provide important information that can be used in the design of video quality metrics. In fact, results in the literature show that video quality metrics that use models based on the characteristics of the HVS have better performance, i.e., give predictions that are better correlated with the values given by human observers (VQEG, 2003).

In this section, we introduce basic aspects of the anatomy and psychophysical features of the HVS that are considered relevant to video processing algorithms and, more specifically, to the design of video quality metrics.

2.1 Anatomy of the HVS

The eyes are far more than a simple camera. A more accurate description would be a self-focusing, self-adjusting for light intensity, and self-cleaning camera that provides a real-time output to a very advanced computer. The main components of the eye are the cornea, the pupil, the lens, and the fluids that fill the eye. A transverse section of the human eye is shown in Fig. 1.

The *optics* of the eye is composed by three major elements: the cornea, the pupil, and the lens. The light (visual stimulus) comes in through the optics and it is projected on the retina – the membrane located on the back of the eye. The optics works just like camera lens and their function is to project a clear and focused image on the retina – the retinal image. Given the physical limitation of the optics, the retinal image is only an approximation of the original image (the visual stimulus). As a result, the retinal image main contain some distortions, among which the most noticeable one is blurring. Since the response of optics is roughly linear, shift-invariant, and low-pass, the resulting retinal image can be approximated by convolving the input visual image with a blurring point spread function (PSF) (Marr, 1982).

The *retina* has the main function of translating the incoming light into nerve signals that can be understood by the brain. It has the shape of a plate and it is composed of many layers of neurons, as depicted in Fig. 2. The light projected on the retina has to pass through several layers before it reaches the photoreceptors cells and is absorbed by the pigment layer.

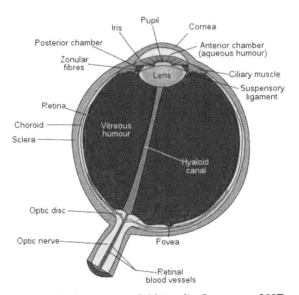

Fig. 1. Transverse section of the human eye (Wikimedia Commons, 2007).

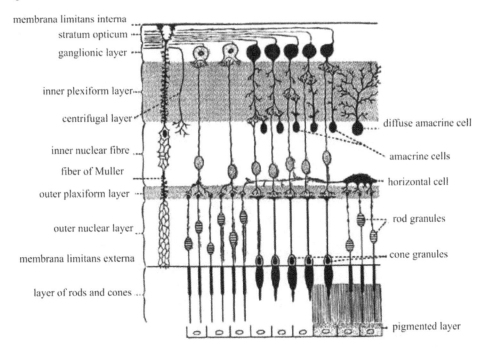

Fig. 2. Plan of retinal neurons. The retina is a stack of several neuronal layers. Light has to pass these layers (from top to bottom) to hit the photoreceptors (layer of rods and cones). The signal propagates through the bipolar and horizontal cells (middle layers) and, then, to the amacrine and ganglion cells. (Adapted from H. Grey (Grey, 1918))

The photoreceptor cells are specialized neurons that convert light energy into signals which can then be understood by the brain. There are two types of photoreceptors cells: *cones* and *rods*. Observe from Fig. 2 that the names are inspired by the shape of the cells. The rods are responsible for vision in low-light conditions. Cones are responsible for vision in normal high-light conditions, color vision, and have the ability to see fine details.

There are three types of cones, which are classified according to the spectral sensitivity of their photochemicals. The tree types are known as *L-cones*, *M-cones*, and *S-cones*, which stand for long, medium, and short wavelengths cones, respectively. Each of them has peak sensitivities around 570nm, 540nm, and 440nm, respectively. These differences are what makes color perception possible. The incoming light from the retina is split among the three types of cones, according to its spectral content. This generates three visual streams that roughly correspond to the three primary colors red, green, and blue.

There are roughly 5 million cones and 100 million rods in a human eye. But their distribution varies largely across the surface of the retina. The center of the retina has the highest density of cones and ganglion cells (neurons that carry the electrical signal from the eye to the brain through the optic nerve). This central area is called *fovea* and is only about half a millimeter in diameter. As we move away from it, the density of both cones and ganglion cells falls off rapidly. Therefore, the fovea is responsible for our fine-detail vision and, as a consequence, we cannot perceive the entire visual stimulus at uniform resolution.

The majority of cones in the retina are L- and M-cones, with S-cones accounting for less than 10% of the total number of cones. Rods, on the other hand, dominate outside the fovea. As a consequence, it is much easier to see dim objects when they are located in the peripheral field of vision. Looking at Fig. 1, we can see that there is a hole or *blind spot*, where the optic nerve is. In this region there are no photoreceptors.

The signal collected from the photoreceptors has to pass through several layers of neurons in the retina (retinal neurons) before being carried off to the brain by the optic nerve. As depicted in Fig. 2, different types of neurons can be found in the retina:

- *Horizontal cells* link receptors and bipolar cells by relatively long connections that run parallel to the retinal layers.
- *Bipolar cells* receive input from the receptors, many of them feeding directly into the retinal ganglion cells.
- *Amacrine cells* link bipolar cells and retinal ganglion cells.
- *Ganglion cells* collect information from bipolar and amacrine cells. Their axons form the optic nerve that leaves the eye through the optic disc and carries the output signal from the retina to other processing centers in the brain.

The signal leaves the eye through the *optic nerve*, formed by the axons of the ganglion cells. A scheme showing central connections of the optic nerves to the brain is depicted in Fig. 3. Observe that the optic nerves from the left and right eye meet at the *optic chiasm*, where the fibers are rearranged. About half of these fibers cross to the opposite side of the brain and the other half stay on the same side. In fact, the corresponding halves of the field of view (right and left) are sent to the left and right halves of the brain. Considering that the retinal images are reversed by the optics of the eye, the right side of the brain processes the left half (of the field of view) of both eyes, while the left side processes the right half of both eyes. This is illustrated by the red and blue lines in Fig. 3.

From the optic chiasm, the fibers are taken to several parts of the brain. Around 90% of them finish at the two *lateral geniculate body*. Besides serving as a relay station for signals from the

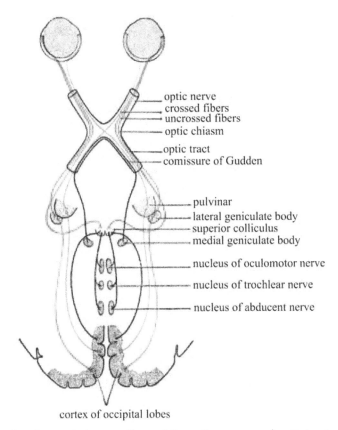

cortex of occipital lobes

Fig. 3. Scheme showing central connections of the optic nerves and optic tracts. (Adapted from H. Grey (Grey, 1918))

retina to the visual cortex, the lateral geniculate body controls how much information is allowed to pass. From there, the fibers are taken to the visual cortex.

The *virtual cortex* is the region of the brain responsible for processing the visual information. It is located on the back of the cerebral hemispheres. The region that receives the information from the lateral geniculate body is called the *primary visual cortex* (also known as V1). In addition to V1, more than 20 other areas receiving visual input have been discovered, but little is known about their functionalities.

V1 is a region specialized on processing information about static and moving objects and recognizing patterns. There is a big variety of cells in V1 that have selective sensitivity to certain types of information. In other words, one particular cell may respond strongly to patterns of a certain orientation or to motion in a certain direction. Others are tuned to particular frequencies, color, velocities, etc. An interesting characteristic of these neurons is the fact that their outputs saturates as the input contrast increases.

The selectivity of the neurons in V1 is the heart of the multichannel organization characteristic of the human vision system. In fact, the neurons in V1 can be modeled as an octave-band Gabor filter bank, where the spatial frequency spectrum (in polar representation) is sampled at octave intervals in the radial frequency dimension and at uniform intervals in the orientation dimension (Marr, 1982). This model is used by several algorithms in image processing and video quality assessment.

2.2 Perceptual features
A number of visual perception phenomena are a consequence of the characteristics of the optics of the human eye. The phenomena described in this section are of particular interest to the area of image processing and, more specifically to video quality.

2.2.1 Foveal and peripheral vision
The densities of the photoreceptors and ganglion cells in the retina are not uniform, increasing towards the center of the retina (fovea) and decreasing on the contrary direction. As a consequence, the resolution of objects in the visual field is also not uniform. The point where the observer fixates is projected on the fovea and, consequently, resolved with the highest resolution. The objects in the peripheral area are resolved with progressively lower resolution (peripheral vision).

2.2.2 Light adaptation
In the real world, the amount of light intensity varies tremendously, from dim (night) to high intensity (sun day). The HVS adapts to this large range by controlling the amount of light that enters the eye. This is done by increasing/decreasing the diameter of the pupils and, at the same time, adjusting the gain of post-receptor neurons in the retina. As a result, instead of coding absolute light intensities, the retina encodes the contrast of the visual stimulus.

The phenomenon that keeps the contrast sensitivity over a wide range of light intensity is known as Weber's law:

$$\Delta I / I = K$$

where I is the background luminance, ΔI is the just noticeable incremental luminance over the background, and K is a constant called the Weber fraction.

2.2.3 Contrast Sensitivity Functions (CSF)
CSF models the sensitivity of the HVS as a function of the spatial frequency of the visual stimuli. A typical CSF is shown in Fig. 4(a). Spatial contrast sensitivity peaks at 3 cycles per degree (cpd), and declines more rapidly at higher than at lower spatial frequencies. Frequencies higher than 40 cpd (8 cpd scotopic) are undetectable even at maximum contrast. For illustration purposes, consider the image in Fig. 4(b) that corresponds to the intensities of a sinusoidal luminance grating. In this image, the spatial frequency (number of luminance cycles the grating repeats in one degree of visual angle) increases from left to right, while contrast (difference between the maximum and minimum luminance) increases from top to bottom. The shape of the visible lower part of the image gives an indication of our relative sensitivity to different spatial frequencies. If the perception of contrast were determined solely by the image contrast, then the alternating bright and dark bars should appear to have equal height across any horizontal line across the image. However, the bars are observed to be significantly higher at the middle of the image, following the shape of the CSF (see Fig. 4(a)).

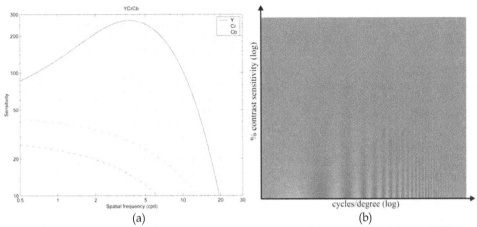

(a)   (b)

Fig. 4. (a) Contrast sensitivity functions for the three channels YCbCr (after Moore, 2002 (Moore, 2002)). (b) Pelli-Robson Chart, where spatial frequency increases from left to right, while contrast increases from top to bottom.

2.2.4 Masking and facilitation

Masking and facilitation are important aspects of the HVS in modeling the interactions between different image components present at the same spatial location. Specifically, these two effects refer to the fact that the presence of one image component (*the mask*) will decrease/ increase the visibility of another image component (*test signal*). The mask generally reduces the visibility of the test signal in comparison with the case where the mask is absent. However, the mask may sometimes facilitate detection as well. Usually, the masking effect is the strongest when the mask and the test signal have similar frequency content and orientations. Most quality metrics incorporate a model for masking and/or facilitation.

2.2.5 Pooling

Pooling refers to the task of arriving at a single measurement of quality from the outputs of the visual streams. It is not quite understood how the HVS performs pooling. But, it is clear that a perceptible distortion may be more annoying in some areas of the scene (such as human faces) than in others. Most quality metrics use the *Minkowski metric* to pool the error signals from the streams with different frequency and orientation selective and arrive at a fidelity measurement (de Ridder, 1992; 2001). The Minkowski metric is also used to combine information across spatial and temporal coordinates.

3. Digital video systems

In this section, we give a brief overview of the available video compression and transmission techniques and their impact on the quality of a digital video.

3.1 Video compression

Video compression (or video coding) is the process of converting a video signal into a format that takes up less storage space or transmission bandwidth. Given the video transmission and storage requirements (up to 270 Mbits/s for Standard Definition and 1.5 Gbit/s for High Definition), video compression is an essential technology for applications such as digital television (terrestrial, cable or satellite transmission), optical storage/reproduction, mobile TV, videoconferencing and Internet video streaming (Poynton, 2003).

There are two types of compression: *lossy* and *lossless* compression (Bosi & Goldberg, 2002). Lossless compression algorithms have the characteristic of assuring perfect reconstruction of the original data. Unfortunately, this type of compression only allows around 2:1 compression ratios, which is not sufficient for video applications. Lossy compression is the type of compression most commonly used for video because it provides much bigger compression ratios. There is, of course, a trade-off: the higher the compression ratio, the lower the quality of the compressed video.

Compression is achieved by removing the redundant information from the video. There are four main types of redundancies that are typically explored by compression algorithms:

- *Perceptual redundancy*: Information of the video that cannot be easily perceived by the human observer and, therefore, can be discarded without significantly altering the quality of the video.
- *Temporal redundancy*: Pixels in successive video frames have great similarity. So, even though motion tend to change the position of blocks of pixels, it does not change their values and therefore their correlation.
- *Spatial redundancy*: There is a significant correlation among pixels around the same neighborhood in a frame.
- *Statistical redundancy*: This type of redundancy is related to the statistical relationship within the video data (bits and bytes).

Each stage of a video compression algorithm is responsible for mainly reducing one type of redundancy. Fig. 5 depicts the functional components in a typical video compression algorithm. Different algorithms differ in what tools are used in each stage. But, most of them share the same principles: motion compensation and block-based transform with subsequent quantization. Currently, there are several standards for video compression, which standardize the decoding process. The encoding process is not fixed, what leaves room for innovation.

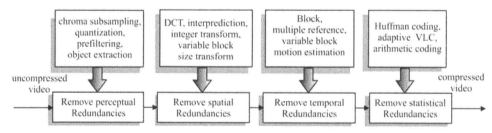

Fig. 5. Functional components in a typical video compression algorithm.

The most popular compression standards were produced by the Motion Picture Experts Group (MPEG) (ITU, 1998) and the Video Coding Experts (VCEG). The MPEG is a working group of the International Organization for Standardization (ISO) and of the International Electrotechnical Commission (IEC), formally known as ISO/IEC – JTC1/SC29/WG11. Among the standards developed by MPEG areMPEG-1,MPEG-2, andMPEG-4. The MPEG-2 is a very popular standard used not only for broadcasting, but also in DVDs (Haskell et al., 1997; ITU, 1998). The main advantage of MPEG-2 is its low cost, given its popularity and the large scale of production. MPEG-2 is also undoubtedly a very mature technology.

The VCEG is a working group of the Telecommunication Standardization Sector of the International Telecommunication Union (ITU-T). Among the standards developed by VCEG are the H.261 and H.263. A joint collaboration between MPEG and VCEG resulted in the development of the H.264, also known as MPEG-4 Part 10 or AVC (Advanced Video Coding) (Richardson, 2003; ITU, 2003). The H.264 represents a major advance in the technology of video compression, providing a considerable reduction of bitrate when compared to previous standards (Lambert et al., Jan. 2006). For the same quality level, H.264 provides a bitrate of about half the bitrate provided by MPEG-2.

3.2 Digital video transmission

Compressed video streams are mainly intended for transmission over communication networks. But, there are different types of video communication and streaming applications. Each one has particular operating conditions and properties. The channels used for video communication may be static or dynamic, packet-switched or circuit-switched. Also, the channels may support a constant or variable bit rate transmission, and may support some form of Quality of Service (QoS) or may only provide best effort support. Finally, the transmission may be point-to-point, multicast, and broadcast.

In most cases, after the video has been digitally compressed, the resulting bitstream is segmented into fixed or variable packets and multiplexed with other data types, such as audio. The next stage is the channel encoder, which will add error protection to the data. The characteristics of the specific video communication application will, of course, have a great impact on the quality of the video displayed at the receiver.

3.3 Common artifacts in digital video systems

An impairment is a property of the video that is perceived as undesirable, whether it is in the original or not. Impairments can be introduced during capture, transmission, storage, and/or display, as well as by any image processing algorithm (e.g. compression) that may be applied along the way (Yuen & Wu, 1998). They can be very complex in their physical descriptions and also in their perceptual descriptions. Most of them have more than one perceptual feature, but it is possible to have impairments that are relatively pure. To differentiate impairments from their perceptual features, we will use the term *artifact* to refer to the perceptual features of impairments and *artifact signal* to refer to the physical signal that produces the artifact.

The most common artifacts present in digital video are:

- *Blockiness* or *blocking* – A type of artifact characterized by a block pattern visible in the picture. It is due to the independent quantization of individual blocks (usually of 8x8 pixels in size) in block-based DCT coding schemes, leading to discontinuities at the boundaries of adjacent blocks. The blocking effect is often the most visible artifact in a compressed video, given its periodicity and the extent of the pattern. More modern codecs, like the H.264, use a deblocking filter to reduce the annoyance caused by this artifact.

- *Blur* or *blurring* – It is characterized for a loss of spatial detail and a reduction of edge sharpness. In the in the compression stage, blurring is introduced by the suppression of the high-frequency coefficients by coarse quantization.
- *Color bleeding* – It is characterized by the smearing of colors between areas of strongly differing chrominance. It results from the suppression of high-frequency coefficients of the chroma components. Due to chroma subsampling, color bleeding extends over an entire macroblock.
- *DCT basis image effect* – It is characterized by the prominence of a single DCT coefficient in a block. At coarse quantization levels, this results in an emphasis of the dominant basis image and reduction of all other basis images.
- *Staircase effect* – These artifacts occurs as a consequence of the fact that DCT basis are best suited for the representation of horizontal and vertical lines. The representation of lines with other orientations require higher-frequency DCT coefficients for accurate reconstruction. Therefore, when higher frequencies are lost, slanted lines appear.
- *Ringing* – Associated with the Gibbs phenomenon. It is more evident along high contrast edges in otherwise smooth areas. It is a direct result of quantization leading to high-frequency irregularities in the reconstruction. Ringing occurs with both luminance and chroma components.
- *Mosquito noise* – Temporal artifact that is seen mainly in smoothly textured regions as luminance/chrominance fluctuations around high contrast edges or moving objects. It is a consequence of the coding differences for the same area of a scene in consecutive frames of a sequence.
- *Flickering* – It occurs when a scene has a high texture content. Texture blocks are compressed with varying quantization factors over time, which results in a visible flickering effect.
- *Packet loss* – It occurs when parts of the video are lost in the digital transmission. As a consequence, parts (blocks) of video are missing for several frames.
- *Jitter* – It is the result of skipping regularly video frames to reduce the amount of video information that the system is required to encode or transmit. This creates motion perceived as a series of distinct snapshots, rather than smooth and continuous motion.

The performance of a particular digital video system can be improved if the type of artifact that is affecting the quality of the video is known (Klein, 1993). This type of information can also be used to enhance the video by reducing or eliminating the identified artifacts (Caviedes & Jung, 2001). In summary, this knowledge makes it possible to implement a complete system for detecting, estimating and correcting artifacts in video sequences. Unfortunately, there is not yet a good understanding of how visible/annoying these artifacts are, how the content influences their visibility/annoyance, and how they combine to produce the overall annoyance. A comprehensive *subjective* study of the most common types of artifacts is still needed.

An effort in this direction has been done by Farias *et al* (Farias, Moore, Foley & Mitra, 2002; Farias et al., 2003a;b; Farias, Foley & Mitra, 2004; Farias, Moore, Foley & Mitra, 2004). Their approach makes use of synthetic artifacts that look like "real" artifacts, yet are simpler, purer, and easier to describe. This approach makes it possible to control the type, proportion, and strength of the artifacts being tested and allows to evaluate the performance of different combination models of the artifact metrics. The results gathered from the psychophysical experiments performed by Farias *et al* show that the synthetic artifacts, besides being visually similar to the real impairments, have similar visibility and annoyance properties. Their results also show that there is an interaction between among different types of artifacts. For example, the presence of noisy artifact signals seem to decrease the perceived strength of the other artifacts, while the presence of blurry artifact signals seem to increase it. The authors also modeled annoyance by combining the artifact perceptual strengths (MSV) using both a Minkowski metric and a linear model (de Ridder, 1992).

4. Subjective video quality assessment

Subjective experiments (also called psychophysical experiments) represent the most accurate way of measuring the quality of a video. In subjective experiments, a number of subjects (observers or participants) are asked to watch a set of test sequences and give judgements about their quality or the annoyance of the impairments. The average of the values collected for each test sequence are known as Mean Observer Score (MOS).

In general, subjective experiments are expensive and time-consuming. The design, execution, and data analysis consume a great amount of the experimenter's time. Running an experiment requires the availability of subjects, equipment, and physical space. As a result, the number of experiments that can be conducted is limited and, therefore, an appropriate methodology should be used to get the most out of the resources.

The International Telecommunication Union (ITU) has recommendations for subjective testing procedures. The two most important documents are the ITU-R Rec. BT.500-11 (ITU-R, 1998), targeted at television applications, and the ITU-T Rec. P.910 (ITU-T, 1999), targeted at multimedia applications. These documents give information regarding the standard viewing conditions, the criteria for selections of observers and test material, assessment procedures, and data analysis methods. Before choosing which method to use, the experimenter should take into account the application in mind and the accuracy objectives.

According to ITU, there are two classes of subjective assessments:

- *Quality assessments* – The judgements given by subjects are in a quality scale, i.e., how good or bad is the quality of the displayed video. These assessments establish the performance of systems under optimum conditions;
- *Impairment assessments* – The judgements given by subjects are in an impairment scale, i.e., how visible or imperceptible are the impairments in the displayed video. These assessments establish the ability of systems to retain quality under non-optimum conditions that relate to transmission.

According to the type of scale, quality or impairment judgements can be classified as *continuous* or *discrete*. Judgements can also be categorical or non-categorical, adjectival or numerical. Depending on the form of presentation of the stimulus (sequences), the assessment method can be classified as *double* or *single* stimulus. In the single stimulus approach the test sequence is presented by itself, while in the double stimulus method a pair of sequences (test sequence and the corresponding reference) are presented together.

The most popular assessment procedures of ITU-R Rec. BT.500-11 are:

- *Double Stimulus Continuous Quality Scale* (DSCQS) – This method is specially useful when the test conditions exhibit the full range of quality. The observer is shown multiple pairs of sequences consisting of a test sequence and the corresponding reference. The sequences have a short duration of around 10s and are presented twice, alternated by each other. The observers are not told which is the reference and which is the test sequence. In each trial, their positions are changed randomly. The observer is asked to assess the overall quality of both sequences by inserting a mark on a vertical scale. Fig. 6 shows a section of a typical score sheet. The continuous scales are divided into five equal lengths, which correspond to the normal ITU five-point quality continuous scale.

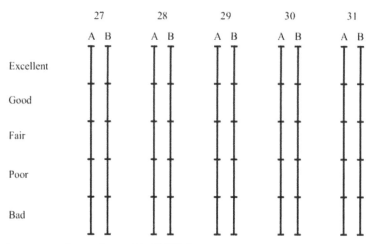

Fig. 6. Continuous quality scale used in DSCQS.

- *Double Stimulus Impairment Scale* (DSIS) – For this method, the reference is always shown before the test sequence and the pair is not repeated. Observers are asked to judge the amount of impairment in the test sequence using a five-level scale. The categories in the scale are 'imperceptible', 'perceptible, but not annoying', 'slightly annoying', 'annoying', and 'very annoying'. This method is adequate for evaluating visible artifacts.
- *Single Stimulus Continuous Quality Evaluation* (SSCQE) – In this method, observers are asked to watch a video (program) of around 20-30 minutes. The content is processed using the conditions under test and the reference is not presented. The observer uses a a slider to continuously rate the quality, as it changes during the presentation. The scale (ruler) goes from 'bad' to 'excellent'.

The most popular assessment procedures of ITU-T Rec. P.910 are:

- *Absolute Category Rating* (ACR) – Also known as Single Stimulus Method (SSM), this method is characterized by the fact that the test sequences are presented one at a time, without the reference. This makes it a very efficient method, compared to DSIS or DSCQS, which have durations of around 2 to 4 times longer. After each presentation, observers are asked to judge the overall quality of the test sequence using a five-level scale. The categories in this scale are 'bad', 'poor', 'fair', 'good', and 'excellent'. A nine-level scale may be used if a higher discriminative power is desired. Also, if additional ratings of each test sequence are needed, repetitions of the same test conditions at different points in time of the test can be used.
- *Degradation Category Rating* (DCR) –This method is identical to the DSIS described earlier.
- *Pair Comparison* (PC) – In this method, all possible pair combinations of all test sequences are shown to viewers, i.e., if there are n test conditions, a total of $n \cdot (n - 1)$

pairs are presented for each reference. The observers have to choose which sequence of the pair he/she thinks has the best quality. This methods allows a very fine distinction between conditions, but also requires a longer period of time when compared to other methods.

Although each assessment method has its own requirements, the following recommendations are valid in most cases:

- The choice of test sequences must take into account the goal of the experiment. The spatial and temporal content of the scenes, for example, are critical parameters. These parameters determine the type and severeness of the impairments present in the test sequences.
- It is important that the set of test scenes spans the full range of quality commonly encountered for the specific conditions under test.
- When a comparison among results from different laboratories is the intention, it is mandatory to use a set of common source sequences to eliminate further sources of variation.
- The test sequences should be presented in a pseudo-random order and, preferably, the experimenter should avoid that sequences generated from the same reference be shown in a subsequent order.
- The viewing conditions, which include the distance from the subject's eye to the monitor and the ambient light, should be set according to the standards.
- The size and the type of monitor or display used in the experiment must be appropriate for the application under test. Callibration of the monitor may be necessary.
- It is best to use the whole screen for displaying the test sequences. In case this is not possible, the sequences must be displayed on a window of the screen, with a 50% grey (Y=U=V=128) background surrounding it.
- Before the experiment starts, the subjects should be tested for visual acuity. After that, written and oral instructions should be given to them, describing the intended application of the system, the type of assessment, the opinion scale, and the presentation methodology.
- At least 15 subjects should be used in the experiment. Preferably, the subjects should not be considered 'experts', i.e., have considerable knowledge in the area of image and video processing.
- Before the actual experiment, indicative results can be obtained by performing a pilot test using only a couple (4-6) of subjects (experts or non-experts).
- A training section with at least five conditions should be included at the beginning of the experimental session. These conditions should be representative of the ones used in the experiment, but should not be taken into account in the statistical analysis of the gathered data. It should be made clear to the observer that the worst quality seen in the training set does not necessarily corresponds to the worst or lowest grade on the scale.
- Include at least two replications (i.e. repetitions of identical conditions) in the experiment. This will help to calculate individual reliability per subject and, if necessary, to discard unreliable results from some subjects.
- Statistical analysis of the gathered data can be performed using standard methods (Snedecor & Cochran, 1989; Hays, 1981; Maxwell & Delaney, 2003; ITU-R, 1998). For each combination of the test variables, the mean value and the standard deviation of the collected assessment grades should be calculated. Subject reliability should also be estimated.

5. Objective video quality metrics

Video quality metrics can be employed to:
- *monitor* video quality;
- *compare* the performance of video processing systems and algorithms; and
- *optimize* the algorithms and parameter settings for a video processing system.

The choice of which type of metric should consider the application and its the requirements and limitations.

In general, video quality metrics can be divided in three different categories according to the availability of the original (reference) video signal:
- *Full Reference* (FR) metric – Original and distorted (or test) videos are available.
- *Reduced Reference* (RR) metric – Besides the distorted video, a description of the original and some parameters are available.
- *No-reference* (NR) metric – Only the distorted video is available.

Figs. 7, 8, and 9 depict the block diagrams corresponding to the full reference, reduced reference, and no-reference video quality metrics, respectively. Observe that on the FR approach the entire reference is available at the measurement point. On the RR approach only part of the reference is available through an auxiliary channel. In this case, the information available at the measurement point generally consists of a set of features extracted from the reference. For the NR approach no information concerning the reference is available at the measuring point.

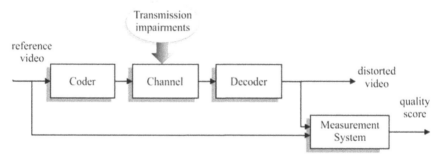

Fig. 7. Block diagram of a full reference video quality assessment system.

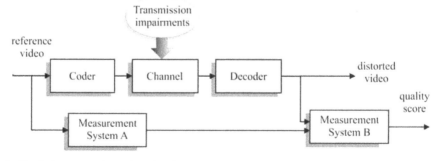

Fig. 8. Block diagram of a reduced reference video quality assessment system.

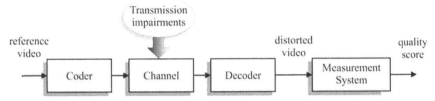

Fig. 9. Block diagram of a no-reference video quality assessment system.

These three classes of metrics are targeted at different applications. FR metrics are more suitable for offline quality measurements, for which a detailed and accurate measurement of the video quality is of higher priority than having immediate results. NR and RR metrics are targeted at real-time applications, where the computational complexity limitations and the lack of access to the reference are the main issues. Comparisons among the performances of several video quality metrics were done by Yubing Wang (Wang, 2006), Eskicioglu and and Fisher (Eskicioglu & Fisher, 1995), Sheikh *et al* (Sheikh et al., 2006), and Avicbas *et al* (Avcibas et al., 2002).

The quality metrics can be classified according to the approach they take for estimating the amount of impairment in a video. There are basically two main approaches. The first one is the *error sensitivity* approach that tries to analyze visible differences between the test and reference videos. This approach is mostly used for full reference metrics, since this is the only type of metric where a pixel-by-pixel difference between the original and test videos can be generated.

The second approach is the *feature extraction* approach that looks for higher-level features that do not belong to the original video to obtain an estimate of the quality of the video. No-reference and reduced reference metrics frequently use the feature extraction approach making use of some a priori knowledge of the features of the original video.

Finally, quality metrics can also be classified according to what type of information they consider when processing the video. Metrics that take into account the how the HVS works are typically called *picture metrics* or perceptual metrics. More simple metrics that only measure the fidelity of the signal without considering its content are called *data metrics*.

In this section, a brief description of a representative set of FR, RR, and NR metrics is presented. Also, a description of data metrics and metrics based on data hiding is presented.

5.1 Data FR fidelity metrics

Data fidelity metrics measure the physical differences between two signals without considering its content. Two of the most popular data fidelity metrics are the mean squared error (MSE) and the peak signal-to-noise ratio (PSNR), which are defined as:

$$\text{MSE} = \frac{1}{N} \sum_{i=1}^{N} (X_i - Y_i)^2, \tag{1}$$

and

$$\text{PSNR} = 10 \cdot \log_{10} \frac{255^2}{MSE}, \tag{2}$$

where N is the total number of pixels in the video, 255 is the maximum intensity value of the images, and X_i and Y_i are the i-th pixels in the original and distorted video, respectively.

Strictly speaking, the MSE measures image differences, i.e. how different two images are. PSNR, on the other hand, measures image fidelity, i.e. how close two images are. In both cases, one of the pictures is always the reference (uncorrupted original) and the other is the test or distorted sequence.

The MSE and PSNR are very popular in the image processing community because of their physical significance and of their simplicity, but over the years they have been widely criticized for not correlating well with the perceived quality measurement (Teo & Heeger, 1994; Eskicioglu & Fisher, 1995; Eckert & Bradley, 1998; Girod, 1993; Winkler, 1999). More specifically, it has been shown that simple metrics like PSNR and MSE can only predict subjective rating with a reasonable accuracy, as long as the comparisons are made for the same content, the same technique or the same type of artifact (Eskicioglu & Fisher, 1995).

One of the major reasons why these simple metrics do not perform as desired is because they do not incorporate any HVS features in their computation. In fact, it has been discovered that in the primary visual cortex of mammals, an image is not represented in the pixel domain, but in a rather different manner. The measurements produced by metrics like MSE or PSNR are simply based on a pixel to pixel comparison of the data, without considering what is the content. These simple metrics do not consider, for example, what are the relationships among pixels in an image (or frames). They also do not consider how the spatial and frequency content of the impairments are perceived by human observers.

5.2 Full reference video quality metrics

In general, full reference (FR) metrics have the best performance among the three types of metrics. This is mainly due to the availability of the reference video. Also, since FR are intended for off-line applications, they can be more computational complex and incorporate several aspects of the HVS. The major drawback of the full reference approach is the fact that a large amount of reference information has to be provided at the final comparison point. Also, a very precise spatial and temporal alignment of reference and impaired videos is needed to guarantee the accuracy of the metric.

A large number of FR metrics are *error sensitivity* metrics, which attempt to analyze and quantify the error signal in a way that simulates the human quality judgement. Some examples include the works by Daly (Daly, 1993), Lubin (Lubin, 1995), Teo and Heeger (Teo & Heeger, 1994), Watson (Watson, 1990; 1998;Watson et al., 2001), Van den Branden Lambrecht and Kunt (van den Branden Lambrecht & Kunt, 1998), and Winkler (Winkler, 1999). The group of *full reference* metrics that uses a *feature extraction* approach is much smaller and includes the works of Algazi and Hiwasa (Algazi & Hiwasa, 1993), Pessoa *et al.* (Pessoa et al., 1998), and Wolf and Pinson (Wolf & Pinson, 1999). In this section, we present a brief description of a representative set of full reference video quality metrics.

5.2.1 Visible Differences Predictor (VDP)

The full reference model proposed by Daly (Daly, 1993; 1992) is known as visible differences predictor (VDP). The general approach of the model consists of finding what limits the visual sensitivity and taking this into account when analysing the differences between distorted and reference videos. The main sensitivity limitations (or variations) considered by the model are *light level, spatial frequency*, and *signal content*. Each of these sensitivity variations corresponds to one of the stages of the model, as described below:

* Amplitude non-linearity – It is well known that sensitivity and perception of lightness are non-linear functions of luminance. The amplitude non-linearity stage of the VDP

describes the sensitivity variations as a function of the gray scale. It is based on a model of the early retina network.

- Contrast Sensitivity Function (CSF) – The CSF describes the variations in the visual sensitivity as a function of spatial frequency. The CSF stage changes the input as a function of light adaptation, noise, color, accommodation, eccentricity, and image size.
- Multiple detection mechanism – It is modeled with four subcomponents:
  - Spatial cortex transform – It models the frequency selectivity of the visual system and creates the framework for multiple detection mechanisms. This is modeled by a hierarchy of filters modified from Watson's cortex transform (Watson, 1987) that separates the image into spatial levels followed by six orientation levels.
  - Masking function – Models the magnitude of the masking effect.
  - Psychometric function – Describes the details of the threshold.
  - Probability summation – Combines the responses of all detection mechanisms into an unified perceptual response.

A simplified block-diagram of the VDP is depicted in Fig. 10. The output of Daly's metric is a probability-of-detection map, which indicates the areas where the reference and test images differ in a perceptual sense.

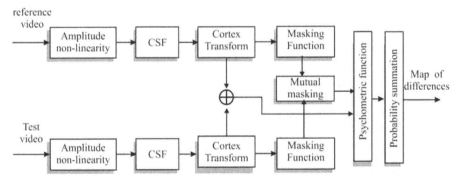

Fig. 10. Block diagram of the visible differences predictor (VDP) (Daly, 1993; 1992).

5.2.2 Sarnoff JND model

The Sarnoff JND model is based on multi-scale spatial vision model proposed by Lubin (Lubin, 1993; 1995). The model takes into account color and temporal variation. Like the metric by Daly, it is designed to predict the probability of detection of artifacts in an image. But, it uses the concept of *just noticeable differences* (JNDs) that are visibility thresholds for changes in images.

The JND unit of measure is defined such that 1 JND corresponds to a 75% chance that an observer viewing the two images detects the difference. JND values above 1 are calculated incrementally. For example, if image A is 1 JND higher than Image B, and image C is 1 JND higher than image A, then image C is 2 JNDs higher than image B. In terms of probability of detection, a 2 JND difference corresponds to 93.75% chance of discrimination, while a 3 JND difference corresponds to 98.44%.

The block diagram of the Sarnoff JND model is depicted in Fig. 11. First, the picture is transformed to the CIE L*u*v* uniform color space (Poynton, 2003). Next, each sequence is filtered and down-sampled using a Gaussian pyramid operation (Burt & Adelson, 1983).

Then, the normalization stage sets the overall gain with a time-dependent average luminance, modelling the HVS insensitivity to overall light level.

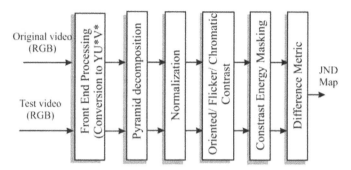

Fig. 11. Block diagram of the Sarnoff JND (Lubin, 1993; 1995).

After normalization, contrast measures are obtained. At each pyramid level, the contrast arrays are calculated by dividing the local difference of the pixel values by the local sum. The result is, then, scaled to be 1 when the image contrast is at the human detection threshold. This gives the definition of 1 JND, which is used on subsequent stages. This scaled contrast arrays are then passed to the contrast energy masking stage in order to desensitize to image "busyness". Then, test and reference are compared to produce the JND map.

5.2.3 Structural Similarity and Image Quality (SSIM)

The Structural SIMilarity and Image Quality (SSIM) (Wang et al., 2004) is based on the idea that natural images are highly "structured". In other words, image signals have strong relationships amongst themselves, which carry information about the structures of the objects in the scene.

To estimate the similarity between a test image and the corresponding reference, the SSIM algorithm measures the luminance $l(x,y)$, contrast $c(x,y)$, and structure $s(x,y)$ of the test image y and the corresponding reference image x, using the following expressions:

$$l(x,y) = \frac{2\mu_x\mu_y + C_1}{\mu_x^2 + \mu_y^2 + C_1},$$
(3)

$$c(x,y) = \frac{2\sigma_x\sigma_y + C_2}{\sigma_x^2 + \sigma_y^2 + C_2},$$
(4)

and

$$s(x,y) = \frac{\sigma_{xy} + C_3}{\sigma_x\sigma_y + C_3},$$
(5)

where C_1, C_2, and C_3 are small constants given by $C_1 = (K_1 \cdot L)^2$, $C_2 = (K_2 \cdot L)^2$, and $C_3 = C_2/2$. L is the dynamic range of the pixel values (for 8 bits/pixel gray scale images, L = 255), $K_1 \ll 1$, and $K_2 \ll 1$.

The general formula of the SSIM metric is given by

$$SSIM(x,y) = [l(x,y)]^\alpha \cdot [c(x,y)]^\beta \cdot [s(x,y)]^\gamma , \tag{6}$$

where α, β, and γ are parameters that define the relative importance of the luminance, contrast, and structure components. If $\alpha = \beta = \gamma = 1$, the above equation is reduced to

$$SSIM(x,y) = \frac{(2\mu_x\mu_y + C_1)(2\sigma_{xy} + C_2)}{(\mu_x^2 + \mu_y^2 + C_1)(\sigma_x^2 + \sigma_y^2 + C_2)}. \tag{7}$$

The SSIM has a range of values varying between '0' and '1', with '1' being the best value possible. A block diagram of the SSIM algorithm is depicted in Fig. 12. A study of the performance of SSIM has shown that this simple metric presents good results (Sheikh et al., 2006).

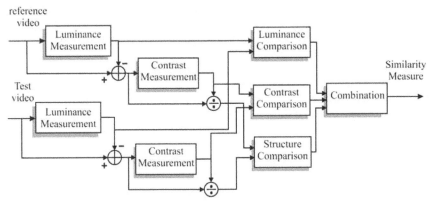

Fig. 12. Block diagram of the SSIM algorithm (Wang et al., 2004).

5.2.4 NTIA Video Quality Metric (VQM)
The video quality metric (VQM) is a metric proposed by Wolf and Pinson from the National Telecommunications and Information Administration (NTIA) (Wolf & Pinson, 1999; Pinson & Wolf, 2004). This metric has recently been adopted by ANSI as a standard for objective video quality. In VQEG Phase II (VQEG, 2003), VQM presented a very good correlation with subjective scores. VQM presented one of the best performances among the competitors.

The algorithm used by VQM includes measurements for the perceptual effects of several video impairments, such as blurring, jerky/unnatural motion, global noise, block distortion, and color distortion. These measurements are combined into a single metric that gives a prediction of the overall quality. The VQM algorithm can be divided into the following stages:

- Calibration – This first stage has the goal of calibrating the video in preparation for the feature extraction stage. With this propose, it estimates and corrects the spatial and temporal shifts, as well as the contrast and brightness offsets, of the processed video sequence with respect to the original video sequence.
- Extraction of quality features – In this stage, the set of quality features that characterizes perceptual changes in the spatial, temporal, and chrominance domains are extracted from spatial-temporal sub-regions of the video sequence. For this, a perceptual filter is

applied to the video to enhance a particular type of property, such as edge information. Features are extracted from spatio-temporal (ST) subregions using a mathematical function and, then, a visibility threshold is applied to these features.

- Estimation of quality parameters – In this stage, a set of quality parameters that describe the perceptual changes is calculated by comparing features extracted from the processed video with those extracted from the reference video.

- Quality estimation – The final step consists of calculating an overall quality metric using a linear combination of parameters calculated in previous stages.

5.3 Reduced reference video quality metrics

Reduced reference (RR) video quality metrics require only partial information about the reference video. To help evaluate the quality of the video, certain features or physical measures are extracted from the reference and transmitted to the receiver as a *side information*. One of the interesting characteristics of RR metrics is the possibility of choosing the amount of side information. In practice, the exact amount of information will be dictated by the characteristics of the side channel that is used to transmit the auxiliary data or, similarly, by the available storage to cache them. Bit rates of the reduced-reference channel can go from zero (for no-reference metrics) to 15 kbps, 80 kbps, or 256 kbps (VQEG, 2009).

Metrics in this class may be less accurate than the *full reference* metrics, but they are also less complex, and make real-time implementations more affordable. Nevertheless, synchronization between the original and impaired data is still necessary. Works in this area include the work by Webster *et al.* (Webster et al., 1993), Brètillon *et al.* (Bretillon et al., 2000), Gunawan and Ghanbari (Gunawan & Ghanbari, 2005), and the work by Carnec *et al.* (Carnec et al., 2003). In this section, we describe the RR metrics by Webster *et al.* and Gunawan and Ghanbari.

5.3.1 Objective video quality assessment system based on human perception

One of the earliest *reduced reference* metrics was proposed by Webster *et al.* (Webster et al., 1993). Their metric is a *feature extraction* metric that estimates the amount of impairment in a video by extracting localized spatial and temporal activity features using especially designed filters. The block-diagram of this metric is depicted in Fig. 13.

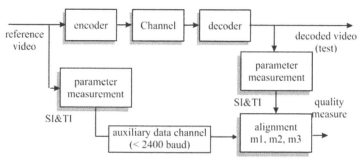

Fig. 13. Block diagram of Webster's algorithm (Webster et al., 1993).

The spatial information (SI) feature corresponds to the the standard deviation of edgeenhanced frames, assuming that degradation will modify the edge statistics in the frames. The temporal information (TI) feature corresponds to the standard deviation of difference frames, i.e., the amount of perceived motion in the video scene. Three comparison metrics are derived from the SI and TI features of the reference and the distorted videos. The metrics for the reference video are transmitted over the RR channel. The size of the RR data depends upon the size of the window over which SI & TI features are calculated.

5.3.2 Local Harmonic Strength (LHS) metric

The work by Gunawan and Ghanbari (Gunawan & Ghanbari, 2005) proposes a RR video quality metric that is based on a *local harmonic strength* (LHS) feature. The harmonic strength can be interpreted as a spatial activity measure, estimated in terms of vertical/horizontal edges of the picture. In summary, the quality measure is based on harmonic gain and loss estimates obtained from a discriminative analysis of the LHS feature computed on gradient images. A simplified block diagram of the LHS RR video quality metric is depicted in Fig. 14.

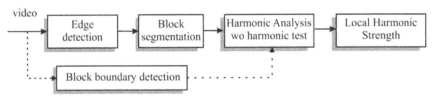

Fig. 14. Block diagram of the LHS algorithm stage of the metric (Gunawan & Ghanbari, 2008; 2005).

The first step of the algorithm is a simple edge-detection stage (3 × 3 Sobel operator) that generates a gradient image. This resulting image is, then, processed by a non-overlap block segmentation algorithm, with a block size large enough to account for any vertical or horizontal activity within the blocks (typically 32 × 32 pixels). An optional alignment with the DCT blocks may also be included to increase the precision of the algorithm.

The LHS is calculated as the accumulated strength of the harmonic frequencies of the blocks on the pictures. Since non-overlapped blocks on a picture are also identified by their spatial location, the collected features from all blocks are organized as a matrix. This matrix has a size which is 32 × 32 smaller than the full resolution picture. LHS matrix features from test and reference pictures are computed separately, and then compared to each other.

The harmonical analysis is performed on the segmented blocks of the gradient image. For this step, a 2-D Fast Fourier Transform (FFT) is applied to each block. The resulting image reveals the appearance of frequency components at certain interval along the two principle axes (horizontal and vertical axes). These frequencies are known as harmonics. The harmonic analysis, then, isolates and accumulates the harmonic components of the resulting FFT spectrum, estimating the value of the LHS feature.

The discriminative analysis is performed after all features from the reference and test images are calculated. Applied to the blocks, the analysis will differentiate between an increase (gain) or decrease (loss) in their strengths, giving an insight on how degradations are distributed over the frame/image. The two quality features produced, namely *harmonic gain* and *harmonic loss*, correspond to blockiness and blurriness on the test image, respectively. To produce a single overall quality measure, spatial collapsing functions (e.g. arithmetic average) are used.

In a more recent algorithm, the author improved the performance of the algorithm by compressing the side information (Gunawan & Ghanbari, 2008), what results in a reduction of the amount of data that needs to be transmitted or stored.

5.4 No-reference video quality metrics

Requiring the reference video or even a small portion of it becomes a serious impediment in many real-time transmission applications. In this case, it becomes essential to develop ways of blindly estimating the quality of a video using a *no-reference* video quality metric. It turns out that, although human observers can usually assess the quality of a video without using the reference, designing a *no-reference* metric is a very difficult task. Considering the difficulties faced by the *full reference* video quality metrics (Eskicioglu & Fisher, 1995; Martens & Meesters, 1997; Rohaly, 2000; VQEG, 2003), this is no surprise.

Except for the metric by Gastaldo *et al.* that uses a neural network (Gastaldo et al., 2001),most of the proposed metrics are *feature extraction* metrics that estimate features of the video. Due to the difficulties encountered in designing NR reference metrics, several metrics rely on one or two features to estimate quality. In most cases, the features used in the algorithms are *artifact signals*, with the most popular being blockiness, blurriness, and ringing. For example, the metrics by Wu *et al.* and Wang *et al.* estimate quality based solely on a blockiness measurement (Wang et al., 2000; Wu & Yuen, 1997; Keimel et al., 2009). The metrics by Farias and Mitra (Farias & Mitra, 2005) and by Caviedes and Jung (Caviedes & Jung, 2001) use four and five artifacts, respectively. In this section, we describe the metrics by Farias and Mitra (Farias & Mitra, 2005) and Oprea *et al.* (Oprea et al., 2009).

5.4.1 No-reference video quality metric based on artifact measurements

As a representation of the metrics based on artifact measurements, we will describe the algorithm proposed by Farias and Mitra (Farias & Mitra, 2005). This approach is based on the assumption that the perceived quality of a video can be affected by a variety of artifacts and that the strengths of these artifacts contribute to the overall annoyance (Ahumada & Null, 1993).

The multidimensional approach requires a good knowledge of the types of artifacts present in digital videos and an extensive study of the most relevant artifacts. The authors performed a series of psychophysical experiments to understand how artifacts depend on the physical properties of the video and how they combine to produce the overall annoyance.

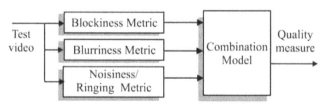

Fig. 15. Block diagram of the *no-reference* metric proposed by Farias and Mitra (Farias & Mitra, 2005).

The block diagram of the metric is as depicted in 15. The algorithm is composed by a set of three artifact metrics (artifact physical strength measurements) for estimating *blockiness*, *blurriness*, *ringing/noisiness*. The metrics are simple enough to be used in real-time applications, as briefly described below.

- The blockiness metric is a modification of the metric by Vlachos (Vlachos, 2000). It estimates the blockiness signal strength by comparing the cross-correlation of pixels inside (intra) and outside (inter) the borders of the coding blocking structure of a frame.

- The blurriness metric is based on the idea that blur makes the edges larger or less sharp (Marziliano et al., 2004; Lu, 2001; Ong et al., 2003). The algorithm measures blurriness by estimating the width of the edges in the frame.
- The noisiness/ringing metric is based on the work by Lee (Lee & Hoppel, 1989) that uses the well known fact that the noise variance of an image can be estimated by the local variance of a flat area. To reduce the content effect a cascade of 1-D filters was used as a pre-processing stage (Olsen, 1993).

To evaluate the performance of each artefact metric, their ability to detect and estimate the artifact signal strength is tested using test sequences containing only the artifact being measured, artifacts other than the artifact being measured, and a combination of all artifacts. The outputs of the individual metrics are also compared to artifact perceptual strengths gathered from psychophysical experiments. A model for overall annoyance is obtained based on a combination of the artifact metrics using a Minkowski metric.

5.4.2 Perceptual video quality assessment based on salient region detection

A recent work by Oprea *et al.* (Oprea et al., 2009) proposes a video quality metric that weighs the distortion measurements on the perceptual importance of the region where it is located.

The first step of this algorithm is to find which are the perceptually important areas of the video frame. For this, the model estimates key features that attract attention: color contrast, object size, orientation, and eccentricity. The measurement of these features will determine which are the important (or salient) areas, producing a saliency map. It is worth pointing out that extracting saliency from video sequences is a complex task because both the spatial extent and dynamic evolution of regions should be considered.

For the detected *salient* areas, a distortion measure is computed using a specialized no-reference metric. The metric considered by the algorithm is a blurriness metric. The blurriness algorithm is based on previous algorithms that estimate the blur by measuring the width of the edges in a frame (Marziliano et al., 2004).

An experiment performed by the authors revealed that the metric has a correlation of about 85% with subjective scores. The algorithm has, nevertheless, limitations concerning the fact that the saliency maps are calculated for the frames individually.

5.5 Metrics using data hiding

An alternative way of implementing a video quality metrics is to use embedding techniques (Sugimoto et al., 1998; Farias, Mitra, Carli & Neri, 2002; Holliman & Young, 2002). The idea consists of embedding in the original video the necessary information to estimate its quality at the time of display. One example of metrics that uses this approach is the work by Farias *et al* (Farias, Mitra, Carli & Neri, 2002). Fig. 16 depicts the block diagram of this video quality assessment system.

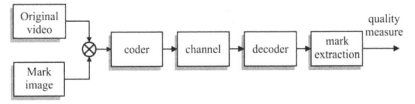

Fig. 16. Block diagram of the video quality assessment system based on data hiding.

At the transmitter, the mark is embedded in each frame of the video using a spread-spectrum technique (Cox et al., 1997). The embedding procedure can be summarized as follows. A pseudo random algorithm is first used to generate pseudo-noise (PN) images $\mathbf{p} = p(i, j, k)$, with values -1 or 1 and zero mean. The final mark to be embedded, $\mathbf{w}$, is obtained by multiplying the binary image, $\mathbf{m}$, by the PN image $\mathbf{p}$. Only one binary image is used for all frames, but the PN images vary from frame to frame.

Then, the logarithm of the luminance of the video frame, $\mathbf{y}$, is taken and the DCT transform, $\mathbf{LY}$, is computed. The mark, $\mathbf{w}$, is multiplied by a scaling factor, α, before being added to the luminance DCT coefficients. After the embedding, the DCT coefficients are given by the following expression:

$$LY'(i,j,k) = \begin{cases} LY(i,j,k) + \alpha \cdot w(i,j,k), & 120 \leq i \leq 240, \ 120 \leq j \leq 240 ; \\ LY(i,j,k), & \text{elsewhere.} \end{cases} \qquad (8)$$

where i and j are the frequency coordinates and k is the temporal coordinate (index of the frame). For the purpose of assessing the quality of a video, the mark is inserted in the mid-frequencies.

The scaling factor, α, is used to vary the strength of the mark. An increase in the value of α increases the robustness of the mark, but also decreases the quality of the video. After the mark is inserted, the exponential of the video is taken and then the inverse DCT (IDCT). The video is then coded (compressed) and sent over the communication channel.

The process of extracting the mark from the received video is summarized as follows. First, the logarithm of the luminance of the received video, $\mathbf{y''}$, is first taken and its DCT calculated. Then, we multiply the mid-frequency DCT coefficients where the mark was inserted by the corresponding pseudo-noise image. Considering that $p(i, j, k) \cdot p(i, j, k) = 1$ because $p(i, j, k)$ is either -1 or +1, we obtain:

$$LY''(i,j,k) \cdot p(i,j,k) = LY(i,j,k) \cdot p(i,j,k) + \alpha \cdot m(i,j), \qquad (9)$$

The result of Eq.(9) is then averaged for a chosen number of frames N_f to eliminate the noise (PN signal) introduced by the spread spectrum embedding algorithm. The extracted binary mark is obtained by taking the sign of this average, as given by the following expression:

$$m_r(i,j) = \text{sgn}\left(\frac{1}{N_f} \sum_{k=1}^{N_f} LY(i,j,k) \cdot p(i,j,k) + \alpha \cdot m(i,j,k) \right), \qquad (10)$$

Since the PN matrix has zero-mean, the sum $\sum_{k=1}^{N_f} LY(i,j,k) \cdot p(i,j,k)$ approaches zero for a large value of N_f. In general, for $N_f \geq 10$ the mark is recovered perfectly, i.e., $\mathbf{m}_r = \mathbf{m}$. When errors are added by compression or transmission, $Y'' = Y' + \eta$ and the extracted mark $\mathbf{m}_r$ is an approximation of $\mathbf{m}$. A measure of the degradation of the mark is given by the Total Square Error (TSE) between the extracted mark $\mathbf{m}_r$ and the original binary image:

$$E_{tse} = \sum_i \sum_j [m(i,j) - m_r(i,j)]^2. \qquad (11)$$

The less the amount of errors caused by processing, compression or transmission, the smaller E_{tse} is. On the other hand, the more degraded the video, the higher E_{tse} is. Therefore, the measure given by E_{tse} can be used as an estimate of the degradation of the host video.

6. The work of the video quality experts group

The Video Quality Experts Group (VQEG) was formed in October 1997 in Turin, Italy, to address video quality issues. Since then, it has been conducting formal evaluations of video quality metrics on common test material.

The first task of VQEG was to perform a validation of full reference video quality metrics targeted at TV applications (FR-TV). VQEG outlined, designed and executed a test program to compare subjective video quality evaluations to the predictions of a number of proposed objective metrics (VQEG, 1999). The result of the test was inconclusive (VQEG, 2000). From this first phase, a database of test sequences and their corresponding subjective rating was made available publicly.

In 2003, the second phase of the FR-TV test was completed (VQEG, 2003). The results of these tests have become part of two ITU recommendations (ITU-T, 2004b; a). Contrary to what happened in the first phase, this time the best metrics reached a correlation of around 94% with the subjective scores. The PSNR had a performance of around 70%.

After concluding the FR-TV tests, VQEG conducted a round of tests to evaluate video quality metrics targeted at multimedia applications. The videos considered for this phase had lower bitrates and smaller frames sizes. Besides that, a larger number of codecs and transmission conditions were considered. But, at this first phase the audio signal was not tested. On the 19th of September 2008, the Final Report of VQEGs Multimedia Phase I was released (VQEG, 2008). The correlation results for the submitted FR, RR, and NR metrics were of about 80%, 78%, and 56%, respectively. PSNR had a correlation of around 65%. VQEG has already started working on the second phase of the multimedia tests. In the second phase, both audio and video signals will be tested (simultaneously).

VQEG is currently finishing the tests for evaluation of reduced- and no-reference video quality metrics for television applications ("RR/NR-TV"). The draft report is currently available and the final report should be made available by the time of this publication. VQEG is also working on the evaluation of metrics to be used with High Definition TV (HDTV) content.

One more recent development of VQEG is the test for "hybrid metrics". These metrics estimate quality by looking at not only the decoded video, but also the encoded bitstream. These metrics are targeted at applications like broadcasting, lab applications, live monitoring in network (bitstream) or at end-user (hybrid no reference).

In June 2009, a new activity of VQEG has been launched. It's named Joint Effort Group (JEG) and it consists of an alternative collaborative action. The idea is to work jointly on both mandatory actions to validate metrics (subjective dataset completion and metrics design).

7. Conclusions and new perspectives

In this chapter, we introduced several aspects of video quality. We described the anatomy of the Human Visual System (HVS), discussing a number of phenomena of visual perception that are of particular relevance to video quality. We briefly introduced the main characteristics of modern digital video systems, focusing on the errors (artifacts) commonly present in digital video applications.

We described both objective and subjective methods for assessing video quality. For the subjective methods, we discussed the most common techniques standardized by ITU. We also discussed the main ideas used in the design of objective metric algorithms, listing a representative set of video quality metrics (FR, RR, and NR). Finally, we discussed the work of the Video Quality Experts Group (VQEG).

It is worth point out that, although much has been done in the last ten years in the area of video quality metrics, there are still a lot of challenges to be solved. Most of the achievements have been in the development of full-reference video quality metrics that evaluate compression artifacts. Much remains to be done, for example, in the area of no-reference and reduced-reference quality metrics.

Also, there has been a growing interest in metrics that estimate the quality of video digitally transmitted over wired or wireless channels/networks. This is due to the popularity of video delivery services over IP networks (e.g. internet streaming and IPTV) or wireless channel (e.g. mobile TV). Another area that has attracted attention is the area of multimedia quality. So far, very few metrics have addressed the issue of simultaneously measuring the quality of all medias involved (e.g. video, audio, text). There is also been an interest in 3D video and HDTV applications.

A new trend in video quality design is the development of *hybrid metrics*, which are metrics that use a combination of packet information, bitstream or decoded video as input (Verscheure et al., 1999; Kanumuri, Cosman, Reibman & Vaishampayan, 2006; Kanumuri, Subramanian, Cosman & Reibman, 2006). The idea here is to also consider parameters extracted from the transport stream and the bitstream (without decoding) in the computation of quality estimation. The main advantage of this approach is the lower bandwidth and processing requirements, when compared to metrics that only consider the fully decoded video.

8. References

Ahumada, A. J., J. & Null, C. (1993). Image quality: a multidimensional problem, *Digital Images and Human Vision* pp. 141–148.

Algazi, V. & Hiwasa, N. (1993). Perceptual criteria and design alternatives for low bit rate video coding, *Proc. 27th Asilomar Conf. on Signals, Systems and Computers*, Vol. 2, Pacific Grove, California, USA, pp. 831–835.

Avcibas, I., Avcba, I., Sankur, B. & Sayood, K. (2002). Statistical evaluation of image quality measures, *Journal of Electronic Imaging* 11: 206–223.

Bosi, M. & Goldberg, R. E. (2002). *Introduction to Digital Audio Coding and Standards*, Springer International Series in Engineering and Computer Science.

Bretillon, P.,Montard, N., Baina, J. & Goudezeune, G. (2000). Quality meter and digital television applications, *Proc. SPIE Conference on Visual Communications and Image Processing*, Vol. 4067, Perth,WA, Australia, pp. 780–90.

Burt, P. J. & Adelson, E. H. (1983). The laplacian pyramid as a compact image code, *IEEE Transactions on Communications* COM-31, 4: 532–540.

Carnec, M., Le Callet, P. & Barba, D. (2003). New perceptual quality assessment method with reduced reference for compressed images, *Proc. SPIE Conference on Visual Communications and Image Processing*, Vol. 5150, Lugano, Switzerland, pp. 1582–93.

Caviedes, J. & Jung, J. (2001). No-reference metric for a video quality control loop, *Proc. Int. Conf. on Information Systems, Analysis and Synthesis*, Vol. 13.

Cox, I., Kilian, J., Leighton, F. & Shamoon, T. (1997). Secure spread spectrum watermarking for multimedia, *IEEE Trans. on Image Processing* 6(12).

Daly, S. (1992). The visible difference predictor: An algorithm for the assessment of image fidelity, *Proc. SPIE Conference on Human Vision and Electronic Imaging XII*, p. 2.

Daly, S. (1993). The visible differences predictor: an algorithm for the assessment of image fidelity, *in* A. B.Watson (ed.), *Digital Images and Human Vision*, MIT Press, Cambridge, Massachusetts, pp. 179–206.

de Ridder, H. (1992). Minkowski-metrics as a combination rule for digital-image-coding impairments, *Proc. SPIE Conference on Human Vision, Visual Processing and Digital Display III*, Vol. 1666, San Jose, CA, USA, pp. 16–26.

de Ridder, H. (2001). Cognitive issues in image quality measurement, *Electronic Imaging* 10(1): 47–55.

Eckert,M. & Bradley, A. (1998). Perceptual quality metrics applied to still image compression, *Signal Processing* 70: 177–200.

Eskicioglu, E. & Fisher, P. (1995). Image quality measures and their performance, *IEEE Trans. Image Processing* 43(12): 2959–2965.

Farias, M., Foley, J. &Mitra, S. (2003a). Perceptual contributions of blocky, blurry and noisy artifacts to overall annoyance, *Proc. IEEE International Conference on Multimedia & Expo*, Vol. 1, Baltimore, MD, USA, pp. 529–532.

Farias, M., Foley, J. & Mitra, S. (2003b). Some properties of synthetic blocky and blurry artifacts, *Proc. SPIE Conference on Human Vision and Electronic Imaging*, Vol. 5007, Santa Clara, CA, USA, pp. 128–136.

Farias, M., Foley, J. & Mitra, S. (2004). Detectability and annoyance of synthetic blurring and ringing in video sequences, *Proc. IEEE International Conference on Acoustics, Speech, and Signal Processing*, IEEE, Montreal, Canada.

Farias, M. & Mitra, S. (2005). No-reference video quality metric based on artifact measurements, *Proc. IEEE Intl. Conf. on Image Processing*, pp. III: 141–144.

Farias, M., Mitra, S., Carli, M. & Neri, A. (2002). A comparison between an objective quality measure and the mean annoyance values of watermarked videos, *Proc. IEEE Intl. Conf. on Image Processing*, Vol. 3, Rochester, NY, pp. 469 –472.

Farias, M., Moore, M., Foley, J. & Mitra, S. (2002). Detectability and annoyance of synthetic blocky and blurry artifacts, *Proc. SID International Symposium*, Vol. XXXIII, Number II, Boston, MA, USA, pp. 708–712.

Farias, M., Moore, M., Foley, J. & Mitra, S. (2004). Perceptual contributions of blocky, blurry, and fuzzy impairments to overall annoyance, *Proc. SPIE Conference on Human Vision and Electronic Imaging*, San Jose, CA, USA.

Gastaldo, P., Rovetta, S. & Zunino, R. (2001). Objective assessment of MPEG video quality: a neural-network approach, *Proc. International Joint Conference on Neural Networks*, Vol. 2, pp. 1432–1437.

Girod, B. (1993). What's wrong with mean-squared error?, *in* A. B. Watson (ed.), *Digital Images and Human Vision*, MIT Press, Cambridge, Massachusetts, pp. 207–220.

Grey, H. (1918). Anatomy of the human body. All images are online and are public domain. URL: *http://www.bartley.com/107/*

Gunawan, I. & Ghanbari, M. (2005). Image quality assessment based on harmonics gain/loss information, *Image Processing, 2005. ICIP 2005. IEEE International Conference on*, Vol. 1, pp. I–429–32.

Gunawan, I. & Ghanbari, M. (2008). Efficient reduced-reference video quality meter, *Broadcasting, IEEE Transactions on* 54(3): 669–679.

Haskell, B. G., Puri, A. & Netravali, A. N. (1997). *Digital video: An Introduction to MPEG-2*, Digital multimedia standards, Chapman & Hall: International Thomson Pub., New York, NY, USA.

Hays, W. (1981). *Statistics for the social sciences*, 3 edn, LLH Technology Publishing, Madison Avenue, New York, N.Y.

Holliman, M. & Young, M. (2002). Watermarking for automatic quality monitoring, *Proc. SPIE Conference on Security and Watermarking of Multimedia Contents*, Vol. 4675, San Jose, CA, USA.

ITU (1998). *ISO/IEC 13818: Generic coding of moving pictures and associated audio (MPEG-2)*.

ITU (2003). *Recommendation ITU-T H.264: Advanced Video Coding for Generic Audiovisual Services*.

Kanumuri, S., Cosman, P., Reibman, A. & Vaishampayan, V. (2006). Modeling packet-loss visibility in mpeg-2 video, *Multimedia, IEEE Transactions on* 8(2): 341–355.

Kanumuri, S., Subramanian, S., Cosman, P. & Reibman, A. (2006). Predicting h.264 packet loss visibility using a generalized linear model, *Image Processing, 2006 IEEE International Conference on*, pp. 2245–2248.

Keimel, C., Oelbaum, T. & Diepold, K. (2009). No-reference video quality evaluation for highdefinition video, *Acoustics, Speech, and Signal Processing, IEEE International Conference on* pp. 1145–1148.

Klein, S. (1993). Image quality and image compression: A psychophysicist's viewpoint, *in* A. B. Watson (ed.), *Digital Images and Human Vision*, MIT Press, Cambridge, Massachusetts, pp. 73–88.

Lambert, P., de Neve, W., de Neve, P., Moerman, I., Demeester, P. & de Walle, R. V. (Jan. 2006). Rate-distortion performance of h.264/avc compared to state-of-the-art video codecs, *Circuits and Systems for Video Technology, IEEE Transactions on* 16(1): 134–140.

Lee, J. & Hoppel, K. (1989). Noise modeling and estimation of remotely-sensed images, *Proc. International Geoscience and Remote Sensing*, Vol. 2, Vancouver, Canada, pp. 1005–1008.

Lu, J. (2001). Image analysis for video artifact estimation and measurement, *Proc. SPIE Conference on Machine Vision Applications in Industrial Inspection IX*, Vol. 4301, San Jose, CA, USA, pp. 166–174.

Lubin, J. (1993). The use of psychophysical data and models in the analysis of display system performance, *in* A. B. Watson (ed.), *Digital Images and Human Vision*, MIT Press, Cambridge, Massachusetts, pp. 163–178.

Lubin, J. (1995). A visual discrimination model for imaging system design and evaluation, *in* E. Peli (ed.), *Vision models for target detection and recognition*, World Scientific Publishing, Singapore.

Marr, D. (1982). Vision: A Computational Investigation into the Human Representation and Processing of Visual Information, Freeman.

Martens, J. & Meesters, L. (1997). Image dissimilarity, *Signal Processing* 70: 1164–1175.

Marziliano, P., Dufaux, F., Winkler, S. & Ebrahimi, T. (2004). Perceptual blur and ringing metrics: Application to JPEG2000, *Signal Processing: Image Communication* 19(2): 163–172.

Maxwell, S. E. & Delaney, H. D. (2003). *Designing experiments and analyzing data: A model comparison perspective*, Lawrence Erlbaum Associates, Mahwah, NJ.

ITU-R (1998). *Recommendation BT.500-8: Methodology for subjective assessment of the quality of television pictures*.

ITU-T (1999). *Recommendation P.910: Subjective Video Quality Assessment Methods for Multimedia Applications.*

ITU-T (2004a). *Objective perceptual video quality measurement techniques for standard definition digital broadcast television in the presence of a full reference.*

ITU-T (2004b). *Recommendation J.144: Objective perceptual video quality measurement techniques for digital cable television in the presence of a full reference.*

Moore, M. S. (2002). *Psychophysical Measurement and Prediction of Digital Video Quality*, PhD thesis, University of California Santa Barbara.

Olsen, S. I. (1993). Estimation of noise in images: an evaluation, *CVGIP-Graphical Models & Image Processing* 55(4): 319–23.

Ong, E.-P., Lin, W., Lu, Z., Yao, S., Yang, X. & Jinag, L. (2003). No-reference JPEG2000, *Proc. IEEE International Conference on Multimedia and Expo*, Vol. 1, Baltimore, USA, pp. 545–548.

Oprea, C., Pirnog, I., Paleologu, C. & Udrea, M. (2009). Perceptual video quality assessment based on salient region detection, *Telecommunications, 2009. AICT '09. Fifth Advanced International Conference on*, pp. 232–236.

Pessoa, A. C. F., Falcao, A. X., Silva, A., Nishihara, R. M. & Lotufo, R. A. (1998). Video quality assessment using objective parameters based on image segmentation, *Proc. SBT/IEEE International Telecommunications Symposium*, Vol. 2, Sao Paulo, Brazil, pp. 498–503.

Pinson, M. & Wolf, S. (2004). A new standardized method for objectively measuring video quality, *Broadcasting, IEEE Transactions on* 50(3): 312–322.

Poynton, C. (2003). Digital Video and HDTV - Algorithms and Interfaces, 5th edn, Morgan Kaufmann.

Richardson, I. E. (2003). *H.264 and MPEG-4 Video Compression*, John Wiley & Sons, New York, NY, USA.

Rohaly, A. M. al., e. (2000). Final report from the video quality experts group on the validation of objective models of video quality assessment, *Technical report*, Video Quality Experts Group.

Sheikh, H., Sabir, M. & Bovik, A. (2006). A statistical evaluation of recent full reference image quality assessment algorithms, *Image Processing, IEEE Transactions on* 15(11): 3440–3451.

Snedecor, G. W. & Cochran, W. G. (1989). *Statistical methods*, 8th edn, Iowa State University Press,

Ames. Sugimoto, O., Kawada, R.,Wada, M. & Matsumoto, S. (1998). Objective measurement scheme for perceived picture quality degradation caused by MPEG encoding without any reference pictures, *Proc. SPIE Conference on Human Vision and Electronic Imaging*, Vol. 4310, San Jose, CA, USA, pp. 932–939.

Teo, P. C. & Heeger, D. J. (1994). Perceptual image distortion, *Proc. IEEE International Conference on Image Processing*, Vol. 2, Austin, TX , USA, pp. 982–986.

van den Branden Lambrecht, C. J. & Kunt, M. (1998). Characterization of human visual sensitivity for video imaging applications, *Signal Processing* 67(3): 255–69.

Verscheure, O., Frossard, P. & Hamdi, M. (1999). User-oriented qos analysis in mpeg-2 video delivery, *Real-Time Imaging* 5(5): 305–314.

Vlachos, T. (2000). Detection of blocking artifacts in compressed video, *Electronics Letters* 36(13): 1106–1108.

VQEG (1999). *VQEG subjective test plan (Phase 1)*. ftp://ftp.crc.ca/crc/vqeg/phase1-docs.

VQEG (2000). Final report from the video quality experts group on the validation of objective models of video quality assessment, *Technical report*, http://www.vqeg.org.

VQEG (2003). Final report from the video quality experts group on the validation of objective models of video quality assessment - Phase II, *Technical report*, http://ftp.crc.ca/test/pub/crc/vqeg/.

VQEG (2008). Final report of vqegs multimedia phase i validation test, *Technical report*, http://www.vqeg.org.

VQEG (2009). Rrnr-tv group - test plan draft version 2, *Technical report*, http://www.vqeg.org.

Wang, Y. (2006). Survey of objective video quality measurements, *Technical Report T1A1.5/96- 110*, Worcester Polytechnic Institute.

Wang, Z., Bovik, A. C., Sheikh, H. R., Member, S., Simoncelli, E. P. &Member, S. (2004). Image quality assessment: From error visibility to structural similarity, *IEEE Transactions on Image Processing* 13: 600–612.

Wang, Z., Bovik, A. & Evan, B. (2000). Blind measurement of blocking artifacts in images, *Proc. IEEE International Conference on Image Processing*, Vol. 3, pp. 981–984.

Watson, A. (1987). The cortex transform: rapid computation of simulated neural images, *Computer Vision, Graphics, and Image Processing* 39(3): 311–327.

Watson, A. B. (1990). Perceptual-components architecture for digital video, *Journal of the Optical Society of America, A-Optics & Image Science* 7(10): 1943–54.

Watson, A. B. (1998). Towards a visual quality metric for digital video, *Proc. European Signal Processing Conference*, Vol. 2, Island of Rhodes, Greece.

Watson, A. B., James, H. &McGowan, J. F. (2001). Digital video quality metric based on human vision, *Journal of Electronic Imaging* 10(1): 20–9.

Webster, A. A., Jones, C. T., Pinson, M. H., Voran, S. D. & Wolf, S. (1993). An objective video quality assessment system based on human perception, *Proc. SPIE Conference on Human Vision, Visual Processing, and Digital Display IV*, Vol. 1913, San Jose, CA, USA, pp. 15–26.

Winkler, S. (1999). A perceptual distortion metric for digital color video, *Proc. SPIE Conference on Human Vision and Electronic Imaging*, Vol. 3644, San Jose, CA, USA, pp. 175–184.

Wolf, S. & Pinson,M. H. (1999). Spatial-temporal distortion metric for in-service quality monitoring of any digital video system, *Proc. SPIE Conference on Multimedia Systems and Applications II*, Vol. 3845, Boston, MA, USA, pp. 266–77.

Wolf, S., Pinson, M. H., Voran, S. D. & Webster, A. A. (1991). Objective quality assessment of digitally transmitted video, *Proc. IEEE Pacific Rim Conference on Communications, Computers and Signal Processing*, Victoria, BC, Canada, pp. 477–82 vol.

Wu, H. & Yuen, M. (1997). A generalized block-edge impairment metric for video coding, *IEEE Signal Processing Letters* 4(11): 317–320.

Yuen, M. & Wu, H. R. (1998). A survey of hybrid MC/DPCM/DCT video coding distortions, *Signal Processing* 70(3): 247–78.

10

Reliable and Repeatable Power Measurements in DVB-T Systems

Leopoldo Angrisani[1], Domenico Capriglione[2],
Luigi Ferrigno[2] and Gianfranco Miele[2]
[1]Dept. of Computer Science and Control Systems, University of Naples
Federico II via Claudio 21, 80125 Napoli,
[2]Dept. of Automation, Electromagnetism, Information Engineering and
Industrial Mathematics, University of Cassino,
via G. Di Biasio, 43 03043 Cassino (Fr),
Italy

1. Introduction

Development and diffusion of digital video broadcasting (DVB) standards have revolutionized the television transmission; whether via satellite (DVB–S), via cable (DVB–C), or terrestrial (DVB–T), the number of services it can offer is able to satisfy the expectation of more demanding customers (ETSI, 2004), (Fischer, 2004). Since many countries in the world suffer from poor coverage of satellite and cable TV, DVB–T is playing a more significant role with respect to the other standards. DVB–T broadcasting networks are, in fact, growing very rapidly. A consequent and pressing need of performance assessment and large scale monitoring of DVB–T systems and apparatuses is thus posed. To reach this goal, a new set of measurements is required and a large number of parameters has to be taken into account, especially due to the complexity characterizing the DVB–T modulation process.

European Telecommunications Standards Institute (ETSI) specifies the parameters and quantities to be measured, and recommends the procedures to be adopted as well as test beds and laboratory equipments to be arranged (ETSI, 2004-2). Power measurement is, in particular, of primary concern: radiofrequency (RF) and intermediate frequency (IF) signal power, noise power, RF and IF power spectrum, should be measured as accurately as possible. Many advantages are connected with this practice, such as better optimization of transmitted power level, thus avoiding waste of energy and reducing the probability of interference with other systems that operate in the same coverage area, and reliable estimation of radiated emissions for verifying compliance limits applied in the regions of interest. Moreover, ETSI suggests the type of instrument to be used for power measurement, such as spectrum analyzer or power meter equipped with a proper sensor and a band-pass filter suitably tuned to the DVB–T frequency band. The former has to be equipped with a specific personality addressed to the integration of the input signal power spectrum on a certain frequency range (channel power measurement), the latter allows only peak and average power to be measured.

Several types of spectrum analyzer and power meter are available on the market. Most of them are general-purpose instruments, and not specifically designed to analyze DVB-T signals. They exhibit relevant accuracy and repeatability problems in the presence of noise-like signals characterized by high peak to average power ratio (PAR), like DVB–T signals. In addition, they are not suited for large scale monitoring of DVB–T networks, where small size, light weight and low cost are critical constraints.

To give an answer to the cited needs, the scientific community has focused the attention on the definition and implementation of new digital signal processing (DSP) based methods for power measurement in DVB–T systems (Angrisani et al., 2006), (Angrisani et al., 2007), (Angrisani et al., 2008), (Angrisani et al., 2009). In particular, the methods based on power spectral density (PSD) estimators have seemed to be the most appropriate. They exploit straightforward measurement algorithms working on the achieved PSD to provide the desired value of the parameter or quantity of interest. Both non-parametric and parametric estimation algorithms have been considered. An overview of their performance in terms of metrological features, computational burden and memory needs if implemented on a real DSP hardware architecture is given hereinafter.

2. Power measurement in DVB-T systems

For assessing the performance of DVB-T systems and apparatuses, a new set of measurements is required. Many parameters and quantities have, in fact, to be evaluated, pointed out by ETSI in the ETSI TR 101 290 technical report (ETSI, 2004-2), called Digital Video Broadcasting Measurements (DVB-M). ETSI also recommends the procedures to be adopted for arranging test-beds or measurement systems.

A list of the measurement parameters and quantities defined for the DVB-T OFDM environment is shown in Table 1, and full referenced in (ETSI, 2004-2). All of them are keys for evaluating the correct operation of DVB-T systems and apparatuses, and each of them is addressed to a specific purpose. The technical report describes this purpose, where the parameter or the quantity has to be evaluated and in which manner. For the sake of clarity, it reports a schematic block diagram of a DVB-T transmitter and receiver, in which all the measurement interfaces are marked with a letter.

As it can clearly be noted from Table 1, power measurement is of great concern. RF and intermediate frequency (IF) signal power, noise power as well as RF and IF power spectrum are, in fact, relevant quantities to be measured as accurately as possible.

There are several RF power measurement instruments available in the market. They can be divided in two main categories: power meters and spectrum analyzers. Even though suggested by (ETSI, 2004-2), all of them suffer from a number of problems when measuring the power of a noise–like signal with a high PAR, as the DVB-T signal. The problems may dramatically worsen if the measurement is carried out in the field and with the aim of a large scale monitoring.

With regard to power meters, they are typically wideband instruments, and as such they must be connected to one or more calibrated band-pass filters centered at the central frequency of the DVB-T signals to be measured and with an appropriate bandwidth. Moreover, their metrological performance strongly depends on the power sensor they rely on. Several power sensors designed to measure different parameters and characterized by different frequency ranges are available on the market. Even though the choice is wide, not all power sensors are suitable to operate with signals characterized by a high PAR, as explained in (Agilent, 2003).

Measurement parameter	T	N	R
RF frequency accuracy (precision)	X		
Selectivity			X
AFC capture range			X
Phase noise of local oscillators	X		X
RF/IF signal power	X		X
Noise power			X
RF and IF spectrum	X		
Receiver sensitivity/ dynamic range for a Gaussian channel			X
Equivalent Noise Degradation (END)			X
Linearity characterization (shoulder attenuation)	X		
Power efficiency	X		
Coherent interferer			X
BER vs. C/N ratio by variation of transmitter power	X		X
BER vs. C/N ratio by variation of Gaussian noise power	X		X
BER before Viterbi (inner) decoder			X
BER before RS (outer) decoder			X
BER after RS (outer) decoder			X
I/Q analysis	X		X
Overall signal delay	X		
SFN synchronization		X	
Channel characteristics		X	

Table 1. DVB-T measurement parameters and their applicability

Differently from power meters, spectrum analyzers are narrowband instruments, and they are characterized by a more complex architecture. They allow different measurements on different RF signals. Their performance depends on several parameters like the resolution bandwidth (RBW), video bandwidth (VBW), detectors, etc. In particular, the detectors play a very important role because they can emphasize some signal characteristics giving unreliable measurement results. This is especially true when the signals involved are noise-like, as the DVB-T signal. To mitigate this problem, some suggestions described in (Agilent, 2003-2) can be followed.

In many cases, power meters and spectrum analyzers are expressly designed to be used only in laboratories; their performance drastically reduces when used in other environments, especially in the field. But, the fundamental problem that can limit their use is their cost. The total financial investment turns to be prohibitive for any interested company if a great number of instruments is needed, as when a large scale monitoring of DVB-T systems and apparatuses has to be pursued.

3. Nonparametric estimation for power measurement in DVB-T systems

In this chapter the most widely used correlation and spectrum estimation methods belonging to the nonparametric techniques, as well as their properties, are presented. They do not assume a particular functional form, but allow the form of the estimator to be determined entirely by the data. These methods are based on the discrete-time Fourier transform of either the signal segment (direct approach) or its autocorrelation sequence (indirect approach). Since the choice of an inappropriate signal model will lead to erroneous results, the successful application of parametric techniques, without sufficient a priori information, is very difficult in practice. In the following two major nonparametric algorithms for PSD estimation have been taken into account (Angrisani L. et al., 2003). The first is based on the Welch method of averaged periodograms, which is also known as the WOSA estimator; the second applies wavelet thresholding techniques to the logarithm of the multitaper estimator.

3.1 WOSA Estimator
The WOSA estimator is computationally one of the most efficient methods of PSD estimation, particularly for long data records (Jokinen H. et al., 2000). This method is based on the division of the acquired signal x(n) into smaller units called segments, which may overlap or be disjoint. The samples in a segment are weighted through a window function to reduce undesirable effects related to spectral leakage. For each segment, a periodogram is calculated.

$$S_x^i(f) = \frac{T_S}{N_S U}\left|\sum_{n=0}^{N_S-1} x^i(n)\omega(n)e^{-j2\pi f n T_S}\right|^2 \tag{1}$$

Variable f stands for frequency, $x^i(n)$ are the samples of the i-th segment, $\omega(n)$ accounts for the window coefficients, N_S denotes the number of samples in a segment, U is a coefficient given by

$$U = \frac{1}{N_S}\sum_{n=0}^{N_S-1}\omega^2(n) \tag{2}$$

and is used to remove the window effect from the total signal power, and T_S represents the sampling period. The PSD estimate $S_x(f)$ is then computed by averaging the periodogram estimates

$$S_x(f) = \frac{1}{K}\sum_{i=0}^{K-1}S_x^i(f) \tag{3}$$

where K represents the number of segments and is given by

$$K = \frac{N - N_S}{N_S - N_P} + 1 \tag{4}$$

where N stands for the total number of acquired samples, and N_P is the number of the overlapped samples between two successive segments. Overlap ratio r is defined as the percentage of ratio between the number of the overlapped samples and the number of samples in a segment, i.e.,

$$r = 100\frac{N_P}{N_S}\%. \tag{5}$$

It is worth noting that proper use of the WOSA estimator imposes the optimal choice of two parameters: 1) window function $\omega(\cdot)$ and 2) overlap ratio r. The periodogram in (2) can be easily evaluated over a grid of equally spaced frequencies through a standard fast Fourier transform (FFT) algorithm (Welch P. D. 1967).

3.2 Multitaper estimation and wavelet thresholding

The idea is to calculate a certain number H of PSD estimates, each using a different window function, which is also called data taper and applied to the whole acquired signal, and then to average them together (Moulin P., 1994). If all data tapers are orthogonal, the resulting multitaper estimator can exhibit good performance, in terms of reduced bias and variance, particularly for signals characterized by a high dynamic range and/or rapid variations, such as those that are peculiar to DVB-T systems.

The multitaper estimator has the following form:

$$S_x(f) = \frac{1}{H}\sum_{i=0}^{H-1} S_x^i(f) \tag{6}$$

where the terms $S_x^i(f)$ called eigenspectra are given by

$$S_x^i(f) = \left|\sum_{n=0}^{N-1} x(n)h_i(n)e^{-j2\pi f n T_s}\right| \tag{7}$$

where $\{h_i(n) : n = 0,...,N-1; i=1,..., H\}$ denotes a set of orthonormal data tapers. A convenient set of easily computable orthonormal data tapers is the set of sine tapers, the ith of which is

$$h_i(n) = \left(\frac{2}{N+1}\right)^{1/2}\sin\left(\frac{(i+1)\pi n}{N+1}\right). \tag{8}$$

A standard FFT algorithm proves to be appropriated in evaluating the eigenspectra over a grid of equally spaced frequencies (Walden et al., 1998).

Provided that H is equal to or greater than 5, it can be demonstrated that random variable $\eta(f)$, as given by

$$\eta(f) = \log\frac{S_x(f)}{S(f)} - \psi(H) + \log H \tag{9}$$

has Gaussian distribution with zero mean and variance σ^2_η equal to $\psi'(H)$; S(f) represents the true PSD, and $\psi(\cdot)$ and $\psi'(\cdot)$ denote the digamma and trigamma functions, respectively (Moulin P., 1994). If we let

$$Y(f) = \log S_x(f) - \psi(H) + \log H \tag{10}$$

we have

$$Y(f) = \log S(f) + \eta(f) \tag{11}$$

i.e., the logarithm of the multitaper estimator, plus a known constant, can be written as the true log spectrum plus approximately Gaussian noise with zero mean value and known variance σ^2_{η}.

These conditions make wavelet thresholding techniques particularly suitable to remove noise and, thus, to produce a smooth estimate of the logarithm of the PSD. In particular, after evaluating the discrete wavelet transform (DWT) of Y(f) computed according to (10), the resulting wavelet coefficients, which are also Gaussian distributed, can be subjected to a thresholding procedure, and the aforementioned smooth estimate can be obtained by applying the inverse DWT to the thresholded coefficients (Walden et al., 1998). A soft threshold function $\delta(\alpha,T)$ is suggested, and it is defined by

$$\delta(\alpha,T) = \text{sgn}(\alpha) \begin{cases} |\alpha| - T, & \text{if } |\alpha| > T \\ 0, & \text{otherwise} \end{cases} \qquad (12)$$

where α denotes the generic wavelet coefficient, and T is the threshold level. In (Donoho D. L. & Johnstone I. M., 1994), Donoho and Johnstone demonstrated that, in the presence of Gaussian noise with zero mean value and variance σ^2_{η}, the optimal value of T is

$$T = \sigma_n \sqrt{2 \times \log N} \qquad (13)$$

where N, which is the number of samples, must be of power of two.

In addition, in this case, the right choice of two parameters, i.e., the number of data tapers H and the mother wavelet $\zeta(\cdot)$ for DWT and inverse DWT evaluation, has to be made to gain a sound spectral estimation.

3.3 Performance optimization and assessment

To optimally choose window function $\omega(\cdot)$ and overlap ratio r for the WOSA estimator and the number of data tapers H and mother wavelet $\zeta(\cdot)$ for the multitaper estimator, a suitable simulation stage has been designed. Regarding r, all values ranging from 0% up to 90%, with a step of 10%, have been considered. As for $\omega(\cdot)$, a large set of functions, which differ from one another in relevant spectral characteristics, has been arranged; the set includes most windows defined in (Reljin I. et al., 1998), such as Hanning, Blackman, MS-3FT, MS-4FT, FD-3FT, and FD-4FT, and the new window proposed in (Jokinen H. et al., 2000), which is referred to as Ollila. Concerning H, the considered values range from 5 up to 50, with a step of 5. In addition, various mother wavelets characterized by different vanishing moments (db3, db8, sym3, sym8, coif1, coif5, bior2.2, and bior2.8) have been enlisted (Daubechies I., 1992).

A number of numerical tests have, in particular, been executed in the Matlab 7 environment, with the aim of minimizing the following figures of merit:

1. experimental standard deviation characterizing both total (σ_T) and channel (σ_C) power measurement results;
2. difference between the mean value of the results provided by the method and the imposed value, which is considered as reference, for both total (Δ_T) and channel (Δ_C) power.

The channel power is obtained by integrating the PSD over the frequency interval that is centered at the tune frequency and as wide as the nominal spacing of the channel itself

(ETSI, 2004). Instead the total power is evaluated integrating the PSD over the whole frequency span analyzed from zero up to half of the adopted sample rate f_S (f_S=1/T_s).
DVB-T reference signals have first been generated. To this aim, the analytical expression for the PSD of a DVB-T signal given by

$$S_X(f) = \sum_{k=-(K-1)/2}^{(K-1)/2} \left[\frac{\sin\left(\pi\left(f - f_k\right)\left(\Delta + T_u\right)\right)}{\pi\left(f - f_k\right)\left(\Delta + T_u\right)} \right]^2 \quad f_k = f_c + \frac{k}{T_u} \tag{14}$$

has been considered, where f_c is the RF signal central frequency, K is the number of transmitted carriers, Δ is the duration of the guard interval, and T_u is the time duration of the useful part of a DVB-T symbol (the useful part does not include the guard interval) (ETSI, 2004). Moreover, the approximate method in the frequency domain presented in (Percival D. B., 1992) has been adopted. It assures accurate time-domain realizations of a zero-mean Gaussian process, which is characterized by a known PSD.
The following DVB-T transmission settings have been imposed: 8K transmission mode (K=6817 and T_u=896 μs) and 1/4 (Δ=224 μs) and 1/32 (Δ=28 μs) guard intervals. In addition, three values of the oversampling factor (considered as the ratio between the sample rate and the RF signal central frequency) have been simulated, and the hypothesis of the acquired records covering one DVB-T symbol has been held. For each transmission setting and oversampling factor value, 50 different realizations (test signals) have been produced.
The obtained results are given in Tables 2 and 3 for the multitaper and WOSA estimators, respectively. Each pair of round brackets describes the couple ($\zeta(\cdot)$ − H or $\omega(\cdot)$ − r) that minimizes the related figure of merit. The last row of both tables quantifies the computation burden in terms of mean processing time on a common Pentium IV computer.
From the analysis of the results, some considerations can be drawn.
- Both estimators have assured good repeatability; the experimental standard deviation is always lower than 0.20%.
- Repeatability improves upon the widening of the guard interval, and the oversampling factor seems to have no influence.
- The WOSA estimator exhibits better performance in terms of Δ_T and Δ_C.
- Measurement time peculiar to the multitaper estimator is much longer than that taken by the WOSA estimator.
The WOSA estimator has given a better trade-off between metrological performance and measurement time, thus confirming the outcomes presented in (Angrisani L. et al., 2006). This is the reason the multitaper estimator has no longer been considered in the subsequent stages of the work.
To fix the minimum hardware requirements of the data acquisition system (DAS) to be adopted in the experiments on emulated and actual DVB-T signals described in the succeeding sections, further tests have been carried out. The sensitivity of the proposed method to the effective number of bits (ENOB) and acquired record length has been assessed. The obtained results are given in Figs. 1 and 2; they refer to a guard interval equal to 224 μs. In particular, Fig. 1 shows the values of σ_C [Fig. 1(a)], Δ_C [Fig. 1(b)], and Δ_T [Fig. 1(c)] versus ENOB for three values of the oversampling factor; Fig. 1(d) presents the estimated PSD for the considered values of ENOB. With regard to σ_T, values very similar to those characterizing σ_C have been experienced. Fig. 2 shows the values of σ_T [Fig. 2(a)] and Δ_T [Fig. 2(b)] versus the acquired record length for the same values of the oversampling factor. With regard to σ_C and Δ_C, values very similar to those characterizing σ_T and Δ_T, respectively, have been experienced.

Figure of merit	Guard interval [μs]	Oversampling factor		
		~3	~6	~12
σ_T [%]	28	0,148 (sym8,10)	0,176 (db3,25)	0,151 (db3,25)
	224	0,129 (coif1,50)	0,097 (coif1,50)	0,117 (db3,25)
σ_C [%]	28	0,148 (sym8,10)	0,176 (db3,25)	0,151 (db3,25)
	224	0,129 (coif1,50)	0,097 (coif1,50)	0,117 (db3,25)
Δ_T [%]	28	0,1104 (bior2.8,50)	0,1252 (bior2.8,50)	0,6335 (bior2.8,50)
	224	0,1509 (bior2.8,50)	0,1050 (bior2.8,50)	0,1237 (bior2.8,50)
Δ_C [%]	28	0,1105 (bior2.8,50)	0,1253 (bior2.8,50)	0,6336 (bior2.8,50)
	224	0,1509 (bior2.8,50)	0,1050 (bior2.8,50)	0,1238 (bior2.8,50)
Measurement time [s]	28	12,55	59,46	280,53
	224	53,61	280,58	1168,20

Table 2. Results obtained in the simulation stage: multitaper estimator is involved.

Figure of merit	Guard interval [μs]	Oversampling factor		
		~3	~6	~12
σ_T [%]	28	0,149 (Ollila,70)	0.181 (Ollila,50)	0,148 (Ollila,30)
	224	0,130 (blackman,60)	0,098 (hanning,50)	0,092 (Ollila,50)
σ_C [%]	28	0,149 (Ollila,70)	0,181 (Ollila,50)	0,148 (Ollila,30)
	224	0,130 (blackman,60)	0,098 (hanning,50)	0,092 (Ollila,50)
Δ_T [%]	28	0,0015 (FD3FT,30)	5,4091e-4 (FD3FT,30)	0,0017 (FD4FT,60)
	224	0,0068 (blackman,40)	0,0028 (MS3FT,10)	0,0020 (MS4FT,60)
Δ_C [%]	28	0,0015 (FD3FT,30)	6,0611e-4 (FD3FT,30)	0,0012 (FD4FT,60)
	224	0,0068 (blackman,40)	0,0017 (MS3FT,10)	0,0020 (MS4FT,60)
Measurement time [s]	28	0,032	0,052	0,096
	224	0,053	0,094	0,177

Table 3. Results obtained in the simulation stage: WOSA estimator is involved.

Looking at Fig. 1, it is possible to establish that 1) an ENOB equal to or greater than six grants an experimental standard deviation in both total (σ_T) and channel (σ_C) power measurements of less than 0.15%, and 2) Δ_C does not seem to be affected by vertical quantization, as, on the contrary, Δ_T does. Furthermore, Fig. 2 clearly evidences that σ_T improves upon the widening of the record length, whereas satisfying values of Δ_T can be achieved if the record lengths covering greater than one half of the DVB-T symbol are considered.

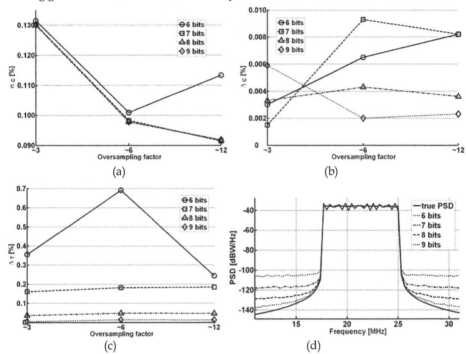

Fig. 1. Simulation stage: a) σ_C, b) Δ_C, and c) Δ_T versus ENOB for three values of the oversampling factor; d) estimated PSD for the considered values of ENOB.

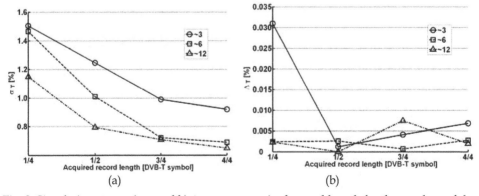

Fig. 2. Simulation stage: a) σ_T and b) Δ_T versus acquired record length for three values of the oversampling factor.

These considerations match well with the typical characteristics of the data acquisition systems available on the market today. High values of the sample rate, required to optimally acquire RF or IF DVB-T signals, are often associated with ENOB not lower than 6 bits.

Further an emulation stage has been designed and applied, with the aim of assessing the performance of the proposed method in the presence of a real DAS and comparing it with that assured by competitive measurement solutions that are already available on the market. Stemming from past experience documented in (Angrisani L. et al., 2006), a suitable measurement station, which is sketched in Fig. 3, has been set up. It has included the following: 1) a processing and control unit, i.e., a personal computer, on which the measurement algorithm has run; 2) an RF signal generator equipped with DVB-T personalities Agilent Technologies E4438C (with an output frequency range of 250 kHz–6 GHz); 3) a traditional spectrum analyzer [express spectrum analyzer (ESA)] Agilent Technologies E4402B (with an input frequency range of 9 kHz–3 GHz); 4) a VSA Agilent Technologies E4406A (with an input frequency range of 7 MHz–4 GHz); 5) a real-time spectrum analyzer (RSA) Tektronix RSA3408A (with an input frequency range of dc–8 GHz); 6) an RF power meter (PM) Agilent Technologies N1911A equipped with two probes N1921A (with an input frequency range of 50 MHz–18 GHz) and E9304A (with an input frequency range of 6 kHz–6 GHz); and 7) a DAS LeCroy SDA6000A (with 6-GHz bandwidth and 20-GS/s maximum sample rate). They are all interconnected through an IEEE-488 interface bus. The function generator has provided 8-MHz-bandwidth DVB-T test signals characterized by an RF central frequency equal to 610 MHz, a nominal total power of -20 dBm, and a 64-state quadrature amplitude modulation (QAM) scheme. Moreover, the same transmission settings considered in the previous stage have been imposed.

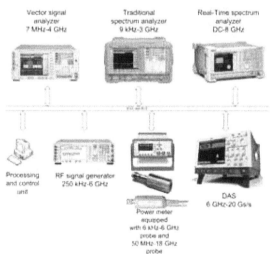

Fig. 3. Measurement station for performance assessment.

A preliminary characterization of cables and connectors utilized in the measurement station has been carried out through the vector network analyzer ANRITSU 37347C (with an input frequency range of 40 MHz–20 GHz), which is equipped with a 3650 SMA 3.5-mm calibration kit (Anritsu, 2003). The mean value and experimental standard deviation of 100 attenuation measures obtained in the interval of 606–614 MHz are given in Table 4.

	Mean attenuation	Experimental standard deviation
Power meter	0.829150	0.000039
Spectrum analyzers	0.834860	0.000019
Oscilloscope	0.834140	0.000014

Table 4. Characterization results of cables and connectors utilized in the measurement station of Fig. 3.

Different operative conditions of the DAS, in terms of vertical resolution (7 and 8 bits nominal) and observation period (1/4, 1/2, 3/4, and 1 DVB-T symbol), have been considered. For each operative condition and transmission setting, 50 sample records have been acquired and analyzed through the proposed method. Examining the obtained results given in Table 5 and Fig. 4, it can be noted that two conditions hold.

1. Higher sampling factors do not seem to affect the method's metrological performance; the same is true if vertical resolution is considered.
2. Performance enhancement can be noticed both in the presence of acquired records covering increasingly longer observation periods.

Successively, 50 repeated measurements of total and channel power have been executed by means of PM and spectrum analyzers (ESA, VSA, and RSA), respectively. Table 6 accounts for the results provided by the PM, whereas Table 7 enlists those that are peculiar to the analyzers. As an example, Fig. 5 sketches a typical PSD estimated by the proposed method [Fig. 5(a)], ESA [Fig. 5(b)], VSA [Fig. 5(c)], and RSA [Fig. 5(d)].

With regard to total power, three considerations can be drawn.

1. Results furnished by the PM are different for the two probes adopted.
2. Experimental standard deviation peculiar to the PM is slightly better than that assured by the proposed method.
3. PM outcomes concur with the total power measurement results of the proposed method; a confidence level equal to 99% is considered (Agilent, 2005).

As for the channel power, it is worth stressing that two conditions hold.

1. The proposed method exhibits satisfying repeatability. The related experimental standard deviation is better than that characterizing ESA, VSA, and RSA results.

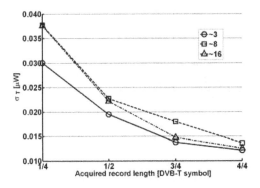

Fig. 4. Emulation stage: σ_T versus acquired record length for three values of the oversampling factor.

8k transmission mode, 64-QAM modulation scheme, 8 bit vertical resolution				
		Oversampling factor		
Figure of Merit	Guard Interval [μs]	~3	~8	~16
σ_T [μW]	28	0.012	0.014	0.013
	224	0.0094	0.017	0.011
σ_C [μW]	28	0.012	0.014	0.013
	224	0.0094	0.017	0.011
P_T [μW]	28	9.931	10.024	9.937
	224	10.142	10.163	10.144
P_C [μW]	28	9.890	9.989	9.895
	224	10.1030	10.125	10.105
8k transmission mode, 64-QAM modulation scheme, 7 bit vertical resolution				
		Oversampling factor		
Figure of Merit	Guard Interval [μs]	~3	~8	~16
σ_T [μW]	28	0.011	0.034	0.014
	224	0.011	0.029	0.015
σ_C [μW]	28	0.011	0.032	0.014
	224	0.011	0.028	0.016
P_T [μW]	28	10.148	10.162	10.157
	224	10.079	10.098	10.097
P_C [μW]	28	9.971	9.985	9.980
	224	9.899	9.919	9.916

Table 5. Total and channel power measures provided by the proposed method. The acquired record covers a single DVB-T symbol.

Transmission Settings 8k, 64-QAM, 610 MHz central frequency			
PM	Guard Interval [μs]	P_{PM} [μW]	σ_{PM} [μW]
N1921A PROBE	28	9.9444	0.0018
	224	9.9630	0.0020
E9304A PROBE	28	8.0402	0.0060
	224	7.95910	0.00086

Table 6. Mean values (PPM) and experimental standard deviations (σPM) of total power measures provided by the PM equipped with N1921A and E9304A probes.

2. ESA,VSA, and RSA outcomes concur with the channel power measurement results of the proposed method; a confidence level equal to 99% is considered (Agilent, 2004), (Agilent, 2001), (Tektronix, 2006).

Finally, a number of experiments on real DVB-T signals have been carried out through the optimized method. The signals have been radiated by two MEDIASET DVB-T multiplexers operating on the UHF 38 (610-MHz RF central frequency) and UHF 55 (746-MHz RF central frequency) channels, respectively.

A simplified measurement station, as sketched in Fig. 6, has been adopted. With respect to that used in the emulation stage, the function generator has been replaced by a suitable amplified antenna, the VSA and RSA have been removed, and a power splitter has been added. Cables, connectors, and a power splitter have been characterized through the

Transmission Settings: 8k, 64-QAM, 610 MHz central frequency					
Instrument		RBW [kHz]	Guard Interval [μs]	P_{SA} [μW]	σ_{SA} [μW]
ESA		100	28	10.322	0.074
		100	224	10.656	0.080
		30	28	10.376	0.068
		30	224	10.142	0.070
VSA		0.871	28	10.506	0.036
		0.871	224	10.218	0.023
		30	28	10.162	0.099
		30	224	9.52	0.12
RSA	SPECTRUM ANALYZERS	50	28	9.311	0.044
		50	224	9.318	0.042
		30	28	9.158	0.041
		30	224	9.042	0.044
	REAL TIME MODE		28	9.177	0.097
			224	9.088	0.081

Table 7. Mean values (P_{SA}) and experimental standard deviations (σ_{SA}) of channel power measures provided by ESA, VSA and RSA; different settings of their resolution bandwidth have been considered.

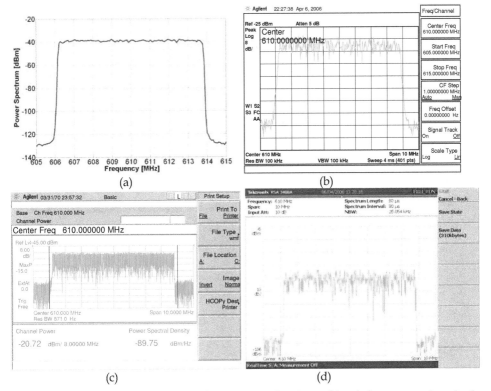

Fig. 5. Power spectrum of an emulated DVB T signal estimated by a) the proposed method, b) ESA, c) VSA and d) RSA.

aforementioned vector network analyzer. The mean value and experimental standard
deviation of 100 attenuation measures obtained in the UHF 38 and UHF 55 channels are
given in Table 8.
As an example, Fig. 7(a) and (b) shows the power spectrum of a DVB-T signal, which is
radiated by the MEDIASET multiplexer operating on UHF 55, as estimated by the proposed
method and ESA, respectively. Channel power measurement results are summarized in
Table 9; good agreement can be appreciated, confirming the efficacy of the proposal
(Angrisani L. et al., 2008).

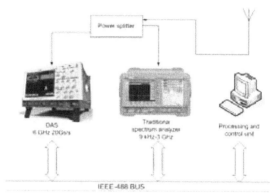

Fig. 6. Measurement station for the experiments on real DVB-T signals.

	UHF Channel	Mean attenuation [dB]	Experimental standard deviation [dB]
DAS	38	-4.703	0.032
	55	-5.403	0.042
Traditional Spectrum Analyzer	38	-19.393	0.021
	55	-19.3886	0.0086

Table 8. Characterization results of cables and connectors utilized in the measurement
station of Fig. 6.

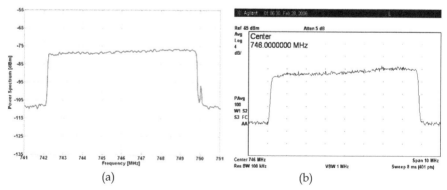

(a)   (b)

Fig. 7. Power spectrum of a real DVB T signal measured by the a) proposed method and b)
ESA.

8k transmission mode, 64-QAM, 28µs guard interval		
	UHF Channel 38 610 MHz	UHF Channel 55 746 MHz
Proposed Method	90.94 nW	93.07 nW
Traditional Spectrum Analyzer	94.06 nW	93.23 nW

Table 9. Experimental results.

4. Parametric estimation for power measurement in DVB-T systems

Parametric estimation methods suppose that the analyzed signal is the output of a model, which is represented as a linear system driven by a noise sequence ε_n. They evaluate the PSD of the signal by estimating the parameters (coefficients) of the linear system that hypothetically "generates" the signal. Among the various methods, autoregressive (AR) approaches are widespread. The computational burden related to AR approaches is, in fact, significantly less than that required to implement moving average (MA) or autoregressive moving average (ARMA) parameter estimation algorithms (Marple, 1980).

A stationary autoregressive process of order p, i.e., AR(p), satisfies

$$x_n = -\sum_{m=1}^{p} a_{p,m} x_{n-m} + \varepsilon_n \tag{15}$$

where $a_{p,1}, a_{p,2},..., a_{p,p}$ are fixed coefficients, and $\{\varepsilon_n\}$ is a white noise process with variance σ^2_p. The PSD of the stationary process described by AR(p) is totally described by the model parameters and the variance of the white noise process. It is given by

$$S(f) = \frac{\sigma_p^2 T_S}{\left|1 + \displaystyle\sum_{m=1}^{p} a_{p,m} e^{-j2\pi m f T_s}\right|^2} \quad |f| \le f_N \tag{16}$$

where $T_S = 1/f_S$ is the sampling interval, and $f_N = 1/(2T_S)$ is the Nyquist frequency. Consequently, with known p, it is necessary to properly estimate the p+1 parameters $a_{p,1}, a_{p,2},..., a_{p,p}$ and σ^2_p. To reach this goal, the relationship between the AR parameters and the autocorrelation sequence (known or estimated) of x_n has to be fixed, as described here.

4.1 Yule–Walker equations

Achieving the expectations on the product $x_n x^*_{n-k}$, the autocorrelation sequence is evaluated as

$$R_{xx}(k) = E\left[x_n x_{n-k}^*\right] = -\sum_{m=1}^{p} a_{p,m} R_{xx}(k-m) + E\left[\varepsilon_n x_{n-k}^*\right]. \tag{17}$$

The plausible fact that $E[\varepsilon_n x^*_{n-k}] = 0$, for $k > 0$, implies that

$$E\left[\varepsilon_n x_n^*\right] = E\left[\varepsilon_n \left(-\sum_{m=1}^{p} a_{p,m}^* x_{n-m}^* + \varepsilon_n^*\right)\right] =$$
$$= -\sum_{m=1}^{p} a_{p,m}^* E\left[\varepsilon_n x_{n-m}\right] + \sigma_p^2 = \sigma_p^2 \tag{18}$$

Hence, the evaluation of (18) for k=0,1,...,p makes it possible to obtain the so-called augmented Yule–Walker equations

$$
\overbrace{\begin{bmatrix} R_{xx}(0) & R_{xx}(-1) & L & R_{xx}(-p) \\ R_{xx}(1) & R_{xx}(0) & L & R_{xx}(-p+1) \\ M & M & O & M \\ R_{xx}(p) & R_{xx}(p-1) & L & R_{xx}(0) \end{bmatrix}}^{R_p} \overbrace{\begin{bmatrix} 1 \\ a_{p,1} \\ M \\ a_{p,p} \end{bmatrix}}^{A_p} = \overbrace{\begin{bmatrix} \sigma_p^2 \\ 0 \\ M \\ 0 \end{bmatrix}}^{\Sigma_p} .
\tag{19}
$$

If we have no stationary process $\{x_n\}$ but we are in the presence of a time series that is a realization of a portion $x_1, x_2, ..., x_N$ of any discrete-parameter stationary process, replacing $R_{xx}(k)$ with

$$
\hat{R}_{xx}(k) = \frac{1}{N}\sum_{i=0}^{N-k} x_i x_{i+k}^* \qquad \text{for } k=0,...,p
\tag{20}
$$

it is possible to solve system (19) by inversion.

4.2 Levinson–Durbin algorithm

To avoid the matrix inversion, which is a time-consuming task and is performed using Gaussian elimination, that requires operations of order p^3, which are denoted as $o(p^3)$, the system (19) can be solved through Levinson-Durbin recursions (Kay & Marple, 1981), (Marple, 1980), which require only $o(p^2)$ operations. The algorithm proceeds with recursively computing the AR parameters for order k from the AR parameters previously determined for order k−1.

In particular, the recursive algorithm is initialized by

$$
a_{1,1} = -\frac{R_{xx}(1)}{R_{xx}(0)}
\tag{21}
$$

$$
\sigma_1^2 = \left(1 - |a_{1,1}|^2\right) R_{xx}(0)
\tag{22}
$$

and the recursion for k = 2, 3,..., p is given by

$$
a_{k,k} = -\frac{R_{xx}(k) + \sum_{m=1}^{k-1} a_{k-1,m} R_{xx}(k-m)}{\sigma_{k-1}^2}
\tag{23}
$$

$$
a_{k,m} = a_{k-1,m} + a_{k,k} a_{k-1,k-m}^*, \qquad 1 \le m \le k-1
\tag{24}
$$

$$
\sigma_k^2 = \sigma_{k-1}^2 \left(1 - |a_{k,k}|^2\right)
\tag{25}
$$

where $a_{k,k}$ is the reflection coefficient (Kay & Marple, 1981).

This algorithm is useful when the correct model order is not known a priori since (21)–(25) can be used to successfully generate higher order models until the modeling error σ^2_k is reduced to a desired value.

4.3 Forward linear prediction algorithm

In the literature, several least-squares estimation procedures that directly operate on the data to yield better AR parameter estimates can be found. These techniques often produce better AR spectra than that obtained with the Yule–Walker approach.

Assume that the sequence $x_0,\ldots, x_{N-1}$ is used to find the p-th-order AR parameter estimates. The forward linear predictor is (Makhoul, 1975)

$$\hat{x}_n = -\sum_{k=1}^{p} a_{p,k} x_{n-k}.$$ (26)

It is possible now to define the forward linear prediction error

$$e_p(n) = x_n - \hat{x}_n = \sum_{k=0}^{p} a_{p,k} x_{n-k} \quad \text{for } p \le n \le N\text{-}1$$ (27)

where $a_{p,0}=1$. Therefore, $e_p(n)$, for $n=p$ to $n=N-1$, can be obtained by

$$
\overbrace{\begin{bmatrix} e_p(p) \\ M \\ e_p(N-1) \end{bmatrix}}^{E}
=
\overbrace{\begin{bmatrix} x_p & L & x_0 \\ M & & M \\ x_{N-1} & L & x_{N-p-1} \end{bmatrix}}^{X_p}
\overbrace{\begin{bmatrix} 1 \\ a_{p,1} \\ M \\ a_{p,p} \end{bmatrix}}^{A}
$$ (28)

where X_p is an $(N-p)\times(p+1)$ Toeplitz matrix.

The approach followed to estimate $a_{p,k}$ consists of minimizing a sum of $e_p(n)$ called prediction error energy, i.e.,

$$SS_p = \sum_{n=p}^{N-1} |e_p(n)|^2 = \sum_{n=p}^{N-1} \left| \sum_{k=0}^{p} a_{p,k} x_{n-k} \right|^2 = E^H E.$$ (29)

Using an alternative description of the N−p error equation (28) such as

$$E = \overbrace{\begin{bmatrix} y & X \end{bmatrix}}^{X_p} \overbrace{\begin{bmatrix} 1 \\ a \end{bmatrix}}^{A}$$ (30)

where $y = [x_p,\ldots, x_{N-1}]^T$, $a = [a_{p,1},\ldots, a_{p,p}]^T$, and $X = \begin{bmatrix} x_{p-1} & L & x_0 \\ M & & M \\ x_{N-2} & L & x_{N-p-1} \end{bmatrix}$ the prediction error

energy (29) may be expressed as

$$SS_p = E^H E = y^H y + y^H X a + a^H X^H y + a^H X^H X a.$$ (31)

To minimize SS_p, this term must be set to zero (Marple, 1987), i.e.,

$$X^H y + X^H X a = 0_p,$$ (32)

where 0_p is the all-zeros vector, obtaining

$$SS_{p,min} = y^H y + y^H X a. \tag{33}$$

Equations (32) and (33) may be combined into a single set of

$$\begin{bmatrix} y^H y & y^H X \\ X^H y & X^H X \end{bmatrix} \begin{bmatrix} 1 \\ a \end{bmatrix} = \begin{bmatrix} y & X \end{bmatrix}^H \begin{bmatrix} y & X \end{bmatrix} \begin{bmatrix} 1 \\ a \end{bmatrix} =$$
$$= \left(X_p \right)^H X_p \begin{bmatrix} 1 \\ a \end{bmatrix} = \begin{bmatrix} SS_{p,min} \\ 0_p \end{bmatrix} \tag{34}$$

These equations form the normal equations of the least squares analysis. This method is called the covariance method (Makhoul, 1975). Due to the particular properties of $(X_p)^H X_p$, it is possible to develop a fast algorithm that is similar to that of the Levinson algorithm. The original fast algorithm for solving the covariance normal equations was developed by Morf et al. (Morf et al, 1977), and further computational reduction was studied by Marple and reported in (Marple, 1987), producing an algorithm that requires $o(p^2)$ operations.

4.4 Burg algorithm

This is the most popular approach for AR parameter estimation with N data samples and was introduced by Burg in 1967 (Burg, 1967). It may be viewed as a constrained least-squares minimization.

The approach followed to estimate $a_{k,k}$ consists of minimizing a sum of forward and backward linear prediction error energies, i.e.,

$$SS_p = \sum_{n=p}^{N-1} \left[\left| e_p(n) \right|^2 + \left| b_p(n) \right|^2 \right] \tag{35}$$

where $e_p(n)$ is defined by (27), and $b_p(n)$ is the backward linear prediction error, which is given by

$$b_p(n) = \sum_{k=0}^{p} a_{p,k}^* x_{n-p+k} \quad \text{for } p \leq n \leq N-1. \tag{36}$$

Note that $a_{p,0}$ is defined as unity.

Substitution of (24) into (27) and (36) yields the following recursive relationship between the forward and backward prediction errors:

$$e_p(n) = e_{p-1}(n) + a_{p,p} b_{p-1}(n-1) \quad \text{for } p \leq n \leq N-1 \tag{37}$$

$$b_p(n) = b_{p-1}(n-1) + a_{p,p}^* e_{p-1}(n) \quad \text{for } p \leq n \leq N-1 \tag{38}$$

and substituting (37) and (38) into (35), SS_p can be written as

$$SS_p = \Gamma_p + 2a_{p,p} \Lambda_p + \Gamma_p a_{p,p}^2 \tag{39}$$

whose coefficients are

$$\Gamma_p = \sum_{n=p}^{N-1} \left[\left| e_{p-1}(n) \right|^2 + \left| b_{p-1}(n-1) \right|^2 \right] \tag{40}$$

$$\Lambda_p = 2 \sum_{n=p}^{N-1} e_{p-1}(n) b_{p-1}^*(n-1). \tag{41}$$

The value of $a_{p,p}$ that minimizes SS_p can easily be calculated by setting the derivative to zero and obtaining

$$a_{p,p} = -\frac{\Lambda_p}{\Gamma_p}. \tag{42}$$

The routine implemented to estimate the AR coefficients is shown in Fig. 2. It needs an initializing step, in which the starting value of the observed forward and backward prediction errors and the innovation variance are chosen using the following relations:

$$e_0(n) = b_0(n) = x_n \tag{43}$$

$$\sigma_0^2 = \frac{1}{N} \sum_{n=1}^{N} |x_n|^2. \tag{44}$$

The Burg algorithm requires a number of operations proportional to p^2.

4.5 Forward and backward linear prediction algorithm

This approach, which was independently proposed by Ulrych and Clayton (Ulrych T. J. & Clayton R. W., 1976). and Nuttal (Nuttal A. H., 1976), is a least-squares procedure for forward and backward predictions, in which the Levinson constraint imposed by Burg is removed.

Noting that (27) and (36) can be summarized by

$$\Delta = \begin{bmatrix} E \\ B^* \end{bmatrix} = \begin{bmatrix} X_p \\ X_p^* J \end{bmatrix} \begin{bmatrix} 1 \\ a \end{bmatrix} \tag{45}$$

where $B = [b_p(p),..., b_p(N-1)]^T$, J is an $(p+1) \times (p+1)$ reflection matrix, and $X_p^* J$ is a Hankel matrix of conjugated data elements, it is possible to rewrite (35) as

$$SS_p = \Delta^H \Delta = E^H E + B^H B. \tag{46}$$

The preceding equation can be minimized with the same procedure used for the covariance method, leading to the set of normal equations

$$\overbrace{\begin{bmatrix} X_p \\ X_p^* J \end{bmatrix}^H \begin{bmatrix} X_p \\ X_p^* J \end{bmatrix}}^{R_p} \begin{bmatrix} 1 \\ a \end{bmatrix} = \begin{bmatrix} SS_{p,min} \\ 0_p \end{bmatrix}. \tag{47}$$

Because the summation range in (35) is identical to that of the covariance method, this least-squares approach is called the modified covariance method. The system (47) can be solved by a matrix inversion that requires a number of operations proportional to p^3, which is one order of magnitude greater than Burg's solution.

Due to the characteristic of the actual structure of the matrix R_p, Marple (Marple, 1980), (Marple, 1987) suggested an algorithm requiring a number of computations proportional to p^2.

4.6 Performance optimization and assessment

The performance of parametric power spectrum estimation methods depends on the model order p. To regulate this parameter to operate with success on DVB-T systems, a suitable simulation stage has been designed and set-up. Once the optimal value of p has been found, a first comparison with the optimized Welch method has been made. Successively further investigation has been carried out in simulation environment, with the aim of evaluating the performance of parametric spectrum estimation methods when they are applied to signals characterized by different quantization levels. Afterwards an emulation stage has been designed and applied with the aim of:

- assessing the performance of the proposed method in the presence of a real DAS;
- comparing it to that assured by competitive measurement solutions already available on the market;
- comparing it to that assured by the optimized Welch method.

Moreover a number of experiments on real DVB-T signals have been carried out through the optimized method, in order to make a comparison with the results obtained in the previous stages. At last the suitability of these methods to be implemented in a low cost DSP platform has been investigated.

As said in the previous paragraph, the performance of PSD AR estimators depends on the polynomial order p. To optimally choose this parameter, a suitable simulation stage has been designed. A number of numerical tests have been executed in the Matlab 7 environment, with the aim of minimizing the same figures of merit defined in the previous section. These tests have been carried out by adopting the same reference signals defined above.

With special regard to AR estimation algorithms, taking into account that higher values of p may introduce spurious details in the estimated spectrum and lower values of p may drive to a highly smoothed spectral estimate (Kay & Marple, 1981), a dual stage optimization procedure has been applied. In the first stage, a rough optimization has been pursued; in particular, a suitable operative range for p has been fixed. The second stage has finely tuned the value of p, within the range previously determined, through the minimization of σ_C and Δ_C.

4.6.1 Rough optimization

Suitable figures of merit, which are addressed to highlight the goodness of the PSD estimates, have been considered. Much attention has been paid to the final prediction error, Akaike's information criterion, and the root mean square error (RMSE); details can be found in (Kay & Marple, 1981) and (Angrisani L. et al., 2003).

Concerning p, two different and consecutive sets have been organized: $\Sigma_1 = \{p \mid 10 \leq p \leq 100\}$ and $\Sigma_2 = \{p \mid 100 < p \leq 5000\}$. In Σ_1, an analysis step of 10 has been adopted, whereas a step of 100 has been considered for Σ_2.

All tests have highlighted quite the same behavior of the three figures of merit; they have reached their minima in strictly overlapping p ranges. For the sake of brevity, Fig. 8 shows only the minimum value of RMSE [Fig. 8(a)] and the corresponding value of p [Fig. 8(b)] versus the observation period expressed as a fraction of the time interval associated with one DVB-T symbol; a guard interval of 224 μs and an oversampling factor of 3 have, in particular, been considered. Very similar outcomes have been attained with a guard interval of 28 μs and two oversampling factors, which are equal to 6 and 12.

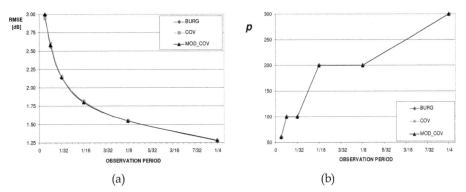

(a)   (b)

Fig. 8. a) Minimum values of RMSE and (b) corresponding values of p versus the observation period, which is expressed as a fraction of the time interval associated with one DVB-T symbol.

From the analysis of the results, some considerations have emerged.

1. The covariance, Burg, and modified covariance estimators reach the lowest RMSE for very similar values of the polynomial order p.
2. RMSE values related to the covariance, Burg, and modified covariance algorithms concur, showing comparable performance in PSD estimation.
3. The values of p that minimize RMSE are significantly high for observation periods that are longer than 1/128 of the time interval associated with one DVB-T symbol.

To fix an operative range of p of practical use, it has been assumed that RMSE values lower than 3 dB assure acceptable performance in channel power measurement (Fig. 9). A threshold of 3 dB has been applied to the results already obtained, thus achieving a strong reduction in the values of p of interest, with a consequent benefit to the computational burden.

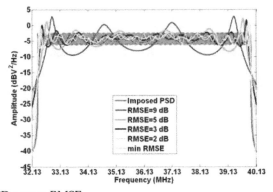

Fig. 9. Estimated PSD versus RMSE.

4.6.2 Fine Optimization

The stage has aimed at fixing the optimal value of p within the operative range established before and comparing the performance granted by the so-optimized covariance, Burg, and modified covariance estimator-based measurement algorithms to that assured by the WOSA-estimator-based algorithm. To reach this goal two figures of merit, σ_C and Δ_C, already defined in paragraph 3, have been minimized.

The obtained values of Δ_C and σ_C and the polynomial order p versus the observation period, which is expressed as a fraction of the time interval associated with one DVB-T symbol, are shown in Fig. 10. An oversampling factor of 3 and a guard interval of 224 μs have been considered. Very similar results have been experienced with a guard interval of 28 μs and two oversampling factors, which are equal to 6 and 12.

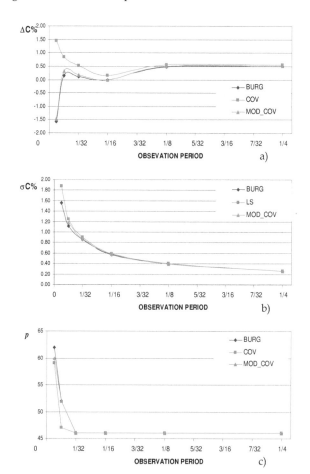

Fig. 10. a) ΔC, b) σC and c) polynomial order p versus the observation period for the considered AR estimator-based measurement algorithms. An oversampling factor equal to 3 and a guard interval equal to 224 μs have been considered.

It is possible to state that the considered AR algorithms grant a very similar performance for both σ_C and Δ_C and that the optimum polynomial order p is equal to 46. In addition, the oversampling factor seems to have no influence; its lowest value (3) is advisable for reducing memory needs.

To fix the minimum hardware requirements of the DAS to be adopted in the experiments on emulated and actual DVB-T signals, the results of which are described in the following, further tests have been carried out. Table 10 gives the estimated σ_C versus the analyzed values of the effective number of bits (ENOB). Observation periods ranging from 1/128 up to 1/4 of the time interval associated with one DVB-T symbol have been considered. σ_C does not seem to be affected by vertical quantization, and the Burg algorithm seems to be more stable if short observation periods are involved.

Estimators	Observation period	ENOB			
		6	7	8	9
BURG	1/128	.1.6	1.6	1.5	1.5
	1/64	1.1	1.1	1.1	1.1
	1/32	0.87	0.86	0.86	0.86
	1/16	0.57	0.56	0.57	0.57
	1/8	0.39	0.39	0.39	0.39
	1/4	0.26	0.26	0.26	0.26
COVARIANCE	1/128	1.8	1.9	2.1	1.9
	1/64	1.3	1.3	1.3	1.2
	1/32	0.90	0.90	0.90	0.90
	1/16	0.59	0.58	0.59	0.59
	1/8	0.40	0.40	0.40	0.40
	1/4	0.26	0.26	0.26	0.26
MODIFIED COVARIANCE	1/128	1.7	1.7	1.7	1.7
	1/64	1.2	1.2	1.2	1.2
	1/32	0.87	0.87	0.87	0.86
	1/16	0.58	0.58	0.58	0.58
	1/8	0.40	0.40	0.40	0.40
	1/4	0.26	0.26	0.26	0.26

Table 10. σ_C% versus ENOB for different observation periods.

Computational burden, in terms of the mean processing time on a common Pentium IV computer, has also been quantified.

The results are given in Table 11. It is possible to note that the measurement time peculiar to the Burg-estimator-based measurement algorithm is lower than that taken by the covariance and modified-covariance-estimator-based algorithms for short observation periods.

The Burg-estimator-based measurement algorithm has shown the best tradeoff between metrological performance and measurement time. This is the reason the covariance- and modified covariance estimator-based algorithms have no longer been considered in the subsequent stages of the work.

8k transmission mode and Δ=224 µs						
	Observation period					
Estimator	1/4	1/8	1/16	1/32	1/64	1/128
Burg	0.062	0.036	0.020	0.010	0.008	0.005
Covariance	0.044	0.028	0.018	0.015	0.008	0.015
Modified Covariance	0.052	0.035	0.024	0.021	0.022	0.023
8k transmission mode and Δ=28 µs						
	Observation period					
Estimator	1/4	1/8	1/16	1/32	1/64	1/128
Burg	0.055	0.033	0.016	0.008	0.006	N/A
Covariance	0.039	0.027	0.017	0.015	0.014	N/A
Modified Covariance	0.046	0.040	0.022	0.019	0.020	N/A

Table 11. Computation time in ms versus the observation period.

An emulation stage has been designed and executed with the aim of assessing the performance of the optimized Burg estimator-based measurement algorithm in the presence of a real DAS and comparing the obtained results to those furnished by the optimized WOSA algorithm. Moreover, all results have been compared to those assured by competitive measurement solutions already available on the market.

Thanks to the experience described in the paragraph 3, a suitable measurement station, sketched in Fig. 11, has been designed and setup.

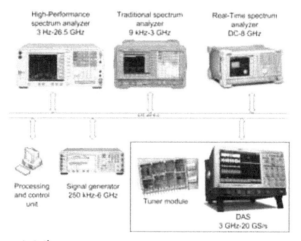

Fig. 11. Measurement station.

It has included:

- a control unit, namely a personal computer (PC);
- a RF signal generator Agilent Technologies E4438C (250 kHz-6 GHz output frequency range), equipped with DVB-T personalities;
- an express spectrum analyzer (ESA) Agilent Technologies E4402B (9 kHz-3 GHz input frequency range);

- a high performance spectrum analyzer (PSA) Agilent Technologies E4440A (3 Hz-26.5 GHz input frequency range);
- a real-time spectrum analyzer (RSA) Tektronix RSA3408A (DC-8 GHz input frequency range);
- a DAS LeCroy WavePro 7300A, (3 GHz bandwidth, 20 GS/s maximum sample rate) coupled to the tuner module for digital terrestrial application described in paragraph 3.

All instruments have been interconnected through an IEEE-488 standard interface bus. The signal generator has provided 8 MHz bandwidth, DVB-T test signals, characterized by a RF center frequency equal to 610 MHz, a nominal total power of -10 dBm and a 64-QAM modulation scheme. Moreover, the same transmission settings considered in the previous stage have been imposed.

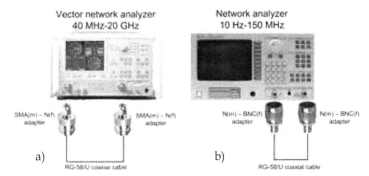

Fig. 12. Measurement bench for the characterization of cables and connectors at a) RF, and b) IF.

A preliminary characterization of cables and connectors utilized in the measurement station has been carried out through the vector network analyzer ANRITSU 37347C (40 MHz-20 GHz input frequency range), equipped with 3650 SMA 3.5 mm calibration kit (Anritsu, 2003), and the spectrum/network analyzer HP 3589A (10 Hz--150 MHz input frequency range) (Agilent, 1991), respectively for RF and IF frequencies. Also the tuner has been characterized.

Different operative conditions of the DAS, in terms of vertical resolution (7- and 8-bit nominal) and observation period (from 1/128 up to 1/4 of the time interval associated with one DVB-T symbol), have been considered; the oversampling factor has been chosen to be equal to 3. For each of them, 100 sample records have been acquired and analyzed both through the Burg- and WOSA-estimator-based measurement algorithms.

The obtained results, which are given in Tables 12–14, have highlighted five conditions.

1. The channel power measures provided by the Burg estimator- based measurement algorithm concur with those furnished by the WOSA-estimator-based algorithm.
2. The channel power measures are influenced by the DAS vertical resolution for both the Burg- and WOSA estimator- based measurement algorithms.
3. Both algorithms exhibit satisfying and comparable repeatability, which is not affected by the DAS vertical resolution and observation period.
4) ESA and PSA outcomes concur with the channel power measurement results of the Burg- and WOSA estimator-based measurement algorithms when a DAS resolution of 8 bits is adopted; a confidence level of 95% is considered.

5. The outcomes of the RSA operating both in normal conditions and as a spectrum analyzer seem to concur with the channel power measurement results of the Burg- and WOSA estimator-based algorithms only for a DAS resolution of 7 bits; a confidence level of 99% is considered.

8 bit DAS resolution							
		Observation period					
Figure of merit	Guard Interval [µs]	1/4	1/8	1/16	1/32	1/64	1/128
P_C [µW]	28	106.41	106.39	106.38	106.52	105.72	N/A
	224	104.87	104.83	104.71	104.68	104.08	102.57
σ_{PC} [µW]	28	0.75	0.75	0.76	0.77	0.78	N/A
	224	0.74	0.74	0.74	0.75	0.75	0.77
7 bit DAS resolution							
		Observation period					
Figure of merit	Guard Interval [µs]	1/4	1/8	1/16	1/32	1/64	1/128
P_C [µW]	28	97.55	97.43	97.31	97.41	96.52	N/A
	224	97.35	97.33	97.12	97.31	96.59	94.92
σ_{PC} [µW]	28	0.69	0.69	0.69	0.70	0.71	N/A
	224	0.71	0.71	0.71	0.72	0.72	0.73

Table 12. Mean values (P_C) and experimental standard deviations (σ_{PC}) of channel power measures provided by the WOSA estimator-based measurement algorithm. DVB-T settings: 8k transmission mode, 64-QAM modulation scheme.

8 bit DAS resolution							
		Observation Period					
Figure of merit	Guard Interval [µs]	1/4	1/8	1/16	1/32	1/64	1/128
P_C [µW]	28	105.65	105.69	105.83	105.90	106.13	N/A
	224	104.30	104.30	104.29	104.27	104.53	104.96
σ_{PC} [µW]	28	0.74	0.75	0.75	0.76	0.78	N/A
	224	0.74	0.74	0.74	0.74	0.75	0.78
7 bit DAS resolution							
		Observation Period					
Figure of merit	Guard Interval [µs]	1/4	1/8	1/16	1/32	1/64	1/128
P_C [µW]	28	96.86	96.76	96.74	96.93	96.99	N/A
	224	96.84	96.83	96.82	96.78	97.01	97.46
σ_{PC} [µW]	28	0.68	0.68	0.69	0.69	0.71	N/A
	224	0.71	0.71	0.71	0.72	0.72	0.74

Table 13. Mean values (P_C) and experimental standard deviations (σ_{PC}) of channel power measures provided by the Burg estimator-based measurement algorithm. DVB-T settings: 8k transmission mode, 64-QAM modulation scheme.

Instrument	Guard Interval [μs]	P_C [μW]	σ_{PC} [μW]
ESA	28	106.63	0.59
	224	106.24	0.63
PSA	28	106.60	0.64
	224	106.77	0.54
RSA	28	92.68	0.66
	224	93.27	0.61
RSA-SA	28	93.40	0.30
	224	93.69	0.31

Table 14. Mean values (P_C) and experimental standard deviations (σ_{PC}) of channel power measures provided by ESA, VSA, RSA and RSA operating as spectrum analyzer. DVB-T settings: 8k transmission mode, 64-QAM modulation scheme.

A number of experiments on real DVB-T signals have been carried out through the optimized algorithm. The signals have been radiated by one MEDIASET DVB-T multiplexer operating on the UHF 38 (610-MHz RF central frequency) channel.

A simplified measurement station has been adopted. With respect to that used in the emulation stage, the function generator has been replaced by a suitable amplified antenna, the PSA and RSA have been removed, and a power splitter has been added (Angrisani L. et al., 2008). The cables, connectors, and power splitter have been characterized through the aforementioned network analyzers.

The channel power measurement results are summarized in Table 15, and a good agreement can be appreciated.

8k transmission mode, 64-QAM, 28μs guard interval UHF Channel 38 (610 MHz)	
	Measured Power [μW]
WOSA estimator-based measurement algorithm	26.75
Burg estimator-based measurement algorithm	26.92
ESA	26.42

Table 15. Experimental results.

5. Implementation issues in DSP-based meters

In order to evaluate the suitability of these methods to be implemented on real cost effective DSP platform two figures of merit have been taken into account:

- memory requirement, intended as the maximum number of samples to be preserved in the hardware memory;
- computational burden, defined as the number of operations (real additions and real multiplications) to be performed for gaining the desired PSD.

5.1 WOSA estimator

It can be demonstrated that an optimized implementation that is able to reduce the memory requirements would have two requirements.

1. A meter memory that is able to preserve, for the whole measurement time, 2M real samples, which are related to the acquired and overlapped buffers, and 2M complex

samples (4M real samples) for the current and averaged FFT. To prevent additional memory requirements, a computational time to perform the current FFT shorter than $M*(1 - r)*T_s$ is desirable, with Ts being the sampling interval.

2. $M*\log_2(M)$ additions and $M*\log_2(M/2)$ multiplications for each FFT calculation performed on M real samples. It is worth stressing that, to achieve a satisfying frequency resolution in PSD estimation, both K and M should sufficiently be high, with a consequent increase in the memory requirement and computational burden.

As an example, let us consider a DVB-T signal with a center frequency of 36.13 MHz, sampled at 100 MS/s. To achieve a good frequency resolution, i.e., 24 kHz, and good metrological performance in the WOSA estimation (with an overlap ratio of 90% [6], [7]), each FFT has to be calculated on 4096 samples, thus requiring 49152 additions and 45056 multiplications. The storage capability of the meter has to allow at least 24576 real samples to be preserved.

The reduction of memory need and computational burden is possible only if the computational time is lower than 40.96 µs (i.e., 4096 samples at 100 MS/s). This is a pressing condition that typically requires the use of expensive multicore platforms.

5.2 Burg estimator

Starting from what Kay and Marple have presented in (Kay & Marple, 1981) and considering the same acquired sequence previously described, it is possible to demonstrate that the minimum number of samples to be stored is 2N+p+2, where p is the selected polynomial order, and the $3Np-p^2-2N-p$ real additions and $3Np-p^2-N+3p$ real multiplications are required for PSD estimation. As for the computational time, the estimation of the current PSD has to take a time interval that is not greater than $N*T_s$, because the whole acquired sequence is involved if real-time operations are pursued.

For N>345, both the computational burden and the required memory depth are higher than those peculiar to the WOSA estimator. To improve this aspect, an optimized implementation called "sequential estimation" that is able to update the PSD estimate whenever a new sample is available can be adopted.

5.3 Sequential Burg estimator

Let us consider (42) for p=k, and denote $a_{k,k}$ as K_k.

Making the time dependence explicit, the following relation is obtained:

$$K_k(N) = -\frac{2\sum_{s=k}^{N} e_{k-1}(s) b_{k-1}^*(s-1)}{\sum_{s=k}^{N} \left[\left| e_{k-1}(s) \right|^2 + \left| b_{k-1}(s-1) \right|^2 \right]} \quad (47)$$

where N is the time index. A time-update recursive formulation for (47) is given by

$$K_k(N+1) = K_k(N) +$$
$$-\frac{\left[K_k(N) \left(\left| e_{k-1}(N) \right|^2 + \left| b_{k-1}(N-1) \right|^2 \right) + 2e_k(N) b_k^*(N-1) \right]}{\sum_{s=k}^{N} \left[\left| e_k(s) \right|^2 + \left| b_k(s-1) \right|^2 \right]}. \quad (48)$$

Equation (48), combined with (24) and (25), for k=1,...,p and initial conditions $e_0(N)=b_0(N)=x_N$, suggests a sequential time-update algorithm for the reflection coefficients. After updating the reflection coefficient K_k, the k + 1 parameters $a_{k,1}$, $a_{k,2}$,..., $a_{k,k}$ and σ^2_k can be calculated using the Levinson–Durbin recursions. The order of complexity involved is $o(p^2)$, which could significantly worsen the overall computational burden if all coefficients and parameters have to be updated whenever a new sample is available.

Significant computational saving is granted by updating the reflection coefficients $K_k(N)$ at each new sample and all the other parameters after a suitable time interval. More specifically, 9p multiplications and 7p additions are required to update the reflection coefficients, whereas p^2 multiplications and p^2 additions are needed for all the other parameters.

As for the memory requirement, the minimum number of samples that the sequential implementation requires to be stored is equal to 7p. The result accounts for p reflection coefficients k_k; p polynomial coefficients $a_{p,m}$; p forward and p backward prediction errors e_k and b_k, respectively; p coefficients Λ_k and p coefficients Γ_k; and p estimates of the noise variance σ^2_k. The obtained value is significantly lower than that required by the non-sequential implementation.

According to the example previously given and considering a value of p equal to 46 (the optimum value previously found), it is possible to assert that 280 samples should be stored in the meter memory, and a computational burden of 360 multiplications and 280 additions should be required to estimate the reflection coefficients.

Hence, it is possible to state that the sequential version of the Burg estimator exhibits better performance than that peculiar to the WOSA estimator and is entitled to be the core of a cost effective DSP-based meter.

6. A cost effective DSP-based DVB-T power meter

In the following the development of a new cost-effective instrument for power measurement in DVB-T systems is proposed. It is based on the improved measurement method sketched in Fig. 13.

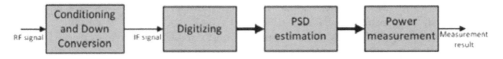

Fig. 13. Simplified block diagram of the proposed measurement method.

After a suitable conditioning and downconversion section, the input signal is digitized and its acquired samples processed in order to estimate its PSD. A proper measurement algorithm, operating on the achieved PSD, finally provides the desired power values.

As for the PSD estimation, the use of Autoregressive (AR) parametric estimators has shown the best trade-off between metrological performance and memory requirements with respect to nonparametric approaches (Angrisani et al., 2009). In addition, as described in (Angrisani et al., 2008-2), efficient implementations of AR parametric PSD estimators have been considered to drastically reduce the measurement time and to limit the memory needs over long observation intervals. A sequential Burg based estimation algorithm has been adopted because it is able to update estimates on data sample by data sample, (Kay & Marple, 1981),

(Marple, 1987) and warrants the best trade-off between computational burden and accuracy, as well as negligible bias and good repeatability.

The core of the proposed instrument is the PSD estimation section that has been implemented on a suitable Field Programmable Gate Array (FPGA) platform. These kinds of digital signal processors are particularly suited for algorithms, such as the sequential implementation of the Burg algorithm, which can exploit the massive parallelism offered by their architecture.

6.1 The hardware

A cost-effective hardware characterizes the meter. It consists of the following sections: (a) the tuner, (b) the analog-to-digital conversion, and (c) the FPGA–based computing platform. A simplified block diagram is depicted in Fig. 14.

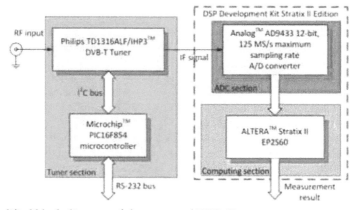

Fig. 14. Simplified block diagram of the proposed DVB–T power meter.

(a) The tuner section down–converts the incoming DVB–T signal, detected by a suitable antenna, to an intermediate frequency (IF) equal to 36.13 MHz. The task is performed by a Philips TD1316ALF/IHP3™ device, which is a single conversion tuner for digital terrestrial applications (NXP, 2006). It is provided with two IF outputs: a narrow-band one, equipped with a surface acoustic wave (SAW) filter and a gain controllable IF-amplifier, and a wideband output without any filter. Both the output circuits are regulated by an internal gain control loop with selectable takeover point settings via I2C bus. An external gain control is also possible if the internal loop is disabled. As far as the narrow-band IF output is concerned, it is possible to select the bandwidth of the SAW filter among 7 MHz and 8 MHz via I2C bus.

All these settings have been controlled and set up by a Microchip™ PIC16F854 microcontroller. It also provides a bus interface conversion between the serial I2C bus of the tuner and a common RS-232 one, allowing a simple connection with PC based environments. In this way, it is possible to set up the DVB–T channel, the SAW filter bandwidth, and the IF amplifier gain.

(b) The analog to digital conversion section is constituted by an Analog™ AD9433. This is a 12–bit monolithic sampling ADC that operates with conversion rates up to 125 MS/s. It is optimized for outstanding dynamic performance in wideband and high IF carrier systems (Analog, 2001).

(c) The computing platform is based on a FPGA chip. In particular the ALTERA™ Stratix II EP2S60 device mounted on the DSP Development Kit Stratix II Edition is considered (Altera, 2007). The chip is a fixed point FPGA that works with operative frequencies from tens of kHz to 400 MHz. This is obtained by using suitable Phase Locked Loops (PLLs) circuits. Other important features of the considered device are the 24176 Adaptive Logic Modules (ALMs), 48352 Adaptive Look-Up Tables (ALUTs), 36 Digital Signal Processing blocks (corresponding to 144 full–precision 18x18–bit multipliers) and 2544192 RAM bits.
The typical cost of the considered FPGA chip is of about $300.

6.2 The firmware
As far as the firmware of the computing platform is concerned, the sequential version of the Burg estimator proposed in (Angrisani et al., 2008-2) and summarized in the block diagram sketched in Fig. 15 is implemented. The firmware operates as follows. After a preliminary initialization phase, not reported in the block diagram, every time a sample is acquired a p-order cycle (i.e. a cycle repeated p times) is started. In each iteration, the estimation of the reflection coefficients (k_i), the σ_i, and the update of the prediction errors is performed. At this

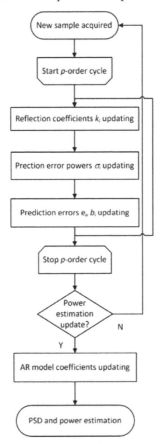

Fig. 15. Block diagram of the implemented FPGA firmware.

stage the user can select if to update the measured power and PSD or not. By updating the desired values of the new coefficients of the p-order model, the estimation of the PSD and channel power is performed, otherwise the p-order cycle begins when a new sample is made available from the ADC.

An order of p equal to 40 has been chosen, and a cascade of 40 sequential blocks implementing the p iterations of the cycle has been realized. The operative frequency of the FPGA device has been set equal to the sampling frequency (100 MS/s). All the implemented blocks warrant a calculation time lower than the sample period (10 ns), thus allowing the real time operation of the instrument. It is worth noting that the firmware architecture realizes a pipeline cascade of computing blocks. This operating way is allowed by the massive parallelism offered by the FPGA architecture. In particular, after a starting latency of 400 ns (i.e. 40 blocks for a sampling time of 10ns) the first measurement result is available. From this time instant on, measurement results are updated each 10 ns.

As far as the hardware resources are concerned, each one of the 40 blocks requires about 4525 ALUTs (Adaptive Look-Up Tables) and 2431 ALMs (Adaptive Logic Modules), thus resulting in a total of 18100 ALUTs and 97240 ALMs for the whole p-order cycle. These values impose the use of a multi-FPGA platform including 4 Stratix II EP2S60 FPGA chips operating in cascade arrangement.

8. References

Agilent (1991). *HP3589A Operator's Guide.* Hewlett--Packard Company. P/N 03589--90021. Santa Clara (CA), USA.

Agilent (2001). *E4406A VSA Series Transmitter Tester User's Guide.* Agilent Technol. P/N E4406-90177. Santa Clara (CA), USA.

Agilent (2003). *AN 1449--2: Fundamentals of RF and Microwave Power Measurements.* Agilent Technologies Inc. EN 5988−9214, Santa Clara (CA), USA.

Agilent (2003-2). *AN 1303: Spectrum Analyzer Measurements and Noise.* Agilent Technologies Inc. EN 5966--4008, Santa Clara (CA), USA.

Agilent (2004) *ESA-E Series Spectrum Analyzers Specification Guide.* Agilent Technol. P/N E4401-90472. Santa Clara (CA) USA.

Agilent (2005). *N1911A and N1912A P-Series Power Meters User's Guide.* Agilent Technol. P/N N1912-90002. Santa Clara (CA) USA.

Altera (2007). Stratix II Device Family Handbook, Altera Corporation. San Jose (CA), USA.

Analog (2001). 12-bit, 105/125 MSps IF sampling A/D converter AD9433, Analog Devices Inc. Norwood (MA), USA.

Angrisani L.; D'Apuzzo M. & D'Arco M. (2003). A new method for power measurements in digital wireless communication systems. *IEEE Trans. Instrum. Meas.*, Vol. 52, No. 4, (Aug. 2003) pp. 1097–1106.

Angrisani L.; Capriglione D.; Ferrigno L. & Miele G. (2006). Reliable and repeatable power measurements in DVB-T systems, *Proceedings IMTC 2006*, pp. 1867–1872, Sorrento, Italy, Apr. 24–27, 2006.

Angrisani L.; Capriglione D.; Ferrigno L. & Miele G. (2007). Power measurement in DVB-T systems: on the suitability of parametric spectral estimation in DSP–based meters., *Proceedings IMTC 2007*, pp. 1–6, Warsaw, Poland, May 1–3, 2007.

Angrisani L.; Capriglione D.; Ferrigno L. & Miele G. (2008). Power measurements in DVB–T systems: New proposal for enhancing reliability and repeatability. *IEEE Trans. Instrum. Meas.*, Vol. 57, No. 10, (Oct. 2008) pp. 2108–2117.

Angrisani L.; Capriglione D.; Ferrigno L. & Miele G. (2008-2) Sequential parametric spectral estimation for power measurements in DVB–T systems, *Proceedings I2MTC 2008*, pp. 314–319, Victoria (BC), Canada, May 2008.

Angrisani L.; Capriglione D.; Ferrigno L. & Miele G. (2009). Power measurement in DVB–T systems: On the suitability of parametric spectral estimation in DSP–based meters. *IEEE Trans. Instrum. Meas.*, Vol. 58, No. 1, (Jan. 2009) pp. 76–86.

Anritsu (2003). Vector Network Analyzers Technical Data Sheet ANRITSU 37100C/37200C/37300C, Rev. C.

Burg J. P. (1967). Maximum Entropy Spectral Analysis, *Proceedings of 37th Meeting Soc. Explor. Geophys.*, Oklahoma City (OK), USA, Oct. 31, 1967.

Daubechies I. (1992). *Ten Lectures on Wavelets*. SIAM, Philadelphia (PA), USA.

Donoho D. L. & Johnstone I. M. (1994). Ideal spatial adaptation by wavelet shrinkage. *Biometrika*, Vol. 81, No. 3, (Aug. 1994) pp. 425–455.

ETSI (2004). *EN 300 744: "Digital Video Broadcasting (DVB); Framing structure, channel coding and modulation for digital terrestrial television (V1.5.1)"*. ETSI Std, Sophia Antipolis, France.

ETSI (2004-2). *TR 101 190: "Digital Video Broadcasting (DVB); Implementation guidelines for DVB terrestrial services; Transmission aspects (V1.2.1)"*. ETSI Std, Sophia Antipolis, France.

Fischer (2004). *Digital Television – A Pratical Guide for Engineers*. Springer–Verlag, ISBN 3540011552, Heidelberg, Germany.

Jokinen H.; Ollila J. & Aumala O. (2004). On windowing effects in estimating averaged periodograms of noisy signals. *Measurement*, Vol. 28, No. 3, (Oct. 2000) pp. 197–207.

Kay S. M. & Marple S. L. (1981). Spectrum analysis—A modern perspective. *Proc. IEEE*, Vol. 69, No. 11, (Nov. 1981) pp. 1380–1419.

Makhoul J. (1975). Linear prediction: A tutorial review. *Proc. IEEE*, Vol. 63, No. 4, (Apr. 1975) pp. 561–580.

Marple L. (1980). A new autoregressive spectrum analysis algorithm. *IEEE Trans. Acoust., Speech, Signal Process.*, Vol. ASSP-28, No. 4, (Aug. 1980) pp. 441–454.

Marple S. L. (1987). *Digital Spectral Analysis With Applications*. Prentice-Hall, Englewood Cliffs (NJ), USA..

Morf M.; Dickinson B.; Kailath T. & Vieira A. (1977). Efficient solution of covariance equations for linear prediction. *IEEE Trans. Acoust., Speech, Signal Process.*, Vol. ASSP-25, No. 5, (Oct. 1977) pp. 429–433.

Moulin P. (1994), Wavelet thresholding techniques for power spectrum estimation. *IEEE Trans. Signal Process.*, Vol. 42, No. 11, (Nov. 1994) pp. 3126–3136.

NXP (2006). TD1300A(L)F mk3 Tuner modules for analog and digital terrestrial (OFDM) applications, NXP Semiconductors. Eindhoven, The Netherlands.

Nuttal A. H. (1976). Spectral analysis of a univariate process with bad data points, via maximum entropy and linear predictive techniques. *Naval Undersea Syst. Cent.*, New London (CT), USA, Tech. Rep. 5303.

Percival D. B. (1992). Simulating Gaussian random processes with specified spectra. *Comput. Sci. Stat.*, Vol. 24, (1992) pp. 534–538.

Reljin I.; Reljin B.; Papic V. & Kostic P. (1998). New window functions generated by means of time convolution—Spectral leakage error, *Proceedings of 9th MELECON*, pp. 878–881, Tel-Aviv, Israel, May 18–20, 1998.

Tektronix (2006). RSA3408A 8 GHz Real-Time Spectrum Analyzer User Manual, Tektronix Inc. 071-1617-01. Beaverton (OR), USA.

Ulrych T. J. & Clayton R. W. (1976). Time series modelling and maximum entropy. *Phys. Earth Planet. Inter.*, Vol. 12, No. 2/3, (Aug. 1976) pp. 188–200.

Walden A. T.; Percival D. B. & McCoy E. (1998). Spectrum estimation by wavelet thresholding of multitaper estimators. *IEEE Trans. Signal Process.*, Vol. 46, No. 12, (Dec. 1998) pp. 3153–3165.

Welch P. D. (1967). The Use of Fast Fourier Transform for the Estimation of Power Spectra: A Method Based on Time Averaging Over Short, Modified Periodograms. *IEEE Transactions on Audio and Electroacoustics*, Vol. AU-15, No. 2, (1967) pp. 70–73.

11

Combined Source and Channel Strategies for Optimized Video Communications

François-Xavier Coudoux[1,2,3], Patrick Corlay[1,2,3],
Marie Zwingelstein-Colin[1,2,3], Mohamed Gharbi[1,2,3],
Charlène Mouton-Goudemand[1,2,3,] and Marc-Georges Gazalet[1,2,3]
[1]*University Lille Nord de France, F-59000 Lille,*
[2]*UVHC, IEMN-DOAE, F-59313 Valenciennes,*
[3]*CNRS, UMR 8520, F-59650 Villeneuve d'Ascq,*
France

1. Introduction

Digital video is becoming more and more popular with the wide deployment of multimedia applications and networks. In the actual context of Universal Media Access (UMA), one of the main challenges is to flexibly deliver video content with the best perceived image quality for end-users having different available resources, access technologies and terminal capabilities. In this chapter, we look in detail at the basic source and channel coding techniques for digital video communication systems, and show how they can be combined efficiently in order to fulfill the quality of service (QoS) constraints of video communication applications. The chapter includes several illustrative examples and references on the related topics.

The chapter begins with an overview of digital video compression basics, including MPEG-2 and H.264/AVC. We discuss the most common coding artifacts due to digital compression, and show how the compressed bitstream is made more sensitive to channel errors (Section 2). Since both compression and channel distortions affect the final perceived video quality, image quality metrics are needed in order to estimate the resulting visual quality. Both subjective and objective metrics are presented briefly and discussed in section 3.

The second half of the chapter concerns channel coding and error control for video communication (Section 4). The most common existing techniques are presented, with a focus on forward error correction (FEC) and the hierarchical modulation, used in the DVB standard, for example. We show that such channel coding schemes can be used to increase the error resilience of compressed video data. For example, scalable video coding can be combined with hierarchical modulation in order to allow the most important information in the compressed video bitstream to be transmitted with better protection against channel distortions. Section 5 explains this concept of scalability, and gives the great benefits of this coding tool for robust video transmission. Since all the various bits of the transmitted video data don't have the same level of importance, unequal error protection (UEP), with its different priority levels can be applied successfully.

For a given application, it is necessary to determine the best combination of lossy compression and channel encoding schemes in order to offer the optimal quality to the end-user. In section 6, we illustrate such a combined source and channel approach by presenting a quality-oriented study for a broadband video distribution system using digital subscriber lines (DSL). Our system allows the coverage area for a given DSL infrastructure to be extended, thus increasing the number of potential end-users. This system applies an adaptation mechanism that determines the "bottleneck" bit-rate at which the reconstructed video has the best quality. First, we detail the complete system architecture, and then we explain how to jointly determine the optimal source and channel coding parameters. Finally, we report our experimental results in order to demonstrate the effectiveness of our system in terms of extended coverage and optimal quality for a given eligibility level. In section 7, we conclude the chapter with a discussion of the current issues and the perspectives for future research on video communications.

2. Digital video compression basics

Digital video signals generally include some redundant information. For still images, the redundancy is spatial and is due to the important correlation between neighboring pixels. In order to reduce this redundancy, lossless data compression can be used, thus allowing a reconstructed image equal to original image to be obtained. The compression ratio obtained with this method is generally very low, close to 2 or 3. Lossy compression insures that a higher compression ratio will be obtained. The deterioration of the reconstructed image is a function of the compression rate, constituting a rate-quality trade-off. Like transmitting still images, transmitting a video stream also requires compressing the video data. This compression is made possible by the video stream's redundancy, both spatial (intra-image) and temporal (inter-image).

To eliminate the redundancy — or, in other words, the correlation — between two images, each image in a video stream is predicted in terms of the previous and/or following images, with only the prediction error being encoded. The first image in the stream (or the group of pictures described below) is always fully encoded without reference to the other images; this is the "Intra" mode. This encoding without reference facilitates the synchronisation of the receiver (i.e., the decoder). The images that follow can be predicted by motion compensation, and the prediction error can be then encoded before being transmitted with motion vectors.

During the encoding process, a video stream is split into a group of pictures (GOP) of a fixed size. The GOP contains:

-   Intra-Picture (I): This is the first frame in each GOP. It is the reference, representing a still image, independent of other pictures.
-   Inter-Picture (P or B): These frames contain the motion-compensated differences. A P-frame is the prediction based on a previous image, while a B-frame is the result of the encoding from two images, one previous and one following. An error in a predicted picture will propagate up to the final image in the GOP. Figure 1 shows the typical structure of a MPEG sequence.

In digital video broadcasting, the widely used video coding standards MPEG-2 (Mitchell et al., 1996) and, more recently, H264/MPEG-4 (Wiegang et al., 2003) are both based on a hybrid encoding method using transformation and motion compensation (Tekalp, 1996), as illustrated in Fig. 2.

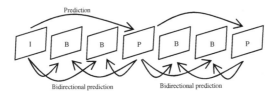

Fig. 1. Structure of MPEG sequence

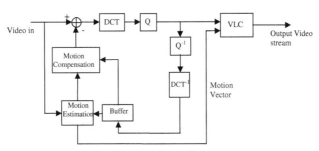

Fig. 2. Hybrid encoding method using transformation and motion compensation

Since the advent of the well-known JPEG algorithms (Pennebaker & Mitchell, 1993), the encoding process has consisted of several steps:

- *Conversion*: The image's color representation is converted into the Y (luminance) and Cr,Cb (chroma) components. The chroma resolution is generally reduced by a factor of 2 both horizontally and vertically.
- *Transformation*: The image is split into blocks, and each block (Intra-Picture or prediction residue) undergoes a discrete cosine transform (DCT). This transform exhibits excellent energy compaction for highly correlated images (Rabbani & Jones, 1991). DCT is independent of the signal to be encoded, and many fast DCT computation algorithms exist. A DCT applied on blocks of 8x8 pixels generates 64 coefficients. The first coefficient represents the constant value (DC), and the others represent waveforms at gradually increasing frequencies. In the most recent H.264 compression standard, the image can be decomposed into blocks of different sizes to adapt to local image statistics, and thus increase encoding efficiency.
- *Quantization*: The amplitudes of the frequency components generated in the previous step are quantized by removing small values. Quantization, which plays a major part in lossy compression, reduces the amount of data needed to represent an image. Since human eye is more sensible to errors in low frequency compared with high frequency (Glenn, 1993), each DCT frequency coefficient is quantized with an adequate step.
- *Scanning*: The quantized DCT coefficients are subjected to zigzag scanning, which arranges the DCT coefficients in order of increasing frequency.
- *Compression*: The resulting data is further compressed using entropic encoding, which is a form of lossless data compression. The entropy encoders compress data by replacing each value, defined by a fixed length, with a corresponding variable length codeword. Since the length of each codeword is an inverse function of its appearance probability, the most common value is represented by the shortest codeword. In JPEG and MPEG2, the entropic encoding is always Huffman encoding.

Typically, in the above encoding process, every 12th frame is an I-frame, and the GOP contains the image string, IBBPBBPBBPBB. The (I) intra-coded frame is split into block of 8 * 8 pixels, and each block is coded independently of the others, using the above encoding process. An Inter-frame (P or B) is divided into 16*16 pixel macro blocks. For each macro block, the motion is estimated in terms of the reference frame, and then the estimation error is compressed.

The H.264/AVC standard allows a compression ratio equal to twice MPEG-2 ratio to be obtained. The H.264/AVC standard is similar to the MPEG-2 standard, but with some rather important differences (Richardson, 2003):

- The intra-coded blocks are predicted in terms of the pixels located above and to the left (causal neighborhood) of those that have previously been encoded and reconstructed. The error prediction is then encoded.
- A deblocking filter is applied to blocks in a decoded video to improve the subjective visual quality.
- The motion is compensated by accounting for different block sizes (16×16, 16×8, 8×16, 8×8, 8×4, 4×8 and 4×4). Using previously-encoded frames as references is much more flexible than past standards, and the precision of the motion compensation is equal to quarter pixel.
- The entropy encoding is enhanced by providing Context-adaptive Binary Arithmetic Coding or Context-adaptive Variable-length Coding for residual data and Exponential-Golomb Coding for many of the syntax elements.

But… what about image quality?

We mentioned in the previous sub-section that digital video compression algorithms use lossy quantization in order to achieve high compression ratios. This quantization results in various kinds of coding artifacts, which may greatly affect the visual quality of the reconstructed video signal, especially for low bit-rate coding. The compression artifacts and their visual significance have been widely studied in the literature. Yuen (1998) provides a comprehensive classification and analysis of most coding artifacts in digital video, compressed using MC/DPCM/block-based DCT hybrid coding methods. In particular, this author shows how the visual impact of coding artifacts is strongly related to the spatial and temporal characteristics, both local and global, of the video sequence, as well as the properties of the human visual system (HVS).

Among the various coding artifacts, *blocking effect* (also called *blockiness*) is the most well-known distortion introduced by video compression algorithms. The blocking effect manifests itself as a discontinuity located at boundaries between adjacent blocks. This spurious phenomenon is due to the fact that common block-based compression algorithms encode adjacent blocks as independent units without taking into account the correlation that exists between them. Hence, at the decoding stage, the quantization error differs from one block to another, resulting in inter-block discontinuities. Figure 3 illustrates this particular coding distortion, which is clearly visible on the face and the building in the background.

This blocking effect is very annoying and mainly affects the visual perception of end-users. The perceptual relevance of this distortion is strongly related to HVS sensitivity: the regular geometric spacing of blocks, the specific horizontal or vertical alignment of block edges, and the spatial frequency of repeated blocks are highly apparent to the human eye. Because of its visual prominence, several methods have been proposed in order to reduce the visibility of the blocking effect in compressed images or sequences. (See the post-processing algorithms proposed by Ramamurthi (1986), Lee (1998) or Coudoux (2001), for example.) Recently, the H.264/AVC codec has introduced a deblocking filter as a standardized tool to reduce the visibility of this coding artifact.

Fig. 3. Illustrative example of the blocking effect (*Foreman* sequence, MPEG-2, QCIF@128Kbps)

Unfortunately, digital image and video impairments are not restricted to coding artifacts, since errors may also occur when transmitting compressed video bitstreams over a noisy channel. Once the video sequence has been compressed by the encoder, the resulting bitstream is typically packetized in the network adaptation layer using transport protocols, such as ATM or TCP/IP, and then the packets are sent over the transmission network.

Different types of impairments can occur in transmissions over noisy channels: packets may be corrupted, or they may be affected by extensive delays that are incompatible with video applications. In all cases, erroneous packets are considered to be lost and are not available for decoding. Depending on the packet size, this loss may corrupt a limited part of a decoded picture, the entire picture or, in the worst case, a complete group of pictures. In the latter case, error concealment techniques can be used at the decoding stage to limit the visual impact of channel errors. In addition, error control mechanisms may fail at the transport level. In this case, errors occur when decoding at the application level. The wide variety of configurations leads to very different visual distortions depending on the kind of corrupted data. Figure 4 shows examples of localized false macroblocks, erroneous or misaligned slices, and frozen parts of pictures. For example, an erroneous VLC may be decoded as a false value and will subsequently result in a localized distortion in the display.

Fig. 4. Examples of visual impairments due to transmission errors (*Foreman* sequence, MPEG-2, QCIF@128Kbps, BER = 10-4)

Visual impairments due to transmission errors generally have a much more severe effect on end-user quality, compared to compression artifacts. In particular, the use of compression techniques based on spatial (e.g., differential encoding of DC coefficient) and temporal (e.g., MC) prediction makes the compressed bitstream very sensitive to channel errors, due to spatial or temporal loss propagation of the corrupted data up to the next synchronization point (e.g., end of slice/intra-frame).

3. Image quality metrics

Digital video quality obviously constitutes one of the key points for any video service to insure a satisfying level of quality for the end-user. For this reason, it is crucial for researchers, broadcasters and network providers to be able to reliably assess and control the perceived video quality. There are two main approaches to image and video quality assessment: the first one relies on subjective evaluation metrics, and the second one is based on objective quality metrics. These two approaches are described in the following sub-sections.

3.1 Subjective metrics

The best way to measure image quality as perceived by a human observer is to use the subjective viewing experience of human observers themselves. The International Telecommunication Union (ITU) has developed and standardized several subjective methods that provide reliable test conditions and measurements. The ITU recommendations, ITU-R Rec. BT.500-11 and ITU-T Rec. P.910, specify:

- the test conditions (e.g., viewing distance, observer selection process, test material),
- the evaluation procedure (e.g., single vs. double stimuli, type of rating scale), and
- the methods for exploiting the data collected (e.g., statistical tools used for accurate analysis of viewers scores).

For example, ITU-R Rec. BT500-11 specifies the Double Stimulus Impairment Scale (DSIS) method shown in Figure 5. With this method, the reference and the test sequence are shown only once, and the observers have to evaluate the corresponding impairment using a five-level impairment scale. A mean opinion score (MOS) is obtained by averaging the evaluations/scores of all observers. More details on subjective video quality assessment are available in the reference books by Wu (2005) and Winkler (2005).

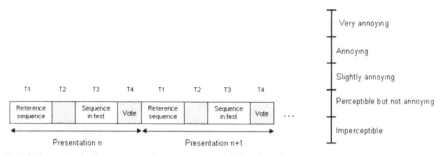

Fig. 5. DSIS method: a) presentation sequence; b) five-level impairment scale

Without any doubt, subjective visual quality assessment is the most correlated with human perception. However, this approach has several drawbacks: it is complex, time-consuming and expensive. Thus, alternative solutions relying on objective metrics are often preferred to such subjective methods. In practice, objective metrics can be used at different places in the broadcasting chain to assess and monitor video quality. They can also be used to optimize the different components of a video communication system, as illustrated later in Section 6.

Nonetheless, in order to be meaningful, objective metrics should be well correlated with the results obtained from the subjective methods.

3.2 Objective metrics

Objective metrics for assessing image and video quality can be divided into three distinct groups:
- signal-based methods,
- structural methods, and
- HVS-based methods.

The most common signal-based method is the Peak Signal-to-Noise Ratio (PSNR), expressed in decibels (dB), and defined as:

$$PSNR(dB) = 10.\log_{10} (d^2/MSE) \tag{1}$$

where d = 255 for 8-bit encoded picture, and MSE is the mean squared error, defined as:

$$MSE = \frac{1}{M.N.T} \sum_{i=1}^{M} \sum_{j=1}^{N} \sum_{k=1}^{T} \left(f_0(i,j,k) - f_d(i,j,k) \right)^2 \tag{2}$$

where f_0 and f_d are the pictures from the original and distorted sequence, respectively. Parameters M and N represent the size (in pixels) of each picture, the video sequence being made up of T pictures. Unfortunately, this objective metric has been shown to be poorly correlated with human visual assessment (Girod, 1993). PSNR-like metrics do not translate the visibility of the distortions, which depend on picture content, the location of the distortions and the HVS masking properties. For example, the two images presented below have the same PSNR numerical value, although the one located on the left side clearly exhibits worst visual quality (especially due to strong blocking artifacts).

Fig. 6. Image compressed by the JPEG algorithm using high-frequency emphasis (left) and Standard Y (right) quantization tables. Both images have the same PSNR: 30.7 dB.

Recently, the Structural SIMilarity (SSIM) method was proposed by Wang et al. (Wang, 2004a). Instead of measuring a simple pixel-by-pixel difference like MSE does, SSIM relies on the fact that human perception depends greatly on the presence of structures inside the video scene: any change in these structures will affect the way that a human observer will perceive the scene. Practically, SSIM is locally computed as a combination of three similarity indicators, one for luminance (based on local means), one for contrast (based on local variance), and one for structural information (based on local covariance). The SSIM values are averaged over the entire image in order to give a single SSIM index by picture. In the case of video sequences, a global note is computed by appropriate weighted averaging of all the pictures in the sequence, as described by Wang et al. (Wang, 2004b). These authors claimed that the SSIM index gives very satisfying correlation results with respect to subjective assessment methods.

Finally, the most preferred methods model Human Visual System (HVS) properties and then integrate them into the objective metric. There has been plenty of research done on HVS-based objective quality metrics since the beginning of 1970s (e.g., Mannos, 1974; Faugeras, 1979; Lukas, 1982). Such methods can be divided into 2 groups:

- *single-channel methods* -- in single-channel methods, the HVS is modelled as a single spatial filter and is characterized by its Contrast Sensitivity Function (CSF). The final metric is generally obtained by weighting the error signal based on HVS sensitivity.

- *multi-channel methods* -- multi-channel methods are more complex because they assume that the visual signal is processed by separate spatial frequency channels. In the past, several multi-channel vision models have been developed by researchers, including Daly (1993) and Watson (2001), for example. These models generally integrate a more complete representation of significant visual phenomena, such as spatiotemporal masking or orientation selectivity. The global score is typically obtained by error pooling using Minkowski summation. Though more complex, these quality metrics provide better prediction accuracy.

Created in 1997, the Video Quality Expert Group (VQEG) has for the last ten years been evaluating the capacity of various video quality metrics to predict subjective quality ratings, as measured by MOS. Many vision-based video quality metrics have been shown to achieve very good correlation scores with MOS, outperforming the PSNR method. In particular, the so-called Video Quality Metric (VQM) has been recently included in two international Recommendations (Pinson, 2004). Nevertheless, for the moment, no method has ever been judged optimal and subjective rating remains the only reference method for accurately evaluating video quality.

4. Channel coding and error control for video communications

Once a digital video has been appropriately coded and compressed (as described in the previous sections), the concern becomes how to reliably transmit this video over a transmission medium — the channel — that by its nature deteriorates the signal quality. This section presents and analyzes the techniques used to improve digital video transmission quality.

For a given compression algorithm, compressed video quality is clearly a monotone increasing function of the bit-rate: the higher the bit-rate, the higher the video quality. In digital communications, transmission quality is measured as the probability of one bit being flipped during the transmission process – a received "1" corresponding to a transmitted "0" and vice-versa. This probability is referred to as the Bit Error Rate (BER). The BER is a monotone decreasing function of the Signal-to-Noise Ratio (SNR) of the transmission, and a monotone increasing function of the bit-rate. Thus, the higher the video bit-rate, the higher the video quality before transmission but also the higher the BER of the transmission (which results in poor quality of the received video). Thus, a good compromise has to be found for the bit-rate so that the overall video quality deterioration (i.e., the deterioration inherent to the compression algorithm and degradation inherent to the transmission) is acceptable.

In the context of digital video transmission — not to be confused with digital communications in general — the main question is " What are the properties that are specific to video in terms of its transmission?". One answer is that all the bits in a digital video bitstream do not have the same importance in terms of video quality, which means that the consequences of transmission failure with respect to the video quality can change dramatically depending on which bit(s) in the bitstream fail.

A few examples

- In Pulse Code Modulation (PCM) source coding, each video sample is quantified and binary coded. Clearly, the loss of the least significant bits (LSB) will only slightly degrade its quality, whereas the loss of the most significant bits (MSB) will lead to totally erroneous reconstructed video signal. Thus, the most significant bits are of greater importance than the least significant bits in terms of video transmission.
- In the Discrete Cosine Transform (DCT) coding used for MPEG formats, high-frequency coefficients generally correspond to fine granularity details in the images, whereas low-frequency coefficients correspond to the structure of the images (Richardson, 2003). Thus, in terms of video transmission, low-frequency coefficients can be considered to be of greater importance than high-frequency coefficients.
- In the packetization and framing process inherent to every digital system, headers are added to the video information in order to insure its proper progress in the network, as well as its decoding at the destination. These headers are of crucial importance, since their loss would involve a transmission or decoding failure of a complete packet of video data (corresponding to from a part of an image to several consecutive images). Thus, in terms of video transmission, headers are of greater importance than the other bits transmitted.

Aware of that some bits are more important than others, recent video compression standards (Richardson, 2003) generally make it possible to partition these bits into several different bitstreams, generally 2 or 3. This means that, from the transmission system design perspective, which is the one covered in this section, the idea is to globally optimize the quality of a video transmission by:

- Partitioning the bits transmitted into several bitstreams of different importance, if this has not already been done at the source coding level (possible with the MPEG-2 or H.264 formats – See Section 5) , then
- Providing a way to give different transmission BERs to these bitstreams, where the values of the BERs shall be adapted to the relative importance of the bitstreams. In the following, we use the term *Unequal Error Protection* (UEP) to speak of the transmission techniques that provide different BERs to different bitstreams in a single video sequence.

UEP transmission techniques can have several different effects. For example, they can either improve the video quality of a given user or, for a fixed video quality, extend the range of users eligible for a video service. For example, in a Asymmetric Digital Subscriber Line (ADSL) environment, the UEP techniques would allow users with a poor-quality subscriber line to benefit video services, which would have been impossible in a traditional transmission environment in which all bits are transmitted with the same BER.

Another desirable feature of UEP digital video transmission systems are their ability to provide a simulcast of different video formats — for example, the Standard Definition (SD) and High Definition (HD) formats. This allows a graceful degradation of the video quality as the channel quality degrades, which is frequently the case in mobile communications. It is also an elegant means of adapting the video quality to the receiver's screen definition level.

Although UEP techniques for the different video bitstreams can be considered at the different layers of the Open System Interconnection (OSI) model, we focus on the techniques that do it at the physical layer. This section is organized as follows. In section 4.1, we review the basic modulation principles, which are used to map digital information onto an analog waveform constituted of a sequence of successive symbols. We also examine how the BER is related to the transmission link's signal-to-noise ratio, as well as to the number of information bits conveyed by each symbol. In section 4.2, we focus on UEP modulation techniques. Two independent types of modulation are presented: hierarchical modulation (e.g., Hierarchical Quadrature Amplitude Modulation (HQAM)) and multi-carrier modulation (e.g., Orthogonal frequency-division multiplexing (OFDM)). We also evoke the possibility of using the two types in combination (e.g., HQAM-OFDM). Since the BER performance achieved by any modulation scheme is generally insufficient in terms of the application requirements, forward error correction (FEC) techniques are usually necessary to insure an acceptable quality of service. In section 4.3, we introduce the FEC principles, as well as the UEP techniques that operate at the FEC layer.

4.1 Modulation basics

This subsection does not aim to cover the subject of modulation exhaustively like (Proakis, 1995) did, but rather to provide the essential information needed to understand the techniques developed in the subsequent subsections.

Modulation is the operation that makes the link between digital information – a sequence of bits at a given bit-rate $1/T_b$, where T_b is the duration of one bit – and an analog waveform appropriate for transmission over a channel. Generally, bits are not transmitted one at a time, but are rather grouped in small quantities (typically 2 to 10 bits), called symbols, which are transmitted sequentially. For a modulation scheme that maps b bits into one symbol, the symbol duration will be $T=b\times T_b$, resulting in a symbol rate of $1/T$ bauds.

As an example, let us consider the rectangular Quadrature Amplitude Modulation with eight modulation levels (8-QAM). A temporal representation of the modulated signal appears in Figure 7a. In this figure, the symbols are formed of $\log_2(8)$ = 3 bits. These bits are used to code the amplitudes of two orthogonal waves of the same frequency, or to code the amplitude A and the phase π of a single wave, since: $x\cos(2\pi f_0 t) + y\cos(2\pi f_0 t) =$

$A\cos(2\pi f_0 t + \Theta)$, where: $A = \sqrt{x^2 + y^2}$, and: $\Theta = \arctan(y/x)$.

A signal-space representation of the signal, called the *constellation*, is a useful visualization tool that facilitates the analytical evaluation of the modulation scheme's performance (Figure 7b). A constellation represents the set of possible values for the amplitude and phase of the sinusoid in the complex plan - 8 points for the 8-QAM constellation. In Figure 7b, the point of the constellation corresponding to each symbol of the transmitted waveform is highlighted in red.

This notion of *symbol* leads to defining a second transmission quality parameter, which is of great practical importance: Symbol Error Rate (SER), or the probability that a symbol will be received erroneously. The relationship between the SER and the BER depends on the way the bits are mapped on each symbol. Generally, this mapping is optimized in order that an erroneous symbol results in no more than one erroneous bit (Gray mapping). Such general cases yield the relation BER = SER/b, where b is the number of bits per symbol. Figure 8 illustrates a Karnaugh-style Gray map for the 8-QAM constellation. If this map was used to construct the modulated signal of Figure 7a, the corresponding transmitted information binary sequence would be ...011110000...

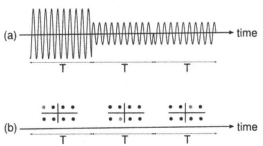

Fig. 7. Different representations of a 8-QAM modulated signal: a) temporal representation; b) signal-space representation (i.e., a constellation)

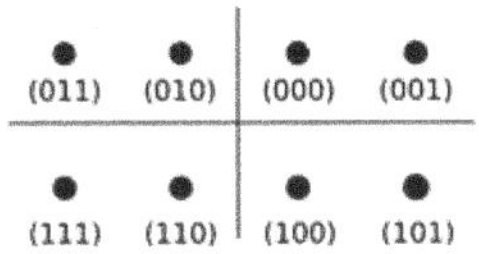

$$
\begin{array}{cccc}
\bullet & \bullet & \bigm| \bullet & \bullet \\
(011) & (010) & (000) & (001) \\[4pt]
\bullet & \bullet & \bigm| \bullet & \bullet \\
(111) & (110) & (100) & (101)
\end{array}
$$

Fig. 8. Karnaugh-style Gray map of a 8-QAM constellation.

For general QAM transmissions over the additive white Gaussian noise channel, the SER can be shown to be related to the distance d between nearest points in the constellation to the noise standard deviation ratio $sigma$, or to the SNR channel and to the number of bits per symbol. This relationship is expressed by the equation (Proakis, 1995):

$SER = 4\beta Q(\alpha)(1 - Q(\alpha))$, where: $\alpha = \sqrt{3SNR/(2^b - 1)}$ and: $\beta = 1 - 2^{-b/2}$. In this equation, the β term represents the average number or nearest neighbors of a constellation point. Figure 9 presents the SER performance of several classical QAM modulations.

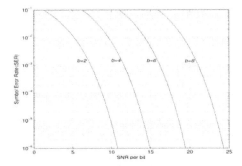

Fig. 9. SER performance of several classic QAM modulations

4.2 Achieving unequal error protection at the modulation level: examples of HQAM, OFDM and HQAM-OFDM combinations

Several possible methods for achieving unequal error protection during modulation are described in this subsection. One possibility is to use hierarchical modulation methods, such as HQAM. The idea of hierarchical modulation comes from the fact that the SER is directly related to the distance between nearest points in the constellation. Figure 10 illustrates the principle, using the example of a two-level 4/8-HQAM and its associated Karnaugh-style Gray map of two highly important bits and two less important bits. As the figure shows, the points are grouped into four clouds, where the distance between two nearest points in a cloud is d_2 and the distance between clouds is $d_1 > d_2$. The map indicates that the least significant bits serve to differentiate between the four points within each cloud and that the two most significant bits serve to differentiate between the clouds. Hence, the BER for the least significant bits is directly related to the distance d_2. For the two most significant bits, the constellation can also be seen as a 4-QAM constellation with distance between points equal to $d_1 + d_2/2$, where $d_2/2$ can be seen as a noise component since it contains no information about these most significant bits.

The ratio $\lambda = d_2/d_1$ controls the bits' relative priority. When $\lambda = 0$, the result is a uniform 4-QAM (the two least significant bits are merely discarded); when $\lambda = 1$, the result is a uniform 8-QAM (equal priority for all bits). When $0 < \lambda < 1$, the most significant bits have a greater priority.

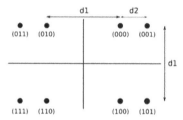

Fig. 10. 8-HQAM constellation and Karnaugh-style Gray map for two most significant bits and one least significant bit

BER analytical expressions have been formulated by Vitthaladevuni (2001) for the class of 4/M-HQAM constellations, in which the number of clouds is 4 (i.e., $\log_2(4)=2$ most significant bits) and the number of points within each cloud is M (i.e., $\log_2(M)$ least significant bits). Clearly, the BER expressions are related to the ratio d_2/d_1, which, in practice, must be chosen appropriately according to the requirements of the video bitstreams. For the 4/16-HQAM constellations, these BERs can be approximated as:

$$BER_{most\_significant} = \frac{1}{4}\left(erfc\left(\frac{d_1}{\sqrt{N_0}}\right) + erfc\left(\frac{d_1 + 2d_2}{\sqrt{N_0}}\right)\right)$$

$$BER_{less\_significant} = \frac{1}{4}\left(erfc\left(\frac{d_2}{\sqrt{N_0}}\right) + erfc\left(\frac{2d_1 + d_2}{\sqrt{N_0}}\right) - erfc\left(\frac{2d_1 + 3d_2}{\sqrt{N_0}}\right)\right)$$

(3)

Figure 11 illustrates these BERs for a 4/16-HQAM constellation as a function of the SNR, for a ratio of lambda=d_2/d_1=0.8.

A second possibility for achieving unequal error protection during modulation is based on multi-carrier modulation methods, such as DMT or OFDM. These methods are used extensively in current digital transmission systems (e.g., DVB, ADSL, Wimax, LTE). In DMT and OFDM, a Quadrature Amplitude Modulation (QAM) is carried out on a sub-channel, using IFFT/FFT processing (Starr, 1999). For a multi-carrier symbol rate $1/T$, the spacing between the sub-channels is also $1/T$, and the overall bandwidth is N/T, where N is half the size of the IFFT/FFT used for processing. One of the key issues in designing efficient DMT systems is the bit-loading algorithm that optimizes the bit and power allocation over the QAM sub-channels, based on their power gains and noise levels.

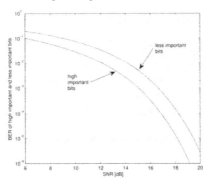

Fig. 11. Approximate BERs of a 4/16-HQAM constellation as a function of the SNR ($\lambda=d_2/d_1=0.8$)

Due to their multi-carrier structure, DMT and OFDM are inherently adapted to provide Frequency Division Multiplexing (FDM) of the different bitstreams. Thus, a natural approach for providing UEP is to multiplex the different streams using FDM, adapting the bit-loading algorithm so that it will provide different BERs for the different bitstreams. Generally, these algorithms assign the "best" sub-carriers to the bits of higher importance, and the other ones to the less important bits, as is suggested by the theoretical water-filling analysis proposed by Starr (1999). Such approaches have been studied by Zheng (2000) and Goudemand (2006), who point out different quality/complexity trade-offs. Figure 12 shows the bit-allocation produced by Zheng's algorithm (2000) for unequal error protection in an ADSL environment, using the European Telecommunications Standards Institute's loop 2 channel model (ETSI, 1996) and two video bitstreams from a data-partitioning MPEG-2 video coder at 6 Mbps (3.6 Mbps for the highly important bitstream and 2.4 Mbps for the less important one). The BERs are 10^{-7} and 10^{-4} respectively.

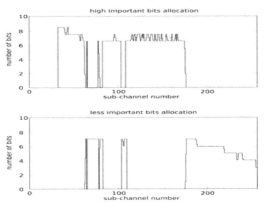

Fig. 12. Bit-allocation result for FDM unequal error protection based on DMT modulation (Goudemand, 2006)

Another possibility for achieving unequal error protection on multi-carrier transmission systems using DMT and OFDM is to combine the two methods described above. This method, called *hierarchical multi-carrier modulation*, involves modulating each sub-carrier using HQAM so that, unlike the pure FDM approach, each sub-channel carries both important and less important bits with embedded unequal error protection. The bit and power allocation over hierarchical multi-carrier modulation minimizes the total transmitted power while maintaining a constant bit-rate and BER for each bitstream. In practice, the bit and power allocation is calculated in two steps, providing two-level unequal error protection. The first step allocates higher priority bits and their corresponding power, and the second one allocates the remaining less important bits (Goudemand1, 2006).

As usual, the bit-loading algorithm must be computationally efficient and must reflect the water-filling principle, in that more bits must be allocated to the sub-channels with the lowest noise levels. Figure 13 shows a typical bit allocation in a hierarchical multi-carrier modulation system.

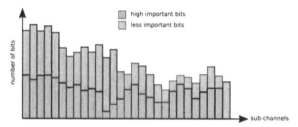

Fig. 13. A typical bit allocation for a hierarchical multi-carrier system

4.3 Achieving unequal error protection at the FEC level

Subsection 4.1 presented our analysis of SER and BER performance in general QAM modulation. This performance is generally insufficient for the needs of video communication. It is thus interesting to compare the bit-rate of a QAM modulation (b bits/symbol) to the maximum bit-rate that could theoretically be transmitted reliably (i.e., at a BER as close to zero as desired) at the same SNR. This maximum bit-rate is known as the channel capacity: $c=\log2(1+SNR)$ bits/symbol (Shannon, 1948). Figure 14 facilitates this comparison. In the figure, the SER is plotted as a function of the ratio bit-rate/channel capacity=b/c for different channel capacity values.

Clearly, satisfactory values of the BER for video transmission (below 10^{-4}) can be achieved at a rate that is very far from the channel capacity. In order to improve transmission efficiency (i.e., in order to achieve sufficiently low BER at rates close to the channel capacity), error correcting codes have to be used. These error correcting codes operate by adding controlled redundancy to the information bits so that only certain bit patterns can be transmitted. The error correcting decoder, which is aware of these patterns, will then be able to detect and even correct some erroneous bits.

Among the class of error correcting codes, linear block codes, also known as Forward Error Correction (FEC) codes, are of practical importance (Costello, 1998). One of them, the Reed-Solomon codes, are used extensively in recent popular communication systems, such as DVB or ADSL. Each Reed-Solomon block code is formed of N bytes, of which K bytes are information bytes and (N-K) bytes are redundancy bytes. Figure 15 illustrates the error correcting capabilities of such codes.

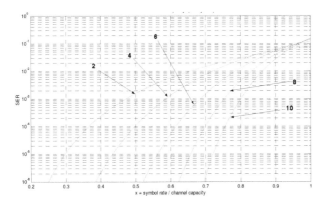

Fig. 14. QAM SER without FEC, as a function of the ratio bit-rate/channel capacity. Parameter: channel capacity (bit/symbol).

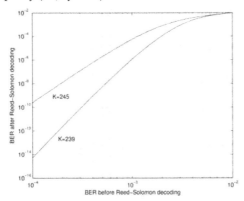

Fig. 15. Error correcting capabilities of some Reed-Solomon codes (N=255,K)

Including FEC in video transmission systems offers new possibilities for achieving UEP. Instead of, or in addition to, providing UEP at the modulation level, UEP can easily be provided at the FEC level by adding different FEC redundancies (and thus different error correction capabilities) to the bits, according to their perceptual importance.

Figure 16 provides a synoptic version of such a UEP approach in the context of a DMT + Reed-Solomon FEC coding, comparing it to a classic DMT + Reed-Solomon FEC coding without UEP.

In this figure, RH and RL, respectively, represent the bit-rates of the bitstreams of higher and lesser importance, and (N_H,K_H) and (N_L,K_L) represent the Reed-Solomon parameters of these two bitstreams. For the classic transmission scheme, $R_0=R_H+R_L$ is the bit-rate, and (N_0,K_0) are the Reed-Solomon parameters. For the two UEP approaches, the DMT modulators are the same, with the same bit and power loading, which makes the BER before Reed-Solomon decoding the same in both approaches.

In order to evaluate the possibilities of this approach to UEP, the cumulative redundancy of the two Reed-Solomon codes, (N_H,K_H) and (N_L,K_L), shall equal the redundancy of (N_0,K_0) (i.e., $R_0.N_0/K_0=R_H.N_H/K_H+R_L.N_L/K_L$). Figure 17 illustrates the relative variations of the BER of the highly important bits (BER_H) versus the relative variations of the BER of the less important bits (BER_L), in terms of the BER of the classic method without UEP (BER_0) for an ADSL environment (ANSI CSA5 test loop) in which $(N_0,K_0)=(255,239)$ and for different proportions of less important bits (10% to 50%).

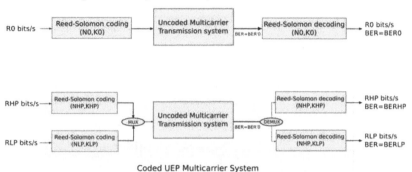

Coded UEP Multicarrier System

Fig. 16. Synoptic version of a DMT system using FEC with UEP and a classic DMT system using FEC without UEP.

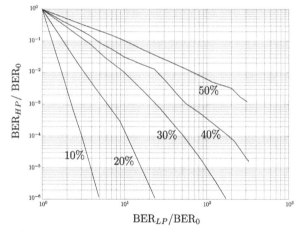

Fig. 17. Evaluation of the possibilities offered by providing unequal error protection at the FEC level.

More sophisticated UEP methods based on error control codes have been explored in the literature. In particular, the UEP methods using multilevel codes and multistage decoding accomplish Unequal Error Protection quite satisfactorily (Wachsmann, 1999; Chui, 2008).

5. Scalability tools

In the previous section, we underlined the fact that UEP with different priority levels can be applied successfully in modern video transmission systems to provide flexibility as well as the QoS level required by end-users. This is true because not all the various bits of the transmitted video data streams have the same importance with respect to reconstructed video quality. Recently, digital video compression standards have introduced the concept of *scalability* to allow video content to be encoded with different levels of resolution and different levels of quality. In this section, we provide a brief overview of the existing scalability modes, as well as the corresponding coding tools.

Typically, video coding standards propose four main scalability modes: SNR scalability, spatial scalability, temporal scalability and data partioning. Each of the modes is presented briefly below, with more detail given for the first and the last modes.

SNR scalability allows the delivery of a video bitstream compressed into several separate layers with the same spatio-temporal resolution but different quality levels. The base layer, which contains a reduced quality version of the encoded video signal, is typically transmitted with a high protection level — for example, using one of the techniques described in Section 4 — to guarantee that video will be decoded even with high error rates. Then, each additional layer enhances the quality of the reconstructed video, but is transmitted with a reduced protection level. Hence, SNR scalability provides graceful degradation of decoded video according to the transmission quality.

A block diagram of a SNR scalable video encoder is shown in Figure 18. First, the base layer is encoded using coarse quantization. Then, this base layer is decoded, and the residual error between the reconstructed base layer and the original video signal, which constitutes the enhancement layer, is computed and then re-encoded during a second encoding stage, using finer quantization.

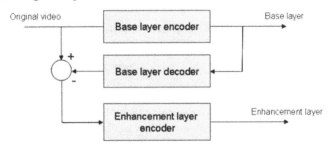

Fig. 18. Block diagram of a SNR scalable video encoder.

Other scalability tools rely on the same basic scheme. With *spatial scalability*, however, the video signal is encoded into separate streams corresponding to different spatial resolutions. The base layer consists of an encoded version of the video signal at lowest spatial resolution. Then, each enhancement layer contains additional data related to higher resolutions.

Temporal scalability allows the simultaneous delivery of video signals with different frame rates.

The last mode, *data partitioning* (DP) (Mathew & Arnold, 1999), is quite similar to SNR scalability. The video signal is encoded into two separate bitstreams, with the additional layer allowing increased video quality if received at the decoding stage. However, data partitioning has the great advantage of being easier to implement. In fact, the DP mode is applied directly to the encoded bitstream and does not require any significant modification of the codec. In MPEG-2, the compressed video bitstream is split into two separate streams: the first one, corresponding to the base layer, contains the most important data for each of the 8x8 encoded blocks, such as low frequencies DCT coefficients or motion vectors. The remaining high frequency DCT coefficients, corresponding to details of each block, constitute the enhancement layer. The priority breakpoint (PBP) parameter marks the place where the bitstream is split into two parts. In the next section, we demonstrate that data partitioning is a great advantage for increasing error resilience, if unequal error protection is applied before transmission.

Since 2003, the scalability concept has been put forward through the design of the scalable video coding (SVC) amendment of the H.264/AVC standard. The SVC technology is based on the coding tools available in H.264/AVC, but includes also specific hierarchical and inter-layer predictive coding techniques. For further details on SVC, see (Schwarz et al., 2007) and (Huang et al., 2007). SVC provides a way to encode a video sequence into a single compressed bit-stream composed of a H.264/AVC compatible base layer and multiple additional layers that enhance spatial resolution, frame rate and quality. It is therefore possible to extract on-the-fly (inside the network or at the terminal) a limited number of layers in order to decode video with given resolution and quality level. Another obvious advantage of SVC is that UEP can be applied efficiently to the different parts of the bit stream having different importance in terms of reconstructed video quality. Hence, using SVC allows supporting a broad range of devices with different capabilities (display resolution, battery power) and access networks. Several papers on SVC applications have been proposed recently in the literature (Schierl et al., 2006) (Kouadio et al., 2008) (Thang et al., 2008). For example, Hellge et al. propose to combine of the spatial and SNR scalability features of SVC with the hierarchical modulation of DVB-H (Hellge et al., 2009). The authors show the benefits of jointly using SVC with hierarchical modulation in terms of error robustness or increased number of services.

6. Application to digital video delivery over digital subscriber lines

In the following Section, we present a complete quality-oriented transmission system for video distribution over DSL, optimized by applying techniques previously described.

The diffusion of audiovisual content, or Video on Demand (VoD), was one of the major objectives in the development of ADSL technology. This technology was initially a huge success for high-speed internet access and gaming. With increased bit-rates, in recent years, there has been a return to one of the original objectives, which was audio and video diffusion through ADSL.

ADSL involves transmission over the physical link portion of the telephone network, called subscriber loop, which connects DSL Multiplexer (DSLAM) located at the central office (CO) and Customer Premises Equipment (CPE) on the Subscriber side. The subscriber loop consists of a twisted-pair copper line. ADSL coexists with voiceband service by using the high frequency band above the one allocated to Plain Old Telephony Services (POTS). This relatively inexpensive technology benefits from the existence of a reliable widespread copper-wire infrastructure. Typically, several customer lines from the same CO ends at the same DSLAM, and the DSLAM outputs are connected to a high-speed Internet backbone line. The modulation used by International Telecommunications Union (ITU) in various standardized versions of ADSL is the DMT (see paragraph 4).

ADSL experiments and knowledge have resulted in several developments (e.g., ADSL1, ADSL2, ADSL2+). Initially, ADSL had a theoretical maximum bit-rate of about 6 Mb/s, which was rapidly multiplied by a factor of almost five in ADSL2+. For a fixed error rate and a fixed transmission power, throughput is strongly dependent on the line characteristics:

- attenuation of the copper line, which depends on line length; and
- noise, including Near End CrossTalk and Far End CrossTalk interference from lines in a same bundle, and impulsive noise.

Unfortunately, high bit-rates are available only to users located near the DSLAM. For users more than 2.5 kilometers from the CO, line attenuation restricts the bit-rate so that it rarely exceeds 4 Mbps. As a result, the subscribers cannot all receive the same bit-rate with the same error rate. If a video is sent with the same bit-rate for all the subscribers, then each subscriber receives the video at a different error rate, which may cause unacceptable visual degradations for a lot of users if the error rate is high. This usually happens for users with limited link capacity below the required bit-rate. In the same way, if the same error rate is set for all subscribers, then the bit-rate must be adapted for each subscriber. Generally, the latter solution is preferable to insure reliability of the received data.

However, in the context of video transmission, it is also necessary to take the real time constraint into account in the video broadcast. All subscribers must be able to receive video simultaneously with an acceptable quality level. To allow this, transcoding is usually done in platform somewhere between the server and the customer. Generally, using transcoding makes it possible, for example, to multicast the video over heterogeneous links. Transcoding is an all-embracing term, which can involve adapting the standard, the format, the bit-rate or the frequency. In this Section, we deal only with transrating, which consists of adapting the video bit-rate to each subscriber loop by removing part of the transmitted video information. Of course, this information removal procedure must be carried out in such a manner that the video received is the least degraded version possible.

In the literature, there are many transrating algorithms that are more, or less, complex. Some are based, for example, on the suppression of high-frequency spatial information (i.e., removal of high-frequency DCT coefficients) (Werner, 1999; Assuncao & Ghanbari, 1997a; Sun et al., 1996; Celandroni et al., 2000). Others are based on the suppression of certain images in order to reduce the display frequency, as in temporal scalability (Horn et al., 1999; Lagendijk et al., 2000). Still others are based on a stronger quantization of predefined image areas (Tudor & Verner, 1997; Assuncao & Ghanbari, 1997a; Assuncao & Ghanbari, 1997b; Sun et al., 1996; Celandroni et al., 2000). These algorithms can be divided into two groups: *closed-loop transrating*, which require a complete decoding and re-encoding of the compressed video source, and *open-loop transrating*, which generally do not resort to a complete decoding, making them much less complex (Assuncao & Ghanbari, 1997a).

In this section, we present a Joint Source and Channel Coding (JSCC) approach for broadband MPEG-2 video distribution over DSL. Originally published by Coudoux et al. (2008), this approach combines a layered hierarchical video transrating scheme with an unequal error protection (UEP) technique and multi-carrier modulation for DSL video distribution in order to optimize the end-to-end video quality. We first highlight the existence of a "bottleneck bandwidth" of the video source after transrating; at this bandwidth, the quality of the video received by the subscriber is optimal. Following that, we present the JSCC system, and then explain the transrating optimization procedure. Finally, we report our simulation results.

6.1 Motivations

Let us consider an example of a MPEG-2 MP@ML single layer video source encoded at 6 Mbps. For the lines not reaching 6 Mbps with a sufficiently low error rate under practical power constraint, decreasing the bit-rate will decrease the transmission error rate. However, this improvement is counterbalanced by the fact that decreasing the bit-rate of the source video (and, as a result, removing some useful video information), increases the deterioration of the quality of the video received. Thus, lowering the bitrate clearly has two contradictory effects on the quality of the video available to the end-user.

Consequently, it can be assumed that, for each subscriber loop that cannot achieve 6 Mbps with appropriate QoS level, there is an ideal bit-rate, called the "bottleneck" bit-rate, at which the overall deterioration is minimal. This minimal deterioration is the result of a compromise between the distortion generated by the bit-rate reduction and the distortion generated by the transmission. Figure 19 illustrates this basic idea.

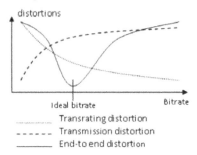

Fig. 19. End-to-end distortion in terms of the overall bit-rate

To insure a minimum level of deterioration, and thus a received video quality threshold, we used a hierarchical video source coding system, coupled with UEP at channel coding level as described in the preceding sections.

6.2 System architecture

Our JSCC system is based on the Data Partitioning (DP) mode used in the MPEG-2 standard, which splits the MPEG-2 bitstream into two hierarchical bitstreams (see Section 5). For simplicity, DP was chosen in order to conform to real-time constraint: indeed, it makes possible to split on-the-fly the incoming video bitstream into two separate ones. The most important bitstream is the base layer containing the most important data (e.g., headers, motion vectors and low-frequency DCT coefficients). The second bitstream is the enhancement layer (EL), containing all the other data, typically high-frequency DCT coefficients. Thus, these two bitstreams can be protected differently against channel errors, using UEP as explained in section 4.

The proposed JSCC system can be decomposed in a four-step adaptation process, as shown in Figure 20:

1. *Estimating the channel* -- The channel-to-noise ratios of the considered line are estimated for each carrier. These ratios are used by the bit- and power-loading algorithm (see Section 4).
2. *Defining the transrating parameters* -- The single layer input video bitstream is transcoded into two video bitstreams. Starting with the estimated channel parameters, the bit-rates of both the base layer bitstream and the enhanced layer bitstream must be determined.
3. *Transrating using data partitioning* -- The MPEG-2 bitstream coming from the very high bit-rate network (from a video server) and received at the CO is transcoded based on the transrating parameters defined in step 2.
4. *Coding and transmission* -- UEP is applied to the two bitstreams. Reed Solomon (RS) codes are used as in the ADSL standard in this step. As explained in section 4, two different RS codes can be applied to the two bitstreams before transmission. The two

bitstreams are then transmitted at fixed BER (with BER1<BER2). The RS code is applied to the base layer, so that the decoded base bitstream can be considered to be error-free at the receiver.

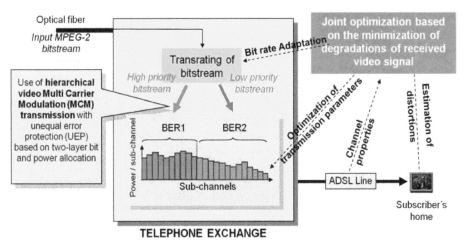

Fig. 20. Overview of the complete JSCC architecture

The first two steps are performed by the ADSL modem during initialization, assuming quasi-static transmission conditions; the last two are specific to our transrating system.

The Data partitioning step uses the Priority Break Point (denoted PBP1 in this chapter) defined in the MPEG-2 standard. PBP1 defines the separation point of the two bitstreams, and its value is related to the number of non-zero DCT coefficients preserved in the base layer (i.e., only the first low-frequency DCT coefficients). PBP1 depends on the number of VLC codes preserved in the base layer after the zigzag serialization MPEG procedure. The JSCC system maintains PBP1 constant in order to insure a minimal video quality level at the receiver side.

As the goal is to reduce the total video bit-rate, we introduce a second Priority Break Point, denoted PBP2 (PBP1≤ PBP2≤127), which defines the point at which the remaining VLC codes are discarded. The extreme values of PBP2 correspond to the situation in which the base layer only is transmitted (PBP2=PBP1) and to the situation in which all the bit-rates are preserved before transrating (PBP2=127). The other intermediate values make it possible to adjust the video bit-rate of the enhanced layer. This adjustment can propagate a quantization error (i.e., drift) and thus lead to a reduction in video quality. However, the quality metric used for determining transrating parameters takes into account of this error (C. Goudemand et al., 2007).

The simulations performed by Goudemand et al. (2006) showed that the optimal value of the PBP2 determines the best compromise between the perceived distortion and the bit-rate reduction obtained. Simulations on different MPEG-2 video sequences transmitted at 6 Mbps were performed with different PBP2 values. From one sequence to another, the bit-rate curves obtained after transrating versus the PBP2 value are very similar. For this reason, the average of these curves was used to determine the video bit-rate after transrating based on PBP2 (Figure 21). As illustrated, the bit-rate increases rapidly from 2.6 to 5.95 Mbps when the PBP2 goes from 64 to 85. Then, from PBP2=85 to 127, the bit-rate increases slowly. This evolution of the bit-rate with PBP2 can be easily explained by the fact that the DCT coefficient's energy decreases as the spatial frequency increases.

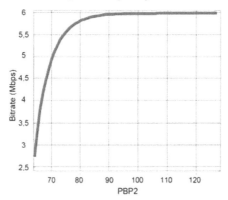

Fig. 21. Evolution of total bit rate as a function of the PBP2 parameter.

We also verified that the bit-rate overhead introduced by data partitioning does not exceed 1.5% of the aggregate video rate and therefore can be neglected. Let us consider our example of a coded sequence at 6 Mbps, transrated with the PBP1 and PBP2 equal to 67 and 85, respectively. According to Figure 21, the bit-rate at PBP1=PBP2=67 is about 4.3 Mbps, which is the base layer bit-rate. With PBP2=85, the bit-rate is 5.95 Mbps, which corresponds to the total bit-rate after transrating (i.e., the total bit-rate of the base and enhanced layers). The bit-rate corresponding to the enhancement layer is therefore equal to 1.65 Mbps.

In order to optimize the overall video quality, it is necessary to have a quality metric which permits to evaluate practically the visual impact of eliminating high-frequency DCT coefficients by transrating. First, let us introduce some features of the quality metric used in our system for the case of still images (i.e., the (I) intra-coded pictures of an MPEG-2 bitstream). Remember that, for the intra-pictures, the DCT coefficients are uniformly quantized. A quantization table defines the quantization step values that were obtained from subjective measurements.

The Normalized Weighted Mean Square Error (NWMSE) quality metric, proposed by Goudemand (2007), is based on the quantization property of the DCT coefficients involved in the MPEG-2 coder. As each quantization step value is related to the importance of the visual impact of the corresponding DCT coefficient, the weights used for this metric are related to these quantization steps. Such WMSE metric has been first introduced by Vandendorpe (1991) in the context of sub-band coding.

In the present case, the reference for calculating the quality metric is the input video sequence compressed at 6 Mbps. First considering the intra-coded pictures, WMSE is typically calculated from the DCT coefficients perceptually weighted according to the contrast sensitivity function (CSF) of the human eye. The weights used in the WMSE computation are inversely proportional to the square of the quantization step values. Therefore, the WMSE of the DCT coefficients can be seen for each block as the MSE of the corresponding quantized values. The perceptual distortion depends only on the error magnitude of the quantized DCT coefficients, independent of the spatial frequencies. The quantized coefficients thus have the same visual importance in the DCT domain. Any additional transrating or transmission distortion can be taken into account in the WMSE of the quantized coefficients.

The previous approach has been extended to (P) and (B) inter-coded pictures, such that WMSE can be computed from quantized DCT coefficients whatever the image type. Normalization is also introduced for each picture type, which depends on the different macroblock types as well as the rate control. However, the suppression of DCT coefficients due to transrating or transmission errors typically results in *drift error* among successive pictures. This phenomenon is accounted for by introducing weighting factors noted W_I, W_P, W_B defined as the average number of frames affected by an error in I, P, B frame, respectively. Finally, the average normalized perceptually weighted MSE of a sequence $NWMSE_{sequence}$ is the weighted sum of the NWMSE averaged for I, P, B frames defined as:

$$NWMSE_{sequence} = W_I E\{NWMSE_{I\,frame}\} + W_P E\{NWMSE_{P\,frame}\} + W_B E\{NWMSE_{B\,frame}\} \qquad (4)$$

6.3 System parameter optimization

The optimization process consists in determining the bit-rate of the two bitstreams, and therefore the values of the two Priority Break Points: PBP1 and PBP2, such that the received video quality (measured thanks to the above metric) is the best. The end-to-end perceptual quality of the video is considered to depend on the total bit-rate. In our JSCC architecture, the two-layer bitstreams received undergoes two independent types of degradations: transrating degradation and transmission degradation. Thus, the total degradation of the system is the sum of these two types, which can be evaluated using the NWMSE quality metric. Figure 22 shows two curves. For a given and fixed value of PBP1, the left side of the figure illustrates the evolution of the total transmission power P with respect to the PBP2.

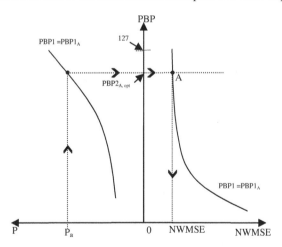

Fig. 22. Proposed approach for the determination of the end-to-end NWMSE

Let us consider the case of a transmission at power P, where P=Pa. This is a case for example in which all the total available power P_a is used for the transmission, making it possible to have the maximum transmission bit-rate. For any value of the PBP1=PBP1$_A$ given, the optimal value of the PBP2=PBP2$_{A,opt}$ is immediately obtained, as shown on the left curve in Figure 22. Thus, the operating point of the system given by (PBP1$_A$, PBP2$_{A,opt}$) can be determined. In addition, the NWMSE is a decreasing function of PBP2, as illustrated on the curve shown on the right side part of Figure 22. Thus, the NWMSE= $NWMSE_A$ can be therefore determined from the value of $PBP2_{opt}$.

If another similar but different value of PBP1 is considered, other curves must be used, such as those in Figure 22. Since the value of PBP1 is unknown, the direct determination of $PBP2_{opt}$ is compromised. If all the values of PBP1 from 64 to 127 are considered, $PBP2_{opt}$ and the NWMSE can be determined for each one of these values. A series of NWMSE values will be obtained. The operating point of the optimal system is thus the couple ($PBP1_{opt}$, $PBP2_{opt}$), which will minimize the global end-to-end NWMSE.

In short, by varying the PBP1 from 64 to 127, determining the optimal value of the PBP2 and the NWMSE for each value of the PBP1, and selecting the couple ($PBP1_{opt}$, $PBP2_{opt}$) that produces the minimal NWMSE, the locus C of all the operating points for the PBP1 values between 64 and 127 can be obtained, as shown in Figure 23.

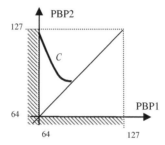

Fig. 23. Evolution of the PBP2 parameter as a function of PBP1, under transmit power constraint (Coudoux et al., 2008).

6.4 Simulation results

Experiments were conducted in two steps: 1) the determination of the optimal transrating parameters and 2) the simulation of the transmission of transrated video sequences over ADSL lines.

The optimal parameters were determined as follows: for each subscriber loop, the transrating couples (PBP1; PBP2) were estimated, which allowed the base and enhancement layers to be transmitted. These parameter couples were obtained using the bit and power allocations at a fixed bit-rate for the two bitstreams, based on the values of PBP1 and PBP2 at a maximum total power of 110 mW as stated in the ADSL standard. The optimal couple was then the one corresponding to the minimum total end-to-end NWMSE.

The simulations were carried out at 6 Mbps initial bit-rate using MPEG-2 (MP@ML) video sequences. ADSL Reed Solomon RS (255, 239) were applied to the base layer, which generated a bit-rate overcost of about 6.7%. The BER of the base layer transmission was fixed at 10^{-6} before RS decoding ($BER_{BL} = 10^{-6}$), which corresponds to about 6.4×10^{-33} after RS decoding. For this reason, the BL transmission was assumed to be error-free. The BER of the enhanced layer transmission was fixed at 10^{-4} ($BER_{HL} = 10^{-4}$) so that visual degradations would be minimized whatever the values of PBP1 and PBP2. The bit and power allocation algorithm used frequency division multiplexing of the two layers, as explained in Section 4. Once the optimal PBP1 and PBP2 parameters for the transmission were determined, the transmission of the video processed with these values was simulated.

For purposes of comparison, the ADSL MPEG-2 transmission was used in our experiments as the reference transmission. Figure 24 represents the evolution of the end-to end NWMSE as a function of the subscriber line length. The European Telecommunications Standards Institute (ETSI) test loop 1 was used (ETSI, 1996). Remember the combined source/channel transrating system described in this section was not designed to improve the quality of the received image on "a good" line, but rather to increase the range of ADSL video transmission. Given this reminder, a single layer ADSL transmission at a BER of 10^{-6} over the 1800 m-long ETSI loop 1 required 2.5 dB more than the authorized ADSL maximum transmission power of 110 mW. In order to reduce the total power to 110 mW without changing all other transmission parameters, it was necessary to reduce the line length by approximately 110 m. The traditional ADSL transmission on the same line was thus limited to 1700 m around the telephone exchange. The solution proposed by the authors led to a slightly degraded transmission in an area with an 1800 m radius, which can possibly be extended if progressive degradations, increasing with the line length, are accepted.

The two-layer JSCC used in these experiments was compared to a single-layer transrating system based on the same principle, but using only one priority break point PBP2=PBP1. With the same average system quality, the two-layer JSCC system led to an increase in the zone covered compared to the single-layer transmission system.

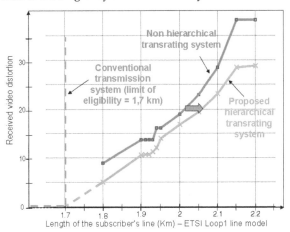

Fig. 24. Evolution of end-to-end perceptual distortions as a function of subscriber's line length (from Coudoux et al., 2008).

7. Conclusion

We demonstrated in this chapter how source and channel coding can be efficiently combined in order to fulfil QoS requirements of modern video communication systems. The underlying philosophy relies on the fact that not all the bits of a compressed video bitstream have the same visual importance. Thus, both digital video compression and transmission parameters should be jointly designed in an end-to-end approach, aiming at delivering the best video quality to the final end-user. We also demonstrated that digital video signals can be encoded into several layers of varying perceptual relevance using scalability tools. Subsequently, if unequal error protection is applied to these layers, the most visually important layers will be the best protected. Such video transmission methods typically increase the flexibility and reliability of video communications in heterogeneous multimedia environments, and produce a better quality of experience for the end-user. The effectiveness of a combined source/channel coding strategy was illustrated for the particular case of DSL video distribution. We showed that the eligibility level of video services can be optimally extended, by transrating the compressed video bitstream available on a distant server for the optimal bit-rate at which the end-user's visual quality is the best. The extension of these results to the case of the scalable extension of the H.264/AVC standard as well as wireless residential networks is currently under consideration in the TOSCANE project (see: http://www.lien.uhp-nancy.fr/lien/index.php?p=toscane).

Combined source and channel coding strategies constitute a promising research topic in the field of video communications. This is particularly true when considering the emergence of new services, such as mobile video streaming on small display devices or 3D-TV, as well as new transmission architectures, such as wireless vision sensor networks, for example. Future work will try to develop more efficient solutions to respond to the new challenges of video communications in terms of error resilience, accessibility, interactivity and universality.

8. References

Chui, J.; Calderbank, A.R. (2008). *Multilevel diversity-embedded space-time codes for video broadcasting over WiMAX*, Proceedings of the IEEE International Conference on Information Theory, pp. 1068-1072, Nice, France, June 2008.

Coudoux, F.-X.; Gazalet, M.G.; Mouton-Goudemand, C.; Corlay & P.; Gharbi, M. (2008). Extended Coverage for DSL Video Distribution Using a Quality-Oriented JSCC Architecture, *IEEE Transactions on Broadcasting*, Volume 54, Issue 3, Sept. 2008, pp. 525 – 531, ISSN: 0018-9316.

Coudoux F.X., Gazalet M., Derviaux C., Corlay P. (2001). Picture quality measurement based on block visibility in discrete cosine transform video sequences, *Journal of Electronic Imaging*, Vol.10(2), pp.498-510.

Daly S. (1993). The visible differences predictor: an algorithm for the assessment of image fidelity. In Watson A.B. (ed.), *Digital Images and Human Vision*, pp. 179-206, MIT Press.

ETSI Technical Report ETR 328 (1996). *Transmission and Multiplexing (TM ; Asymmetric Digital Subscriber Line (ADSL) ; Requirements and Performance*, Reference DTR/TM-06001, November 1996.

Faugeras O.D. (1979). Digital color image processing within the framework of a human visual model, *IEEE Trans. On Acoustics, Speech and Signal Processing*, vol. 22, no. 4, pp. 380-393.

Girod B. (1993). What's wrong with mean-squared error? , in *Visual Factors of Electronic Image Communications*. Cambridge, MA: MIT Press.

Glenn W.E. (1993), *Digital image compression based on visual perception and scene properties, video processing*, SMPTE Journal, pp. 395-397, May 1993

Goudemand, C., Coudoux, F.X., Gazalet, M. (2006). A study on Power and Bit Assignment of Embedded Multi-Carrier Modulation Schemes for Hierarchical Image Transmission over Digital Subscriber Line, *IEICE Transactions on Communications*, Vol. E89, No.7 (July 2006), page numbers (2071-2073).

Goudemand, C.; Gazalet, M.; Coudoux, F.X.; Gharbi, M. (2006). Reduced complexity power minimization algorithm for DMT transmission – Application to layered multimedia services over DSL, *Proceedings of the 13th International Conference of Electronics, Circuits and Systems, ICECS 2006*, pp. 728-731, Nice, France, December 2006.

Goudemand C., Coudoux F.X., Gazalet M.G. (2006). Optimal bit rate adaptation for layered video transmission over spectrally shaped channels using multicarrier modulation, *IEEE ICIP-2006*, pp.13-16, Atlanta, USA.

Goudemand C., Gazalet M.G., Coudoux F.X., Corlay P., Gharbi M. (2007). A Low Complexity Image Quality Metric for Real-Time Open-Loop Transcoding Architectures, *IEEE ICC' 07*, Glasgow.

Huang, H-C., Peng, W-H., Chiang, T., Hang, H-M., "Advances in the Scalable Amendment of H.264/AVC", *IEEE Commun. Mag.*, pp. 68-76, Jan. 2007.

Hellge, C., Mirta, S., Schierl, T., Wiegand, T., „Mobile TV with SVC and Hierarchical Modulation for DVB-H Broadcast Services", *IEEE BMSB*, Bilbao, 13-15 May 2009.

Kouadio, A., Clare, M., Noblet, L., Bottreau, V., "SVC – a highly scalable version of H.264/AVC', EBU Technical Review, 2008.

Lagendijk R.L., Frimout E.D., Biemond J. (2000). Low-Complexity Rate-Distortion Optimal Transcoding of MPEG I-frames, *Signal Processing: Image Communication*, no. 15, p531 – 544.

Lee Y.L., Kim H.C., Park H.W. (1998). Blocking effect reduction of JPEG images by signal adaptive filtering, *IEEE Trans. Image Processing*, vol. 7, no. 2, pp. 229-234.

Lin, S., Costello, D. (1983), *Error Control Coding: Fundamentals and Applications*, Prentice-Hall Series in Computer Applications in Electrical Engineering, ISBN 0-13-283796-X, N.J. 07632.

Lukas F.X., Budrikis Z.L. (1982). Picture quality prediction based on a visual model, *IEEE Transactions on Communications*, vol. 30, no. 7, pp. 1679-1692.

Mannos J.L., Sakrison D.J. (1974). The effects of a visual fidelity criterion on the encoding of images, *IEEE Trans. On Information Theory*, vol. 20;, no. 4, pp. 525-535.

Mathew R., Arnold J.F. (1999), Efficient Layered Video coding using Data Partionning, *Signal Processing: Image Communication*, n°14, 1999.

Mitchell J., Pennebacker W., Fogg C., Le Gall D. (1995). *MPEG Video Standard Compression*, Van Nostrand Reinhold, New York.

Pennebaker W.B., Mitchell J.L. (1993). *JPEG Still Image Data Compression Standard*, Van Nostrand Reinhold, New York.

Pinson M., Wolf S. (2004). A new standardized method for objectively measuring video quality. *IEEE Transactions on Broadcasting*, vol. 50, no. 3, pp 312-322.

Proakis, G.P. (1995). *Digital Communications*, third edition, McGraw-Hill Electrical Engineering Series, ISBN 0-07-051726-6, International Edition.

Rabbani M., Jones P.W. (1991),. *Digital Image Compression Techniques*, SPIE Press, Bellingham

Ramamurthi B., Gersho A. (1986). Nonlinear space variant postprocessing of block coded images, IEEE Trans. Acoust., Speech, Signal Processing, vol. ASSP-34, pp. 1258-1267.

Richardson, I. (2003). H.264 *and MPEG-4 Video Compression: Video Coding for Next Generation Multimedia*, John Wiley & Sons, ISBN 0-470-84837-5.

Schierl, T., Gänger, K., Wiegand, T., Stockhammer, T., "SVC-based multisource streaming for robust video transmission in mobile ad hoc networks", *IEEE Wireless Commun. Mag.*, Special Issue on Multimedia in Wireless/Mobile Ad Hoc Networks, Vol. 13, N°. 5, pp. 96-103, Oct. 2006.

Schwarz, H., Marpe, D., Wiegand, T., "Overview of the Scalable Video Coding extension of the H.264/AVC standard", IEEE Trans. Circuits Syst. Video Technol., Vol. 17, N°. 9, pp. 1103-1120, Sept. 2007.

Shannon, C.E. (1948). A mathematical Theory of Communications, *Bell System Technical Journal*, Vol. 27 (October 1948), page numbers (379-423,623-656).

Starr, T., Cioffi, J.M., Silverman P.J. (1999). *Understanding Digital Subscriber Line Technology*, Prentice Hall PTR, ISBN 0-13-780545-4, N.J. 07458.

Sun H., Kwok W., Zdepski J. (1996). Architectures for MPEG Compressed Bitstream Scaling, *IEEE Transactions on Circuits and Systems for Video Technology*, Vol. 6, No. 2.

Talluri R., Moccagatta I., Nag Y., Gene C. (1999). « Error Concealment by Data Partitioning », *Signal Processing : Image Communication*, No. 14.

Tekalp, M. (1996). *Digital video processing*, Prentice Hall: Signal processing, Chapman&Hall, International Thomson Publishing.

Thang, T-C., Kang, J-W., Yoo, J-J., Ro, Y-M., "Optimal Multilayer Adaptation of SVC Video over Heterogeneous Environments", *Advances in Multimedia*, Volume 2008, Article ID 739192, 8 pages, doi:10.1155/2008/739192

Vandendorpe L. (1991). Optimized quantization for image subband coding, *Signal Processing: Image Commun.*, 4, pp. 65-79.

Vitthaladevuni, P.K.; Alouini, M.S. (2001). BER Computation of 4/M-QAM Hierarchical Constellations, *IEEE Transactions on Broadcasting*, Vol.47, No.3 (September 2001), page numbers (228-239).

Wachsmann, U.; Fischer, F.H; Huber, J.B; (1999). Multilevel Codes: Theoretical Concepts and Practical Design Rules, *IEEE Transactions of Information Theory*, Vol.45, No.5 (July 1999), page numbers (1361-1391).

Wang Z., Bovik A.C., Sheikh H.R., Simoncelli E.P. (2004). Image quality assessment; from error visibility to structural similarity, *IEEE Trans. Image Processing*, vol. 13, no. 4, pp. 300-612.

Wang Z., Lu L., Bovik A. (2004). Video quality assessment based on structural distortion measurement. *Signal Processing: Image Communication*, special issue on objective video quality metrics, vol. 19, pp. 121-132.

Watson A.B., Hu J., McGowan, J.F. (2001). Digital video quality metric based on human vision. *Journal of Electronic Imaging*, vol. 10, no. 1, pp. 20-29.

Werner O. (1999). Requantization for Transcoding of MPEG-2 Intra frames, *IEEE Trans. Image Processing*, Vol. 8, No. 2.

Wiegand T., Sullivan G. J., Bjntegaard G., Luthra A. (2003), Overview of the H.264/AVC video coding standard,. *IEEE Trans. Circuits Syst. Video Techn.* 13(7), pp 560-576 (2003)

Winkler S., *Digital Video Quality: Vision Models and Metrics*, Wiley Press, 2005.

Wu H.R. (Ed.), Rao K.R. (Ed.), *Digital Video Image Quality and Perceptual Coding*, CRC Press, Nov. 2005.

Yuen M., "Coding Artifacts and Visual Distortions", in *Digital Video Image Quality and Perceptual Coding*, H.R. Wu (Ed.), K.R. Rao (Ed.), CRC Press, 2005.

Zheng, H. ; Liu, K.J.R. (2000). Power Minimization for Delivering Integrated Multimedia Services over Digital Subscriber Line, *IEEE Journal of Selected Areas on Communications*, Vol.18, No.6, (June 2000), page numbers 841-849.

Permissions

All chapters in this book were first published in DV, by InTech Open; hereby published with permission under the Creative Commons Attribution License or equivalent. Every chapter published in this book has been scrutinized by our experts. Their significance has been extensively debated. The topics covered herein carry significant findings which will fuel the growth of the discipline. They may even be implemented as practical applications or may be referred to as a beginning point for another development.

The contributors of this book come from diverse backgrounds, making this book a truly international effort. This book will bring forth new frontiers with its revolutionizing research information and detailed analysis of the nascent developments around the world.

We would like to thank all the contributing authors for lending their expertise to make the book truly unique. They have played a crucial role in the development of this book. Without their invaluable contributions this book wouldn't have been possible. They have made vital efforts to compile up to date information on the varied aspects of this subject to make this book a valuable addition to the collection of many professionals and students.

This book was conceptualized with the vision of imparting up-to-date information and advanced data in this field. To ensure the same, a matchless editorial board was set up. Every individual on the board went through rigorous rounds of assessment to prove their worth. After which they invested a large part of their time researching and compiling the most relevant data for our readers.

The editorial board has been involved in producing this book since its inception. They have spent rigorous hours researching and exploring the diverse topics which have resulted in the successful publishing of this book. They have passed on their knowledge of decades through this book. To expedite this challenging task, the publisher supported the team at every step. A small team of assistant editors was also appointed to further simplify the editing procedure and attain best results for the readers.

Apart from the editorial board, the designing team has also invested a significant amount of their time in understanding the subject and creating the most relevant covers. They scrutinized every image to scout for the most suitable representation of the subject and create an appropriate cover for the book.

The publishing team has been an ardent support to the editorial, designing and production team. Their endless efforts to recruit the best for this project, has resulted in the accomplishment of this book. They are a veteran in the field of academics and their pool of knowledge is as vast as their experience in printing. Their expertise and guidance has proved useful at every step. Their uncompromising quality standards have made this book an exceptional effort. Their encouragement from time to time has been an inspiration for everyone.

The publisher and the editorial board hope that this book will prove to be a valuable piece of knowledge for researchers, students, practitioners and scholars across the globe.

List of Contributors

Bernhard Hechenleitner
Salzburg University of Applied Sciences, Austria

O. Eerenberg and P.H.N. de With
NXP Semiconductors Research, CycloMedia Technology / Eindhoven University of Technology, The Netherlands

Tamgnoue Valéry, Véronique Moeyaert, Sébastien Bette and Patrice Mégret
University of Mons (UMONS), Faculty of Engineering, Department of Electromagnetism and Telecommunications, Mons Belgium

Jia-Chyi Wu, Chi-Min Li and Kuo-Hsean Chen
National Taiwan Ocean University Department of Communications, Navigation and Control Engineering, Taiwan

Tetsuya Takiguchi, Jun Adachi and Yasuo Ariki
Kobe University, Japan

Poullin Dominique
ONERA, France

Vandenberghe, Leroux, De Turck, Moerman and Demeester
Ghent University, Belgium

Archana M. Rajurkar
Dept. of Computer Sc. and Engg. M.G.M.'s College of Engineering, Nanded – 431 605

R.C. Joshi
Dept. of Electronics and Computer Engg. Indian Institute of Technology Roorkee, Roorkee - 247 667

Santanu Chaudhary
Dept. of Electrical Engg., Indian Institute of Technology, Delhi, New Delhi

Ramchandra Manthalkar
Dept. of Electronics and Telecommunication Engg. S.G.G.S. Institute of Engineering, and Technology Nanded – 431 605, India

Mylène C. Q. Farias
Department of Computer Science University of Brasília, (UnB) Brazil

Leopoldo Angrisani
Dept. of Computer Science and Control Systems, University of Naples Federico II via Claudio 21, 80125 Napoli

Domenico Capriglione, Luigi Ferrigno and Gianfranco Miele
Dept. of Automation, Electromagnetism, Information Engineering and Industrial Mathematics, University of Cassino, via G. Di Biasio, 43 03043 Cassino (Fr), Italy

François-Xavier Coudoux, Patrick Corlay, Marie Zwingelstein-Colin, Mohamed Gharbi, Charlène Mouton-Goudemand and Marc-Georges Gazalet
University Lille Nord de France, F-59000 Lille

UVHC, IEMN-DOAE, F-59313 Valenciennes CNRS, UMR 8520, F-59650 Villeneuve d'Ascq, France

Index

Printed in the USA
CPSIA information can be obtained
at www.ICGtesting.com
JSHW011435221024
72173JS00004B/818